The Book of Life

Also by J. Krishnamurti

The Book of Life

*Daily Meditations
with Krishnamurti*

J. KRISHNAMURTI

HarperOne
An Imprint of HarperCollins*Publishers*

HarperOne

Grateful acknowledgment is made to Quest Books, Wheaton, IL., for permission to quote from *The Commentaries on Living*, Vols. I, II, and III, by J. Krishnamurti. For information regarding Krishnamurti, contact Krishnamurti Foundation of America, P.O. Box 1560, Ojai, California 93024.

Edited by R. E. Mark Lee

Book design by Claudia Smelser

HarperCollins books may be purchased for educational, business, or sales promotional use. For information, please e-mail the Special Markets Department at SPsales@harpercollins.com.

HarperCollins Web site: http://www.harpercollins.com

HarperCollins®, 📖®, and HarperOne™ are trademarks of HarperCollins Publishers.

Library of Congress Cataloging-in-Publication Data
Krishnamurti, J. (Jiddu)
The book of life : daily meditations with Krishnamurti / J. Krishnamurti. — 1st ed.
ISBN: 978-0-06-064879-4
1. Spiritual life—Meditations. 2. Devotional calendars. I. Title.
BL624.2.K75   1995
181'.4—dc20   94–42158

23 24 25 26 27 LBC 62 61 60 59 58

TABLE *of* CONTENTS

Introduction **vii**

INTRODUCTION

IN 1934 KRISHNAMURTI SAID, "*Why do you want to be students of books instead of students of life? Find out what is true and false in your environment with all its oppressions and its cruelties, and then you will find out what is true.*" Repeatedly he pointed out that the "book of life," which is ever changing with a vitality that cannot be held in thought, was the only one worth "reading," all others being filled with secondhand information. "*The story of mankind is in you, the vast experience, the deep-rooted fears, anxieties, sorrow, pleasure and all the beliefs that man has accumulated throughout the millennia. You are that book.*"

This book, *The Book of Life: Daily Meditations with Krishnamurti,* is arranged in an order somewhat replicating the way Krishnamurti delivered his talks. He usually began with listening and the relationship between the speaker and the audience, and ended with subjects that naturally emerge when life is in order and greater depth begins to surface into consciousness. During his last days in 1985 and 1986 he talked about creativity and the possibility of a totally new way of life. This book has excerpts on those subjects.

Many themes reccurred throughout his teachings. His vision was the whole broad observation of the human condition wherein every aspect of life is interconnected. *The Book of Life* presents passages on a new theme for every week of the year with each topic developed over seven days. These quotations are identified by their source and referenced in the Sources index. Readers who are interested in exploring specific themes in greater depth are invited to go to the full texts of the books from which they are excerpted.

Krishnamurti began speaking publicly in 1929 with a voice that Aldous Huxley described as having "intrinsic authority." His powerful exploration of the nature of truth and freedom has resulted in millions of copies of his talks and dialogues being published and translated into more than forty languages.

Krishnamurti, although shy and retiring, tirelessly gave thousands of talks, delivered without notes or preparation, essentially unfolding one seminal theme: Truth can be discovered by anyone, without the help of any authority and, as life is ever-present, in an instant. His talks span the whole range of personal and social conflict and concern. Observing the depth and scope of our behavior, as it occurs in the moment, becomes the necessary action in transforming ourselves and our society. When asked by someone attending one of his talks why he spoke and what he wanted to accomplish he replied, "*I want to tell you something, perhaps the way to find out what is reality—not the way as a system, but how to set about it. And if you can find this for yourself, there will not be one speaker, there will be all of us talking, all of us expressing that reality in our lives where we are. . . . Truth cannot be accumulated. What is accumulated is always being destroyed; it withers away. Truth can never wither because it can only be found from moment to moment in every thought, in every relationship, in every word, in every gesture, in a smile, in tears. And if you and I can find that and live it—the very living is the finding of it—then we shall not become propagandists; we shall be creative human beings—not perfect human beings, but creative human beings, which is vastly different. And that, I think, is why I am talking, and perhaps that is why you are here listening.*

"*There is only the problem; there is no answer; for in the understanding of the problem lies its dissolution.*" Often, when he was asked a question, Krishnamurti responded, "Let us find out what we mean by . . . ," thus examining the question and opening it up for inquiry rather than immediately giving an answer. For Krishnamurti, probing a question or problem fueled that inquiry rather than simply following a logical and intellectual search for an answer. The extracts in this book are presented to the reader as questions that might have been posed without a prompt from the reader for an immediate answer.

Krishnamurti pointed out that the dialogue with his listeners in the talks that he gave was not intellectual and was not anchored in thoughts and ideals. He said, "*After all, the purpose of these talks is to communicate with each other, and not to impose upon you a certain series of ideas. Ideas never change the mind, never bring about a radical transformation in the mind. But if we can individually communicate with each other at the same time and at the same level, then perhaps there will be an understanding which is not merely propaganda . . . so these talks are not meant to dissuade or to persuade you in any way, either actually or subliminally.*"

◈

In almost all his public talks and dialogues, Krishnamurti used the terms "mankind" or "man" when referring to the whole of humanity. But in the latter part of his life, he frequently interrupted himself to tell his audience, "Please, when I say mankind, I mean the women, too. So don't get mad at me."

Krishnamurti spoke with extraordinary simplicity, and not as a guru or religious teacher with a derivative teaching, special vocabulary, or ties to any organization or sect. Demand for his clear, authentic teachings grew as he traveled the world. From 1930 until his death in 1986, he spoke to ever-larger audiences in Europe, North America, Australia, South America, and India.

This book contains excerpts taken from published and unpublished talks, dialogues, and writings between 1933 and 1968. Among those is the first popular Krishnamurti book, read by the public at large, *Education and the Significance of Life,* written under a large oak tree in Ojai, California, and published in 1953 by Harper & Row, the publisher that was to continue for more than thirty years to publish his works in America. His next book, *The First and Last Freedom,* was also published by Harper & Row, in 1954, and with a long preface by his friend Aldous Huxley.

Commentaries on Living were written between 1949 and 1955 in longhand on pages without margins and with no corrections or erasures. Aldous Huxley had encouraged Krishnamurti to write, and the manuscript, edited by D. Rajagopal, was published in 1956. Essentially it is a chronicle of Krishnamurti's interviews with people who came to be with him and talk, and there is in these pages the feeling of a meeting of two friends talking and exploring without hesitation or fear. The chapters in these books often open with a brief description of the landscape, climate, or nearby animals. From the simplicity of this natural world comes an easy transition to the inner landscape of confusion, anxiety, beliefs—the general and personal concerns people brought to their meetings with Krishnamurti. Some interviews were not published in those first three volumes of *The Commentaries on Living*, and they appear here for the first time. In some of these previously unpublished interviews, Krishnamurti used "thought-feeling" to describe a unitary response.

Life Ahead and *Think on These Things* were edited by Krishnamurti's friend Mary Lutyens in 1963 and 1964 and published by Harper & Row. These two books comprise a compendium of selected and edited questions and answers from talks with young people, and have been so well received that they have come to be regarded as religious and literary classics. They were followed by a body of work that extends to more than fifty books.

Krishnamurti thought himself unimportant and unnecessary to the process of understanding truth, of seeing ourselves. On one occasion he referred to himself as a telephone, a mechanism to be used by a listener. He said, "*What the speaker is saying has very little importance in itself. The really important thing is for the mind to be so effortlessly aware that it is in a state of understanding all the time. If we don't understand and merely listen to words, we invariably go away with a series of concepts or ideas, thereby establishing a pattern to which we then try to adjust ourselves in our daily or so-called spiritual lives.*"

It might be worthwhile, as you read on, to be alert to the way Krishnamurti regarded the relationship between two people searching for the truth. In 1981 he said, "*We are like two friends sitting in the park on a lovely day talking about life, talking about our problems, investigating the very nature of our existence, and asking ourselves seriously why life has become such a great problem, why, though intellectually we are very sophisticated, yet our daily life is such a grind, without any meaning, except survival—which again is rather doubtful. Why has life, everyday existence, become such a torture? We may go to church, follow some leader, political or religious, but the daily life is always a turmoil; though there are certain periods which are occasionally joyful, happy, there is always a cloud of darkness about our life. And these two friends, as we are, you and the speaker, are talking over together in a friendly manner, perhaps with affection, with care, with concern, whether it is at all possible to live our daily life without a single problem."*

◈

JANUARY

Listening

Learning

Authority

Self-Knowledge

◈

Listen with Ease

Have you ever sat very silently, not with your attention fixed on anything, not making an effort to concentrate, but with the mind very quiet, really still? Then you hear everything, don't you? You hear the far off noises as well as those that are nearer and those that are very close by, the immediate sounds—which means really that you are listening to everything. Your mind is not confined to one narrow little channel. If you can listen in this way, listen with ease, without strain, you will find an extraordinary change taking place within you, a change that comes without your volition, without your asking; and in that change there is great beauty and depth of insight.

Putting Aside Screens

How do you listen? Do you listen with your projections, through your projection, through your ambitions, desires, fears, anxieties, through hearing only what you want to hear, only what will be satisfactory, what will gratify, what will give comfort, what will for the moment alleviate your suffering? If you listen through the screen of your desires, then you obviously listen to your own voice; you are listening to your own desires. And is there any other form of listening? Is it not important to find out how to listen not only to what is being said but to everything—to the noise in the streets, to the chatter of birds, to the noise of the tramcar, to the restless sea, to the voice of your husband, to your wife, to your friends, to the cry of a baby? Listening has importance only when one is not projecting one's own desires through which one listens. Can one put aside all these screens through which we listen, and really listen?

Beyond the Noise of Words

Listening is an art not easily come by, but in it there is beauty and great understanding. We listen with the various depths of our being, but our listening is always with a preconception or from a particular point of view. We do not listen simply; there is always the intervening screen of our own thoughts, conclusions, and prejudices. . . . To listen there must be an inward quietness, a freedom from the strain of acquiring, a relaxed attention. This alert yet passive state is able to hear what is beyond the verbal conclusion. Words confuse; they are only the outward means of communication; but to commune beyond the noise of words, there must be in listening an alert passivity. Those who love may listen; but it is extremely rare to find a listener. Most of us are after results, achieving goals; we are forever overcoming and conquering, and so there is no listening. It is only in listening that one hears the song of the words.

Listening Without Thought

I do not know whether you have listened to a bird. To listen to something demands that your mind be quiet—not a mystical quietness, but just quietness. I am telling you something, and to listen to me you have to be quiet, not have all kinds of ideas buzzing in your mind. When you look at a flower, you look at it, not naming it, not classifying it, not saying that it belongs to a certain species—when you do these, you cease to look at it. Therefore, I am saying that it is one of the most difficult things to listen—to listen to the communist, to the socialist, to the congressman, to the capitalist, to anybody, to your wife, to your children, to your neighbor, to the bus conductor, to the bird—just to listen. It is only when you listen without the idea, without thought, that you are directly in contact; and being in contact, you will understand whether what he is saying is true or false; you do not have to discuss.

Listening Brings Freedom

When you make an effort to listen, are you listening? Is not that very effort a distraction that prevents listening? Do you make an effort when you listen to something that gives you delight? . . . You are not aware of the truth, nor do you see the false as the false, as long as your mind is occupied in any way with effort, with comparison, with justification or condemnation. . . .

Listening itself is a complete act; the very act of listening brings its own freedom. But are you really concerned with listening, or with altering the turmoil within? If you would listen . . . in the sense of being aware of your conflicts and contradictions without forcing them into any particular pattern of thought, perhaps they might altogether cease. You see, we are constantly trying to be this or that, to achieve a particular state, to capture one kind of experience and avoid another, so the mind is everlastingly occupied with something; it is never still to listen to the noise of its own struggles and pains. Be simple . . . and don't try to become something or to capture some experience.

Listening Without Effort

You are now listening to me; you are not making an effort to pay attention, you are just listening; and if there is truth in what you hear, you will find a remarkable change taking place in you—a change that is not premeditated or wished for, a transformation, a complete revolution in which the truth alone is master and not the creations of your mind. And if I may suggest it, you should listen in that way to everything—not only to what I am saying, but also to what other people are saying, to the birds, to the whistle of a locomotive, to the noise of the bus going by. You will find that the more you listen to everything, the greater is the silence, and that silence is then not broken by noise. It is only when you are resisting something, when you are putting up a barrier between yourself and that to which you do not want to listen—it is only then that there is a struggle.

Listening to Yourself

QUESTIONER: While I am here listening to you, I seem to understand, but when I am away from here, I don't understand, even though I try to apply what you have been saying.

KRISHNAMURTI: . . . You are listening to yourself, and not to the speaker. If you are listening to the speaker, he becomes your leader, your way to understanding—which is a horror, an abomination, because you have then established the hierarchy of authority. So what you are doing here is listening to yourself. You are looking at the picture the speaker is painting, which is your own picture, not the speaker's. If that much is clear, that you are looking at yourself, then you can say, "Well, I see myself as I am, and I don't want to do anything about it"— and that is the end of it. But if you say, "I see myself as I am, and there must be a change," then you begin to work out of your own understanding—which is entirely different from applying what the speaker is saying. . . . But if, as the speaker is speaking, you are listening to yourself, then out of that listening there is clarity, there is sensitivity; out of that listening the mind becomes healthy, strong. Neither obeying nor resisting, it becomes alive, intense—and it is only such a human being who can create a new generation, a new world.

Look with Intensity

. . . It seems to me that learning is astonishingly difficult, as is listening also. We never actually listen to anything because our mind is not free; our ears are stuffed up with those things that we already know, so listening becomes extraordinarily difficult. I think—or rather, it is a fact—that if one can listen to something with all of one's being, with vigor, with vitality, then the very act of listening is a liberative factor, but unfortunately you never do listen, as you have never learned about it. After all, you only learn when you give your whole being to something. When you give your whole being to mathematics, you learn; but when you are in a state of contradiction, when you do not want to learn but are forced to learn, then it becomes merely a process of accumulation. To learn is like reading a novel with innumerable characters; it requires your full attention, not contradictory attention. If you want to learn about a leaf—a leaf of the spring or a leaf of the summer—you must really look at it, see the symmetry of it, the texture of it, the quality of the living leaf. There is beauty, there is vigor, there is vitality in a single leaf. So to learn about the leaf, the flower, the cloud, the sunset, or a human being, you must look with all intensity.

To Learn, the Mind Must Be Quiet

To discover anything new you must start on your own; you must start on a journey completely denuded, especially of knowledge, because it is very easy, through knowledge and belief, to have experiences; but those experiences are merely the products of self-projection and therefore utterly unreal, false. If you are to discover for yourself what is the new, it is no good carrying the burden of the old, especially knowledge—the knowledge of another, however great. You use knowledge as a means of self-projection, security, and you want to be quite sure that you have the same experiences as the Buddha or the Christ or X. But a man who is protecting himself constantly through knowledge is obviously not a truth-seeker. . . .

For the discovery of truth there is no path. . . . When you want to find something new, when you are experimenting with anything, your mind has to be very quiet, has it not? If your mind is crowded, filled with facts, knowledge, they act as an impediment to the new; the difficulty for most of us is that the mind has become so important, so predominantly significant, that it interferes constantly with anything that may be new, with anything that may exist simultaneously with the known. Thus knowledge and learning are impediments for those who would seek, for those who would try to understand that which is timeless.

Learning Is Not Experience

The word *learning* has great significance. There are two kinds of learning. For most of us learning means the accumulation of knowledge, of experience, of technology, of a skill, of a language. There is also psychological learning, learning through experience, either the immediate experiences of life, which leave a certain residue, of tradition, of the race, of society. There are these two kinds of learning how to meet life: psychological and physiological; outward skill and inward skill. There is really no line of demarcation between the two; they overlap. We are not considering for the moment the skill that we learn through practice, the technological knowledge that we acquire through study. What we are concerned about is the psychological learning that we have acquired through the centuries or inherited as tradition, as knowledge, as experience. This we call learning, but I question whether it is learning at all. I am not talking about learning a skill, a language, a technique, but I am asking whether the mind ever learns psychologically. It has learned, and with what it has learned it meets the challenge of life. It is always translating life or the new challenge according to what it has learned. That is what we are doing. Is that learning? Doesn't learning imply something new, something that I don't know and am learning? If I am merely adding to what I already know, it is no longer learning.

When Is Learning Possible?

To inquire and to learn is the function of the mind. By learning I do not mean the mere cultivation of memory or the accumulation of knowledge, but the capacity to think clearly and sanely without illusion, to start from facts and not from beliefs and ideals. There is no learning if thought originates from conclusions. Merely to acquire information or knowledge is not to learn. Learning implies the love of understanding and the love of doing a thing for itself. Learning is possible only when there is no coercion of any kind. And coercion takes many forms, does it not? There is coercion through influence, through attachment or threat, through persuasive encouragement, or subtle forms of reward.

Most people think that learning is encouraged through comparison, whereas the contrary is the fact. Comparison brings about frustration and merely encourages envy, which is called competition. Like other forms of persuasion, comparison prevents learning and breeds fear.

Learning Is Never Accumulative

Learning is one thing and acquiring knowledge is another. Learning is a continuous process, not a process of addition, not a process which you gather and then from there act. Most of us gather knowledge as memory, as idea, store it up as experience, and from there act. That is, we act from knowledge, technological knowledge, knowledge as experience, knowledge as tradition, knowledge that one has derived through one's particular idiosyncratic tendencies; with that background, with that accumulation as knowledge, as experience, as tradition, we act. In that process there is no learning. Learning is never accumulative; it is a constant movement. I do not know if you have ever gone into this question at all: what is learning and what is the acquisition of knowledge? . . . Learning is never accumulative. You cannot store up learning and then from that storehouse act. You learn as you are going along. Therefore, there is never a moment of retrogression or deterioration or decline.

Learning Has No Past

Wisdom is something that has to be discovered by each one, and it is not the result of knowledge. Knowledge and wisdom do not go together. Wisdom comes when there is the maturity of self-knowing. Without knowing oneself, order is not possible, and therefore there is no virtue.

Now, learning about oneself, and accumulating knowledge about oneself, are two different things. . . . A mind that is acquiring knowledge is never learning. What it is doing is this: It is gathering to itself information, experience as knowledge, and from the background of what it has gathered, it experiences, it learns; and therefore it is never really learning, but always knowing, acquiring.

Learning is always in the active present; it has no past. The moment you say to yourself, "I have learned," it has already become knowledge, and from the background of that knowledge you can accumulate, translate, but you cannot further learn. It is only a mind that is not acquiring, but always learning—it is only such a mind that can understand this whole entity that we call the "me," the self. I have to know myself, the structure, the nature, the significance of the total entity; but I can't do that burdened with my previous knowledge, with my previous experience, or with a mind that is conditioned, for then I am not learning, I am merely interpreting, translating, looking with an eye that is already clouded by the past.

Authority Prevents Learning

We generally learn through study, through books, through experience, or through being instructed. Those are the usual ways of learning. We commit to memory what to do and what not to do, what to think and what not to think, how to feel, how to react. Through experience, through study, through analysis, through probing, through introspective examination, we store up knowledge as memory; and memory then responds to further challenges and demands, from which there is more and more learning. . . . What is learned is committed to memory as knowledge, and that knowledge functions whenever there is a challenge, or whenever we have to do something.

Now I think there is a totally different way of learning, and I am going to talk a little bit about it; but to understand it, and to learn in this different way, you must be completely rid of authority; otherwise, you will merely be instructed, and you will repeat what you have heard. That is why it is very important to understand the nature of authority. Authority prevents learning—learning that is not the accumulation of knowledge as memory. Memory always responds in patterns; there is no freedom. A man who is burdened with knowledge, with instructions, who is weighted down by the things he has learned, is never free. He may be most extraordinarily erudite, but his accumulation of knowledge prevents him from being free, and therefore he is incapable of learning.

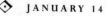

To Destroy Is to Create

To be free, you have to examine authority, the whole skeleton of authority, tearing to pieces the whole dirty thing. And that requires energy, actual physical energy, and also, it demands psychological energy. But the energy is destroyed, is wasted, when one is in conflict. . . . So when there is the understanding of the whole process of conflict, there is the ending of conflict, there is abundance of energy. Then you can proceed, tearing down the house that you have built throughout the centuries and that has no meaning at all.

You know, to destroy is to create. We must destroy, not the buildings, not the social or economic system—this comes about daily—but the psychological, the unconscious and the conscious defenses, securities that one has built up rationally, individually, deeply, and superficially. We must tear through all that to be utterly defenseless, because you must be defenseless to love and have affection. Then you see and understand ambition, authority; and you begin to see when authority is necessary and at what level—the authority of the policeman and no more. Then there is no authority of learning, no authority of knowledge, no authority of capacity, no authority that function assumes and which becomes status. To understand all authority—of the gurus, of the Masters, and others—requires a very sharp mind, a clear brain, not a muddy brain, not a dull brain.

Virtue Has No Authority

Can the mind be free from authority, which means free from fear, so that it is no longer capable of following? If so, this puts an end to imitation, which becomes mechanical. After all, virtue, ethics, is not a repetition of what is good. The moment it becomes mechanical, it ceases to be virtue. Virtue is something that must be from moment to moment, like humility. Humility cannot be cultivated, and a mind that has no humility is incapable of learning. So virtue has no authority. The social morality is no morality at all; it's immoral because it admits competition, greed, ambition, and therefore society is encouraging immorality. Virtue is something that transcends morality. Without virtue there is no order, and order is not according to a pattern, according to a formula. A mind that follows a formula through disciplining itself to achieve virtue creates for itself the problems of immorality.

An external authority that the mind objectifies, apart from the law, as God, as moral, and so on, becomes destructive when the mind is seeking to understand what real virtue is. We have our own authority as experience, as knowledge, which we are trying to follow. There is this constant repetition, imitation, which we all know. Psychological authority—not the authority of the law, the policeman who keeps order—the psychological authority, which each one has, becomes destructive of virtue because virtue is something that is living, moving. As you cannot possibly cultivate humility, as you cannot possibly cultivate love, so also virtue cannot be cultivated; and there is great beauty in that. Virtue is nonmechanical, and without virtue there is no foundation for clear thinking.

The Old Mind Is Bound by Authority

The problem then is: Is it possible for a mind that has been so conditioned—brought up in innumerable sects, religions, and all the superstitions, fears—to break away from itself and thereby bring about a new mind? . . . The old mind is essentially the mind that is bound by authority. I am not using the word *authority* in the legalistic sense; but by that word I mean authority as tradition, authority as knowledge, authority as experience, authority as the means of finding security and remaining in that security, outwardly or inwardly, because, after all, that is what the mind is always seeking—a place where it can be secure, undisturbed. Such authority may be the self-imposed authority of an idea or the so-called religious idea of God, which has no reality to a religious person. An idea is not a fact, it is a fiction. God is a fiction; you may believe in it, but still it is a fiction. But to find God you must completely destroy the fiction, because the old mind is the mind that is frightened, is ambitious, is fearful of death, of living, and of relationship; and it is always, consciously or unconsciously, seeking a permanency, security.

Free at the Beginning

If we can understand the compulsion behind our desire to dominate or to be dominated, then perhaps we can be free from the crippling effects of authority. We crave to be certain, to be right, to be successful, to know; and this desire for certainty, for permanence, builds up within ourselves the authority of personal experience, while outwardly it creates the authority of society, of the family, of religion, and so on. But merely to ignore authority, to shake off its outward symbols, is of very little significance.

To break away from one tradition and conform to another, to leave this leader and follow that, is but a superficial gesture. If we are to be aware of the whole process of authority, if we are to see the inwardness of it, if we are to understand and transcend the desire for certainty, then we must have extensive awareness and insight, we must be free, not at the end, but at the beginning.

Liberation from Ignorance, from Sorrow

We listen with hope and fear; we seek the light of another but are not alertly passive to be able to understand. If the liberated seems to fulfill our desires we accept him; if not, we continue our search for the one who will; what most of us desire is gratification at different levels. What is important is not how to recognize one who is liberated but how to understand yourself. No authority here or hereafter can give you knowledge of yourself; without self-knowledge there is no liberation from ignorance, from sorrow.

Why Do We Follow?

Why do we accept, why do we follow? We follow another's authority, another's experience and then doubt it; this search for authority and its sequel, disillusionment, is a painful process for most of us. We blame or criticize the once accepted authority, the leader, the teacher, but we do not examine our own craving for an authority who can direct our conduct. Once we understand this craving we shall comprehend the significance of doubt.

Authority Corrupts Both
Leader and Follower

Self-awareness is arduous, and since most of us prefer an easy, illusory way, we bring into being the authority that gives shape and pattern to our life. This authority may be the collective, the State; or it may be the personal, the Master, the savior, the guru. Authority of any kind is blinding, it breeds thoughtlessness; and as most of us find that to be thoughtful is to have pain, we give ourselves over to authority. Authority engenders power, and power always becomes centralized and therefore utterly corrupting; it corrupts not only the wielder of power, but also him who follows it. The authority of knowledge and experience is perverting, whether it be vested in the Master, his representative or the priest. It is your own life, this seemingly endless conflict, that is significant, and not the pattern or the leader. The authority of the Master and the priest takes you away from the central issue, which is the conflict within yourself.

Can I Rely on My Experience?

Most of us are satisfied with authority because it gives us a continuity, a certainty, a sense of being protected. But a man who would understand the implications of this deep psychological revolution must be free of authority, must he not? He cannot look to any authority, whether of his own creation or imposed upon him by another. And is this possible? Is it possible for me not to rely on the authority of my own experience? Even when I have rejected all the outward expressions of authority—books, teachers, priests, churches, beliefs—I still have the feeling that at least I can rely on my own judgment, on my own experiences, on my own analysis. But can I rely on my experience, on my judgment, on my analysis? My experience is the result of my conditioning, just as yours is the result of your conditioning, is it not? I may have been brought up as a Muslim or a Buddhist or a Hindu, and my experience will depend on my cultural, economic, social, and religious background, just as yours will. And can I rely on that? Can I rely for guidance, for hope, for the vision which will give me faith in my own judgment, which again is the result of accumulated memories, experiences, the conditioning of the past meeting the present? . . . Now, when I have put all these questions to myself and I am aware of this problem, I see there can only be one state in which reality, newness, can come into being, which brings about a revolution. That state is when the mind is completely empty of the past, when there is no analyzer, no experience, no judgment, no authority of any kind.

Self-Knowledge Is a Process

So, to understand the innumerable problems that each one of us has, is it not essential that there be self-knowledge? And that is one of the most difficult things, self-awareness—which does not mean an isolation, a withdrawal. Obviously, to know oneself is essential; but to know oneself does not imply a withdrawal from relationship. And it would be a mistake, surely, to think that one can know oneself significantly, completely, fully, through isolation, through exclusion, or by going to some psychologist, or to some priest; or that one can learn self-knowledge through a book. Self-knowledge is obviously a process, not an end in itself; and to know oneself, one must be aware of oneself in action, which is relationship. You discover yourself, not in isolation, not in withdrawal, but in relationship—in relationship to society, to your wife, your husband, your brother, to man; but to discover how you react, what your responses are, requires an extraordinary alertness of mind, a keenness of perception.

The Untethered Mind

The transformation of the world is brought about by the transformation of oneself, because the self is the product and a part of the total process of human existence. To transform oneself, self-knowledge is essential; without knowing what you are, there is no basis for right thought, and without knowing yourself there cannot be transformation. One must know oneself as one is, not as one wishes to be, which is merely an ideal and therefore fictitious, unreal; it is only that *which is* that can be transformed, not that which you wish to be. To know oneself as one is requires an extraordinary alertness of mind, because *what is* is constantly undergoing transformation, change; and to follow it swiftly the mind must not be tethered to any particular dogma or belief, to any particular pattern of action. If you would follow anything, it is no good being tethered. To know yourself, there must be the awareness, the alertness of mind in which there is freedom from all beliefs, from all idealization, because beliefs and ideals only give you a color, perverting true perception. If you want to know what you are, you cannot imagine or have belief in something which you are not. If I am greedy, envious, violent, merely having an ideal of non-violence, of non-greed, is of little value. . . . The understanding of what you are, whatever it be—ugly or beautiful, wicked or mischievous—the understanding of what you are, without distortion, is the beginning of virtue. Virtue is essential, for it gives freedom.

Active Self-Knowledge

Without self-knowledge, experience breeds illusion; with self-knowledge, experience, which is the response to challenge, does not leave a cumulative residue as memory. Self-knowledge is the discovery from moment to moment of the ways of the self, its intentions and pursuit, its thoughts and appetites. There can never be "your experience" and "my experience"; the very term "my experience" indicates ignorance and the acceptance of illusion.

Creativeness Through Self-Knowledge

. . . There is no method for self-knowledge. Seeking a method invariably implies the desire to attain some result—and that is what we all want. We follow authority—if not that of a person, then of a system, of an ideology—because we want a result that will be satisfactory, which will give us security. We really do not want to understand ourselves, our impulses and reactions, the whole process of our thinking, the conscious as well as the unconscious; we would rather pursue a system that assures us of a result. But the pursuit of a system is invariably the outcome of our desire for security, for certainty, and the result is obviously not the understanding of oneself. When we follow a method, we must have authorities—the teacher, the guru, the savior, the Master—who will guarantee us what we desire; and surely that is not the way to self-knowledge.

Authority prevents the understanding of oneself, does it not? Under the shelter of an authority, a guide, you may have temporarily a sense of security, a sense of well-being, but that is not the understanding of the total process of oneself. Authority in its very nature prevents the full awareness of oneself and therefore ultimately destroys freedom; in freedom alone can there be creativeness. There can be creativeness only through self-knowledge.

Quiet Mind, Simple Mind

When we are aware of ourselves, is not the whole movement of living a way of uncovering the "me," the ego, the self? The self is a very complex process that can be uncovered only in relationship, in our daily activities, in the way we talk, the way we judge, calculate, the way we condemn others and ourselves. All that reveals the conditioned state of our own thinking, and is it not important to be aware of this whole process? It is only through awareness of what is true from moment to moment that there is discovery of the timeless, the eternal. Without self-knowledge, the eternal cannot be. When we do not know ourselves, the eternal becomes a mere word, a symbol, a speculation, a dogma, a belief, an illusion to which the mind can escape. But if one begins to understand the "me" in all its various activities from day to day, then in that very understanding, without any effort, the nameless, the timeless comes into being. But the timeless is not a reward for self-knowledge. That which is eternal cannot be sought after; the mind cannot acquire it. It comes into being when the mind is quiet, and the mind can be quiet only when it is simple, when it is no longer storing up, condemning, judging, weighing. It is only the simple mind that can understand the real, not the mind that is full of words, knowledge, information. The mind that analyzes, calculates, is not a simple mind.

Self-Knowing

Without knowing yourself, do what you will, there cannot possibly be the state of meditation. I mean by "self-knowing," knowing every thought, every mood, every word, every feeling; knowing the activity of your mind—not knowing the supreme self, the big self; there is no such thing; the higher self, the atma, is still within the field of thought. Thought is the result of your conditioning, thought is the response of your memory—ancestral or immediate. And merely to try to meditate without first establishing deeply, irrevocably, that virtue which comes about through self-knowing is utterly deceptive and absolutely useless.

Please, it is very important for those who are serious to understand this. Because if you cannot do that, your meditation and actual living are divorced, are apart—so wide apart that though you may meditate, taking postures indefinitely, for the rest of your life, you will not see beyond your nose; any posture you take, anything that you do, will have no meaning whatsoever.

. . . It is important to understand what this self-knowing is, just to be aware, without any choice, of the "me" which has its source in a bundle of memories—just to be conscious of it without interpretation, merely to observe the movement of the mind. But that observation is prevented when you are merely accumulating through observation—what to do, what not to do, what to achieve; if you do that, you put an end to the living process of the movement of the mind as the self. That is, I have to observe and see the fact, the actual, the *what is*. If I approach it with an idea, with an opinion—such as "I must not," or "I must," which are the responses of memory—then the movement of *what is* is hindered, is blocked; and therefore, there is no learning.

Creative Emptiness

Can you not just listen to this as the soil receives the seed and see if the mind is capable of being free, empty? It can be empty only by understanding all its own projections, its own activities, not off and on, but from day to day, from moment to moment. Then you will find the answer, then you will see that the change comes without your asking, that the state of creative emptiness is not a thing to be cultivated—it is there, it comes darkly, without any invitation, and only in that state is there a possibility of renewal, newness, revolution.

Self-Knowledge

Right thinking comes with self-knowledge. Without understanding yourself, you have no basis for thought; without self-knowledge what you think is not true.

You and the world are not two different entities with separate problems; you and the world are one. Your problem is the world's problem. You may be the result of certain tendencies, of environmental influences, but you are not different fundamentally from another. Inwardly we are very much alike; we are all driven by greed, ill will, fear, ambition, and so on. Our beliefs, hopes, aspirations have a common basis. We are one; we are one humanity, though the artificial frontiers of economics and politics and prejudice divide us. If you kill another, you are destroying yourself. You are the center of the whole, and without understanding yourself you cannot understand reality.

We have an intellectual knowledge of this unity but we keep knowledge and feeling in different compartments and hence we never experience the extraordinary unity of man.

Relationship Is a Mirror

Self-knowledge is not according to any formula. You may go to a psychologist or a psychoanalyst to find out about yourself, but that is not self-knowledge. Self-knowledge comes into being when we are aware of ourselves in relationship, which shows what we are from moment to moment. Relationship is a mirror in which to see ourselves as we actually are. But most of us are incapable of looking at ourselves as we are in relationship, because we immediately begin to condemn or justify what we see. We judge, we evaluate, we compare, we deny or accept, but we never observe actually *what is,* and for most people this seems to be the most difficult thing to do; yet this alone is the beginning of self-knowledge. If one is able to see oneself as one is in this extraordinary mirror of relationship, which does not distort, if one can just look into this mirror with full attention and see actually *what is,* be aware of it without condemnation, without judgment, without evaluation—and one does this when there is earnest interest—then one will find that the mind is capable of freeing itself from all conditioning; and it is only then that the mind is free to discover that which lies beyond the field of thought.

After all, however learned or however petty the mind may be, it is consciously or unconsciously limited, conditioned, and any extension of this conditioning is still within the field of thought. So freedom is something entirely different.

◇

FEBRUARY

Becoming

Belief

Action

Good and Evil

◇

Becoming Is Strife

Life as we know it, our daily life, is a process of becoming. I am poor and I act with an end in view, which is to become rich. I am ugly and I want to become beautiful. Therefore my life is a process of becoming something. The will to be is the will to become, at different levels of consciousness, in different states, in which there is challenge, response, naming, and recording. Now, this becoming is strife, this becoming is pain, is it not? It is a constant struggle: I am this, and I want to become that.

All Becoming Is Disintegration

The mind has an idea, perhaps pleasurable, and it wants to be like that idea, which is a projection of your desire. You are this, which you do not like, and you want to become that, which you like. The ideal is a self-projection; the opposite is an extension of *what is;* it is not the opposite at all, but a continuity of *what is,* perhaps somewhat modified. The projection is self-willed, and conflict is the struggle towards the projection. . . . You are struggling to become something, and that something is part of yourself. The ideal is your own projection. See how the mind has played a trick upon itself. You are struggling after words, pursuing your own projection, your own shadow. You are violent, and you are struggling to become nonviolent, the ideal; but the ideal is a projection of *what is,* only under a different name.

When you are aware of this trick that you have played upon yourself, then the false as the false is seen. The struggle towards an illusion is the disintegrating factor. All conflict, all becoming is disintegration. When there is an awareness of this trick that the mind has played upon itself, then there is only *what is.* When the mind is stripped of all becoming, of all ideals, of all comparison and condemnation, when its own structure has collapsed, then the *what is* has undergone complete transformation. As long as there is the naming of *what is,* there is relationship between the mind and *what is;* but when this naming process—which is memory, the very structure of the mind— is not, then *what is* is not. In this transformation alone is there integration.

Can the Crude Mind Become Sensitive?

Listen to the question, to the meaning behind the words. Can the crude mind become sensitive? If I say my mind is crude and I try to become sensitive, the very effort to become sensitive is crudity. Please see this. Don't be intrigued, but watch it. Whereas, if I recognize that I am crude without wanting to change, without trying to become sensitive, if I begin to understand what crudeness is, observe it in my life from day to day—the greedy way I eat, the roughness with which I treat people, the pride, the arrogance, the coarseness of my habits and thoughts—then that very observation transforms *what is.*

Similarly, if I am stupid and I say I must become intelligent, the effort to become intelligent is only a greater form of stupidity; because what is important is to understand stupidity. However much I may try to become intelligent, my stupidity will remain. I may acquire the superficial polish of learning, I may be able to quote books, repeat passages from great authors, but basically I shall still be stupid. But if I see and understand stupidity as it expresses itself in my daily life—how I behave toward my servant, how I regard my neighbor, the poor man, the rich man, the clerk—then that very awareness brings about a breaking up of stupidity.

Opportunities for Self-Expansion

. . . Hierarchical structure offers an excellent opportunity for self-expansion. You may want brotherhood, but how can there be brotherhood if you are pursuing spiritual distinctions? You may smile at worldly titles; but when you admit the Master, the savior, the guru in the realm of the spirit, are you not carrying over the worldly attitude? Can there be hierarchical divisions or degrees in spiritual growth, in the understanding of truth, in the realization of God? Love admits no division. Either you love, or do not love; but do not make the lack of love into a long-drawn-out process whose end is love. When you know you do not love, when you are choicelessly aware of that fact, then there is a possibility of transformation; but to sedulously cultivate this distinction between the Master and the pupil, between those who have attained and those who have not, between the savior and the sinner, is to deny love. The exploiter, who is in turn exploited, finds a happy hunting-ground in this darkness and illusion.

. . . Separation between God or reality and yourself is brought about by you, by the mind that clings to the known, to certainty, to security. This separation cannot be bridged over; there is no ritual, no discipline, no sacrifice that can carry you across it; there is no savior, no Master, no guru who can lead you to the real or destroy this separation. The division is not between the real and yourself; it is in yourself.

. . . What is essential is to understand the increasing conflict of desire; and this understanding comes only through self-knowledge and constant awareness of the movements of the self.

Beyond All Experiencing

Understanding of the self requires a great deal of intelligence, a great deal of watchfulness, alertness, watching ceaselessly, so that it does not slip away. I, who am very earnest, want to dissolve the self. When I say that, I know it is possible to dissolve the self. Please be patient. The moment I say "I want to dissolve this," and in the process I follow for the dissolution of that, there is the experiencing of the self; and so, the self is strengthened. So, how is it possible for the self not to experience? One can see that creation is not at all the experience of the self. Creation is when the self is not there, because creation is not intellectual, is not of the mind, is not self-projected, is something beyond all experiencing, as we know it. Is it possible for the mind to be quite still, in a state of nonrecognition, which is, non-experiencing, to be in a state in which creation can take place—which means, when the self is not there, when the self is absent? Am I making myself clear or not? . . . The problem is this, is it not? Any movement of the mind, positive or negative, is an experience which actually strengthens the "me." Is it possible for the mind not to recognize? That can only take place when there is complete silence, but not the silence which is an experience of the self and which therefore strengthens the self.

What Is the Self?

The search for power, position, authority, ambition, and all the rest are the forms of the self in all its different ways. But what is important is to understand the self and I am sure you and I are convinced of it. If I may add here, let us be earnest about this matter; because I feel that if you and I as individuals, not as a group of people belonging to certain classes, certain societies, certain climatic divisions, can understand this and act upon this, then I think there will be real revolution. The moment it becomes universal and better organized, the self takes shelter in that; whereas, if you and I as individuals can love, can carry this out actually in everyday life, then the revolution that is so essential will come into being . . . .

You know what I mean by the self? By that, I mean the idea, the memory, the conclusion, the experience, the various forms of namable and unnamable intentions, the conscious endeavor to be or not to be, the accumulated memory of the unconscious, the racial, the group, the individual, the clan, and the whole of it all, whether it is projected outwardly in action, or projected spiritually as virtue; the striving after all this is the self. In it is included the competition, the desire to be. The whole process of that is the self; and we know actually when we are faced with it, that it is an evil thing. I am using the word *evil* intentionally, because the self is dividing; the self is self-enclosing; its activities, however noble, are separated and isolated. We know all this. We also know that extraordinary are the moments when the self is not there, in which there is no sense of endeavor, of effort, and which happens when there is love.

When There Is Love, Self Is Not

Reality, truth, is not to be recognized. For truth to come, belief, knowledge, experiencing, virtue, pursuit of virtue—which is different from being virtuous—all this must go. The virtuous person who is conscious of pursuing virtue can never find reality. He may be a very decent person; that is entirely different from the man of truth, from the man who understands. To the man of truth, truth has come into being. A virtuous man is a righteous man, and a righteous man can never understand what is truth; because virtue to him is the covering of the self, the strengthening of the self; because he is pursuing virtue. When he says, "I must be without greed," the state in which he is nongreedy and which he experiences, strengthens the self. That is why it is so important to be poor, not only in the things of the world, but also in belief and in knowledge. A man rich with worldly riches, or a man rich in knowledge and belief, will never know anything but darkness, and will be the center of all mischief and misery. But if you and I, as individuals, can see this whole working of the self, then we shall know what love is. I assure you that is the only reformation which can possibly change the world. Love is not the self. Self cannot recognize love. You say, "I love," but then, in the very saying of it, in the very experiencing of it, love is not. But, when you know love, self is not. When there is love, self is not.

Understanding What Is

Surely, a man who is understanding life does not want beliefs. A man who loves has no beliefs—he loves. It is the man who is consumed by the intellect who has beliefs, because intellect is always seeking security, protection; it is always avoiding danger, and therefore it builds ideas, beliefs, ideals, behind which it can take shelter. What would happen if you dealt with violence directly, now? You would be a danger to society; and because the mind foresees the danger, it says, "I will achieve the ideal of nonviolence ten years later"—which is such a fictitious, false process . . . To understand *what is* is more important than to create and follow ideals because ideals are false, and *what is* is the real. To understand *what is* requires an enormous capacity, a swift and unprejudiced mind. It is because we don't want to face and understand *what is* that we invent the many ways of escape and give them lovely names as the ideal, the belief, God. Surely, it is only when I see the false as the false that my mind is capable of perceiving what is true. A mind that is confused in the false can never find the truth. Therefore, I must understand what is false in my relationships, in my ideas, in the things about me, because to perceive the truth requires the understanding of the false. Without removing the causes of ignorance, there cannot be enlightenment; and to seek enlightenment when the mind is un-enlightened is utterly empty, meaningless. Therefore, I must begin to see the false in my relationships with ideas, with people, with things. When the mind sees that which is false, then that which is true comes into being and then there is ecstasy, there is happiness.

What We Believe

Does belief give enthusiasm? Can enthusiasm sustain itself without a belief, and is enthusiasm at all necessary, or is a different kind of energy needed, a different kind of vitality, drive? Most of us have enthusiasm for something or other. We are very keen, very enthusiastic about concerts, about physical exercise, or about going to a picnic. Unless it is nourished all the time by something or other, it fades away and we have a new enthusiasm for other things. Is there a self-sustaining force, energy, which doesn't depend on a belief?

The other question is: Do we need a belief of any kind, and if we do, why is it necessary? That's one of the problems involved. We don't need a belief that there is sunshine, the mountains, the rivers. We don't need a belief that we and our wives quarrel. We don't have to have a belief that life is a terrible misery with its anguish, conflict, and constant ambition; it is a fact. But we demand a belief when we want to escape from a fact into an unreality.

Agitated by Belief

So, your religion, your belief in God, is an escape from actuality, and therefore it is no religion at all. The rich man who accumulates money through cruelty, through dishonesty, through cunning exploitation believes in God; and you also believe in God, you also are cunning, cruel, suspicious, envious. Is God to be found through dishonesty, through deceit, through cunning tricks of the mind? Because you collect all the sacred books and the various symbols of God, does that indicate that you are a religious person? So, religion is not escape from the fact; religion is the understanding of the fact of what you are in your everyday relationships; religion is the manner of your speech, the way you talk, the way you address your servants, the way you treat your wife, your children, and neighbors. As long as you do not understand your relationship with your neighbor, with society, with your wife and children, there must be confusion; and whatever it does, the mind that is confused will only create more confusion, more problems and conflict. A mind that escapes from the actual, from the facts of relationship, shall never find God; a mind that is agitated by belief shall not know truth. But the mind that understands its relationship with property, with people, with ideas, the mind which no longer struggles with the problems which relationship creates, and for which the solution is not withdrawal but the understanding of love—such a mind alone can understand reality.

Beyond Belief

We realize that life is ugly, painful, sorrowful; we want some kind of theory, some kind of speculation or satisfaction, some kind of doctrine, which will explain all this, and so we are caught in explanation, in words, in theories, and gradually beliefs become deeply rooted and unshakable because behind those beliefs, behind those dogmas, there is the constant fear of the unknown. But we never look at that fear; we turn away from it. The stronger the beliefs, the stronger the dogmas. And when we examine these beliefs—the Christian, the Hindu, the Buddhist—we find that they divide people. Each dogma, each belief has a series of rituals, a series of compulsions which bind man and separate man. So, we start with an inquiry to find out what is true, what the significance is of this misery, this struggle, this pain; and we are soon caught up in beliefs, in rituals, in theories.

Belief is corruption because behind belief and morality lurks the mind, the self—the self growing big, powerful and strong. We consider belief in God, the belief in something, as religion. We consider that to believe is to be religious. You understand? If you do not believe, you will be considered an atheist, you will be condemned by society. One society will condemn those who believe in God, and another society will condemn those who do not. They are both the same. So, religion becomes a matter of belief—and belief acts and has a corresponding influence on the mind; the mind then can never be free. But it is only in freedom that you can find out what is true, what is God, not through any belief, because your very belief projects what you think ought to be God, what you think ought to be true.

The Screen of Belief

You believe in God, and another does not believe in God, so your beliefs separate you from each other. Belief throughout the world is organized as Hinduism, Buddhism, or Christianity, and so it divides man from man. We are confused, and we think that through belief we shall clear the confusion; that is, belief is superimposed on the confusion, and we hope that confusion will thereby be cleared away. But belief is merely an escape from the fact of confusion; it does not help us to face and to understand the fact but to run away from the confusion in which we are. To understand the confusion, belief is not necessary, and belief only acts as a screen between ourselves and our problems. So, religion, which is organized belief, becomes a means of escape from *what is,* from the fact of confusion. The man who believes in God, the man who believes in the hereafter, or who has any other form of belief, is escaping from the fact of what he is. Do you not know those who believe in God, who do *puja,* who repeat certain chants and words, and who in their daily life are dominating, cruel, ambitious, cheating, dishonest? Shall they find God? Are they really seeking God? Is God to be found through repetition of words, through belief? But such people believe in God, they worship God, they go to the temple every day, they do everything to avoid the fact of what they are—and such people you consider respectable because they are yourself.

Meeting Life Anew

One of the things, it seems to me, that most of us eagerly accept and take for granted is the question of beliefs. I am not attacking beliefs. What we are trying to do is to find out why we accept beliefs; and if we can understand the motives, the causation of acceptance, then perhaps we may be able not only to understand why we do it, but also be free of it. One can see how political and religious beliefs, national and various other types of beliefs, do separate people, do create conflict, confusion, and antagonism—which is an obvious fact; and yet we are unwilling to give them up. There is the Hindu belief, the Christian belief, the Buddhist—innumerable sectarian and national beliefs, various political ideologies, all contending with one another, trying to convert one another. One can see, obviously, that belief is separating people, creating intolerance; is it possible to live without belief? One can find that out only if one can study oneself in relationship to a belief. Is it possible to live in this world without a belief—not change beliefs, not substitute one belief for another, but be entirely free from *all* beliefs, so that one meets life anew each minute? This, after all, is the truth: to have the capacity of meeting everything anew, from moment to moment, without the conditioning reaction of the past, so that there is not the cumulative effect which acts as a barrier between oneself and that *which is*.

Belief Hinders True Understanding

If we had no belief, what would happen to us? Shouldn't we be very frightened of what might happen? If we had no pattern of action, based on a belief—either in God, or in communism, or in socialism, or in imperialism, or in some kind of religious formula, some dogma in which we are conditioned—we should feel utterly lost, shouldn't we? And is not this acceptance of a belief the covering up of that fear—the fear of being really nothing, of being empty? After all, a cup is useful only when it is empty; and a mind that is filled with beliefs, with dogmas, with assertions, with quotations, is really an uncreative mind; it is merely a repetitive mind. To escape from that fear—that fear of emptiness, that fear of loneliness, that fear of stagnation, of not arriving, not succeeding, not achieving, not being something, not becoming something—is surely one of the reasons, is it not, why we accept beliefs so eagerly and greedily? And, through acceptance of belief, do we understand ourselves? On the contrary. A belief, religious or political, obviously hinders the understanding of ourselves. It acts as a screen through which we look at ourselves. And can we look at ourselves without beliefs? If we remove these beliefs, the many beliefs that one has, is there anything left to look at? If we have no beliefs with which the mind has identified itself, then the mind, without identification, is capable of looking at itself as it is—and then, surely there is the beginning of the understanding of oneself.

 FEBRUARY 14

Direct Observation

Why do ideas take root in our minds? Why do not facts become all-important—not ideas? Why do theories, ideas, become so significant rather than the fact? Is it that we cannot understand the fact, or have not the capacity, or are afraid of facing the fact? Therefore, ideas, speculations, theories are a means of escaping away from the fact . . .

You may run away, you may do all kinds of things; the facts are there—the fact that one is angry, the fact that one is ambitious, the fact that one is sexual, a dozen things. You may suppress them; you may transmute them, which is another form of suppression; you may control them, but they are all suppressed, controlled, disciplined with ideas. . . . Do not ideas waste our energy? Do not ideas dull the mind? You may be clever in speculation, in quotations; but it is obviously a dull mind that quotes, that has read a lot and quotes.

. . . You remove the conflict of the opposite in one stroke if you live with the fact and therefore liberate the energy to face the fact. For most of us, contradiction is an extraordinary field in which the mind is caught. I want to do this, and I do something entirely different; but if I face the fact of wanting to do this, there is no contradiction; and therefore, at one stroke I abolish altogether all sense of the opposite, and my mind then is completely concerned with *what is,* and with the understanding of *what is.*

Action Without Idea

It is only when the mind is free from idea that there can be experiencing. Ideas are not truth; and truth is something that must be experienced directly, from moment to moment. It is not an experience which you want—which is then merely sensation. Only when one can go beyond the bundle of ideas—which is the "me," which is the mind, which has a partial or complete continuity—only when one can go beyond that, when thought is completely silent, is there a state of experiencing. Then one shall know what truth is.

Action Without the Process of Thought

What do we mean by idea? Surely idea is the process of thought. Is it not? Idea is a process of mentation, of thinking; and thinking is always a reaction either of the conscious or of the unconscious. Thinking is a process of verbalization, which is the result of memory; thinking is a process of time. So, when action is based on the process of thinking, such action must inevitably be conditioned, isolated. Idea must oppose idea, idea must be dominated by idea. There is a gap then between action and idea. What we are trying to find out is whether it is possible for action to be without idea. We see how idea separates people. As I have already explained, knowledge and belief are essentially separating qualities. Beliefs never bind people; they always separate people; when action is based on belief or an idea or an ideal, such an action must inevitably be isolated, fragmented. Is it possible to act without the process of thought, thought being a process of time, a process of calculation, a process of self-protection, a process of belief, denial, condemnation, justification. Surely, it must have occurred to you as it has to me, whether action is at all possible without idea.

Do Ideas Limit Action?

Can ideas ever produce action, or do ideas merely mold thought and therefore limit action? When action is compelled by an idea, action can never liberate man. It is extraordinarily important for us to understand this point. If an idea shapes action, then action can never bring about the solution to our miseries because, before it can be put into action, we have first to discover how the idea comes into being.

Ideology Prevents Action

The world is always close to catastrophe. But it seems to be closer now. Seeing this approaching catastrophe, most of us take shelter in idea. We think that this catastrophe, this crisis, can be solved by an ideology. Ideology is always an impediment to direct relationship, which prevents action. We want peace only as an idea, but not as an actuality. We want peace on the verbal level, which is only on the thinking level, though we proudly call it the intellectual level. But the word *peace* is not peace. Peace can only be when the confusion which you and another make ceases. We are attached to the world of ideas and not to peace. We search for new social and political patterns and not for peace; we are concerned with the reconciliation of effects and not in putting aside the cause of war. This search will bring only answers conditioned by the past. This conditioning is what we call knowledge, experience; and the new changing facts are translated, interpreted, according to this knowledge. So, there is conflict between *what is* and the experience that has been. The past, which is knowledge, must ever be in conflict with the fact, which is ever in the present. So, this will not solve the problem but will perpetuate the conditions that have created the problem.

Action Without Ideation

The idea is the result of the thought process, the thought process is the response of memory, and memory is always conditioned. Memory is always in the past, and that memory is given life in the present by a challenge. Memory has no life in itself; it comes to life in the present when confronted by a challenge. And all memory, whether dormant or active, is conditioned, is it not? Therefore there has to be quite a different approach. You have to find out for yourself, inwardly, whether you are acting on an idea, and if there can be action without ideation.

Acting Without
Idea Is the Way of Love

Thought must always be limited by the thinker who is conditioned; the thinker is always conditioned and is never free; if thought occurs, immediately idea follows. Idea in order to act is bound to create more confusion. Knowing all this, is it possible to act without idea? Yes, it is the way of love. Love is not an idea; it is not a sensation; it is not a memory; it is not a feeling of postponement, a self-protective device. We can only be aware of the way of love when we understand the whole process of idea. Now, is it possible to abandon the other ways and know the way of love, which is the only redemption? No other way, political or religious, will solve the problem. This is not a theory which you will have to think over and adopt in your life; it must be actual. . .

. . . When you love, is there idea? Do not accept it; just look at it, examine it, go into it profoundly; because every other way we have tried, and there is no answer to misery. Politicians may promise it; the so-called religious organizations may promise future happiness; but we have not got it now, and the future is relatively unimportant when I am hungry. We have tried every other way; and we can only know the way of love if we know the way of idea and abandon idea, which is to act.

Conflict of the Opposites

I wonder if there is such a thing as evil? Please give your attention, go with me, let us inquire together. We say there is good and evil. There is envy and love, and we say that envy is evil and love is good. Why do we divide life, calling this good and that bad, thereby creating the conflict of the opposites? Not that there is not envy, hate, brutality in the human mind and heart, an absence of compassion, love, but why do we divide life into the thing called good and the thing called evil? Is there not actually only one thing, which is a mind that is inattentive? Surely, when there is complete attention, that is, when the mind is totally aware, alert, watchful, there is no such thing as evil or good; there is only an awakened state. Goodness then is not a quality, not a virtue, it is a state of love. When there is love, there is neither good nor bad, there is only love. When you really love somebody, you are not thinking of good or bad, your whole being is filled with that love. It is only when there is the cessation of complete attention, of love, that there comes the conflict between what I am and what I should be. Then that which I am is evil, and that which I should be is the so-called good.

. . . You watch your own mind and you will see that the moment the mind ceases to think in terms of becoming something, there is a cessation of action which is not stagnation; it is a state of total attention, which is goodness.

Beyond Duality

Are you not aware of it? Are not its actions obvious, its sorrow crushing? Who has created it but each one of us? Who is responsible for it but each one of us? As we have created good, however little, so we have created evil, however vast. Good and evil are part of us and are also independent of us. When we think-feel narrowly, enviously, with greed and hate, we are adding to the evil which turns and rends us. This problem of good and evil, this conflicting problem, is always with us as we are creating it. It has become part of us, this wanting and not wanting, loving and hating, craving and renouncing. We are continually creating this duality in which thought-feeling is caught up. Thought-feeling can go beyond and above good and its opposite only when it understands its cause—craving. In understanding merit and demerit there is freedom from both. Opposites cannot be fused and they are to be transcended through the dissolution of craving. Each opposite must be thought out, felt out, as extensively and deeply as possible, through all the layers of consciousness. Through this thinking out, feeling out, a new comprehension is awakened, which is not the product of craving or of time.

There is evil in the world to which we are contributing as we contribute to the good. Man seems to unite more in hate than in good. A wise man realizes the cause of evil and good, and through understanding frees thought-feeling from it.

Justifying Evil

Obviously the present crisis throughout the world is exceptional, without precedent. There have been crises of varying types at different periods throughout history—social, national, political. Crises come and go; economic recessions, depressions, come, get modified, and continue in a different form. We know that; we are familiar with that process. Surely the present crisis is different, is it not? It is different first because we are dealing not with money nor with tangible things but with ideas. The crisis is exceptional because it is in the field of ideation. We are quarreling with ideas, we are justifying murder; everywhere in the world we are justifying murder as a means to a righteous end, which in itself is unprecedented. Before, evil was recognized to be evil, murder was recognized to be murder, but now murder is a means to achieve a noble result. Murder, whether of one person or of a group of people, is justified, because the murderer, or the group that the murderer represents, justifies it as a means of achieving a result that will be beneficial to man. That is, we sacrifice the present for the future—and it does not matter what means we employ as long as our declared purpose is to produce a result that we say will be beneficial to man. Therefore, the implication is that a wrong means will produce a right end and you justify the wrong means through ideation . . . We have a magnificent structure of ideas to justify evil and surely that is unprecedented. Evil is evil; it cannot bring about good. War is not a means to peace.

Goodness Has No Motive

If I have a motive to be good, does that bring about goodness? Or is goodness something entirely devoid of this urge to be good, which is ever based on a motive? Is good the opposite of bad, the opposite of evil? Every opposite contains the seed of its own opposite, does it not? There is greed, and there is the ideal of nongreed. When the mind pursues nongreed, when it tries to be nongreedy, it is still greedy because it wants to be something. Greed implies desiring, acquiring, expanding; and when the mind sees that it does not pay to be greedy, it wants to be nongreedy, so the motive is still the same, which is to be or to acquire something. When the mind wants not to want, the root of want, of desire, is still there. So goodness is not the opposite of evil; it is a totally different state. And what is that state?

Obviously, goodness has no motive because all motive is based on the self; it is the egocentric movement of the mind. So what do we mean by goodness? Surely, there is goodness only when there is total. Attention has no motive. When there is a motive for attention, is there attention? If I pay attention in order to acquire something, the acquisition, whether it be good or bad, is not attention—it is a distraction. A division. There can be goodness only when there is a totality of attention in which there is no effort to be or not to be.

Human Evolution

Must we know drunkenness to know sobriety? Must you go through hate in order to know what it is to be compassionate? Must you go through wars, destroying yourself and others, to know what peace is? Surely, this is an utterly false way of thinking, is it not? First you assume that there is evolution, growth, a moving from bad to good, and then you fit your thinking into that pattern. Obviously, there is physical growth, the little plant becoming the big tree; there is technological progress, the wheel evolving through centuries into the jet plane. But is there psychological progress, evolution? That is what we are discussing—whether there is a growth, an evolution of the "me," beginning with evil and ending up in good. Through a process of evolution, through time, can the "me," which is the center of evil, ever become noble, good? Obviously not. That which is evil, the psychological "me," will always remain evil. But we do not want to face that. We think that through the process of time, through growth and change, the "I" will ultimately become reality. This is our hope, that is our longing—that the "I" will be made perfect through time. What is this "I," this "me"? It is a name, a form, a bundle of memories, hopes, frustrations, longings, pains, sorrows, passing joys. We want this "me" to continue and become perfect, and so we say that beyond the "me" there is a "super-me," a higher self, a spiritual entity which is timeless, but since we have thought of it, that "spiritual" entity is still within the field of time, is it not? If we can think about it, it is obviously within the field of our reasoning.

 FEBRUARY 26

Freedom from Occupation

Can the mind be free from the past, free from thought—not from the good or bad thought? How do I find out? I can only find out by seeing what the mind is occupied with. If my mind is occupied with the good or occupied with the bad, then it is only concerned with the past, it is occupied with the past. It is not free of the past. So, what is important is to find out how the mind is occupied. If it is occupied at all, it is always occupied with the past because all our consciousness is the past. The past is not only on the surface but on the highest level, and the stress on the unconscious is also the past. . . .

Can the mind be free from occupation? This means—can the mind be completely without being occupied and let memory, the thoughts good and bad, go by without choosing? The moment the mind is occupied with one thought, good or bad, then it is concerned with the past. . . . If you really listen—not just merely verbally, but really profoundly—then you will see that there is stability that is not of the mind, that is the freedom from the past.

Yet, the past can never be put aside. There is a watching of the past as it goes by, but not occupation with the past. So the mind is free to observe and not to choose. Where there is choice in this movement of the river of memory, there is occupation; and the moment the mind is occupied, it is caught in the past; and when the mind is occupied with the past, it is incapable of seeing something real, true, new, original, uncontaminated.

Thinking Begets Effort

"How can I remain free from evil thoughts, evil and wayward thoughts?" Is there the thinker, the one apart from thought, apart from the evil, wayward thoughts? Please watch your own mind. We say, "There is the *I*, the *me* that says, 'This is a wayward thought,' 'This is bad,' 'I must control this thought,' 'I must keep to this thought.'" That is what we know. Is the one, the *I*, the thinker, the judger, the one that judges, the censor, different from all this? Is the *I* different from thought, different from envy, different from evil? The *I* which says that it is different from this evil is everlastingly trying to overcome me, trying to push me away, trying to become something. So you have this struggle, the effort to put away thoughts, not to be wayward.

We have, in the very process of thinking, created this problem of effort. Do you follow? Then you give birth to discipline, controlling thought—the *I* controlling the thought which is not good, the *I* who is trying to become nonenvious, nonviolent, to be this and to be that. So you have brought into being the very process of effort when there is the *I* and the thing that it is controlling. That is the actual fact of our everyday existence.

◇

MARCH

Dependence

Attachment

Relationship

Fear

◇

A Free Mind Has Humility

Have you ever gone into the question of psychological dependence? If you go into it very deeply, you will find that most of us are terribly lonely. Most of us have such shallow, empty minds. Most of us do not know what love means. So, out of that loneliness, out of that insufficiency, out of the privation of life, we are attached to something, attached to the family; we depend upon it. And when the wife or the husband turns away from us, we are jealous. Jealousy is not love; but the love which society acknowledges in the family is made respectable. That is another form of defense, another form of escape from ourselves. So every form of resistance breeds dependence. And a mind that is dependent can never be free.

You need to be free, because you will see that a mind that is free has the essence of humility. Such a mind, which is free and therefore has humility, can learn—not a mind that resists. Learning is an extraordinary thing—to learn, not to accumulate knowledge. Accumulating knowledge is quite a different thing. What we call knowledge is comparatively easy, because that is a movement from the known to the known. But to learn is a movement from the known to the unknown—you learn only like that, do you not?

We Never Question
the Problem of Dependence

Why do we depend? Psychologically, inwardly, we depend on a belief, on a system, on a philosophy; we ask another for a mode of conduct; we seek teachers who will give us a way of life which will lead us to some hope, some happiness. So we are always, are we not, searching for some kind of dependence, security. Is it possible for the mind ever to free itself from this sense of dependence? Which does not mean that the mind must achieve independence—that is only the reaction to dependence. We are not talking of independence, of freedom from a particular state. If we can inquire without the reaction of seeking freedom from a particular state of dependence, then we can go much more deeply into it. . . . We accept the necessity for dependence; we say it is inevitable. We have never questioned the whole issue at all, why each one of us seeks some kind of dependence. Is it not that we really, deep down, demand security, permanency? Being in a state of confusion, we want someone to get us out of that confusion. So, we are always concerned with how to escape or avoid the state in which we are. In the process of avoiding that state, we are bound to create some kind of dependence, which becomes our authority. If we depend on another for our security, for our inward well-being, there arise out of that dependence innumerable problems, and then we try to solve those problems—the problems of attachment. But we never question, we never go into the problem of dependence itself. Perhaps if we can really intelligently, with full awareness, go into this problem, then we may find that dependence is not the issue at all—that it is only a way of escaping from a deeper fact.

There Is Some Deeper Factor
That Makes Us Depend

We know we depend—on our relationship with people or on some idea or on a system of thought. Why?

. . . Actually, I do not think dependence is the problem; I think there is some other deeper factor that makes us depend. And if we can unravel that, then both dependence and the struggle for freedom will have very little significance; then all the problems which arise through dependence will wither away. So, what is the deeper issue? Is it that the mind abhors, fears, the idea of being alone? And does the mind know that state which it avoids? So long as that loneliness is not really understood, felt, penetrated, dissolved—whatever word you may like to use—so long as that sense of loneliness remains, dependence is inevitable, and one can never be free; one can never find out for oneself that which is true, that which is religion.

Become Deeply Aware

Dependence sets going the movement of aloofness and attachment, a constant conflict without comprehension, without a release. You must become aware of the process of attachment and dependence, become aware of it without condemnation, without judgment, and then you will perceive the significance of this conflict of opposites. If you become deeply aware and consciously direct thought to comprehend the full meaning of need, of dependence, your conscious mind will be open and clear about it; and then the subconscious, with its hidden motives, pursuits, and intentions, will project itself into the conscious. When this happens, you must study and understand each intimation of the subconscious. If you do this many times, becoming aware of the projections of the subconscious after the conscious has thought out the problem as clearly as possible, then, even though you give your attention to other matters, the conscious and the subconscious will work out the problem of dependence, or any other problem. Thus, there is established a constant awareness, which will patiently and gently bring about integration; and if your health and diet are all right, this will in turn bring about fullness of being.

Relationship

Relationship based on mutual need brings only conflict. However interdependent we are on each other, we are using each other for a purpose, for an end. With an end in view, relationship is not. You may use me and I may use you. In this usage, we lose contact. A society based on mutual usage is the foundation of violence. When we use another, we have only the picture of the end to be gained. The end, the gain, prevents relationship, communion. In the usage of another, however gratifying and comforting it may be, there is always fear. To avoid this fear, we must possess. From this possession there arises envy, suspicion, and constant conflict. Such a relationship can never bring about happiness.

A society whose structure is based on mere need, whether physiological or psychological, must breed conflict, confusion, and misery. Society is the projection of yourself in relation with another, in which the need and the use are predominant. When you use another for your need, physically or psychologically, in actuality there is no relationship at all; you really have no contact with the other, no communion with the other. How can you have communion with the other when the other is used as a piece of furniture, for your convenience and comfort? So, it is essential to understand the significance of relationship in daily life.

The "Me" Is the Possession

Renunciation, self-sacrifice, is not a gesture of greatness, to be praised and copied. We possess because without possession we are not. Possessions are many and varied. One who possesses no worldly things may be attached to knowledge, to ideas; another may be attached to virtue, another to experience, another to name and fame, and so on. Without possessions, the "me" is not; the "me" *is* the possession, the furniture, the virtue, the name. In its fear of not being, the mind is attached to name, to furniture, to value; and it will drop these in order to be at a higher level, the higher being the more gratifying, the more permanent. The fear of uncertainty, of not being, makes for attachment, for possession. When the possession is unsatisfactory or painful, we renounce it for a more pleasurable attachment. The ultimate gratifying possession is the word *God,* or its substitute, the State.

. . . So long as you are unwilling to be nothing, which in fact you are, you must inevitably breed sorrow and antagonism. The willingness to be nothing is not a matter of renunciation, of enforcement, inner or outer, but of seeing the truth of *what is*. Seeing the truth of *what is* brings freedom from the fear of insecurity, the fear which breeds attachment and leads to the illusion of detachment, renunciation. The love of *what is* is the beginning of wisdom. Love alone shares, it alone can commune; but renunciation and self-sacrifice are the ways of isolation and illusion.

To Exploit Is to Be Exploited

As most of us seek power in one form or another, the hierarchical principle is established, the novice and the initiate, the pupil and the Master, and even among the Masters there are degrees of spiritual growth. Most of us love to exploit and be exploited, and this system offers the means, whether hidden or open. To exploit is to be exploited. The desire to use others for your psychological necessities makes for dependence, and when you depend you must hold, possess; and what you possess possesses you. Without dependence, subtle or gross, without possessing things, people, and ideas, you are empty, a thing of no importance. You want to be something, and to avoid the gnawing fear of being nothing you belong to this or that organization, to this or that ideology, to this church or that temple; so you are exploited, and you in your turn exploit.

The Cultivation of Detachment

There is only attachment; there is no such thing as detachment. The mind invents detachment as a reaction to the pain of attachment. When you react to attachment by becoming "detached," you are attached to something else. So that whole process is one of attachment. You are attached to your wife or your husband, to your children, to ideas, to tradition, to authority, and so on; and your reaction to that attachment is detachment. The cultivation of detachment is the outcome of sorrow, pain. You want to escape from the pain of attachment, and your escape is to find something to which you think you can be attached. So there is only attachment, and it is a stupid mind that cultivates detachment. All the books say, "Be detached," but what is the truth of the matter? If you observe your own mind, you will see an extraordinary thing—that through cultivating detachment, your mind is becoming attached to something else.

Attachment Is Self-Deception

We are the things we possess, we are that to which we are attached. Attachment has no nobility. Attachment to knowledge is not different from any other gratifying addiction. Attachment is self-absorption, whether at the lowest or at the highest level. Attachment is self-deception, it is an escape from the hollowness of the self. The things to which we are attached—property, people, ideas—become all-important, for without the many things which fill its emptiness, the self is not. The fear of not being makes for possession; and fear breeds illusion, the bondage to conclusions. Conclusions, material or ideational, prevent the fruition of intelligence, the freedom in which alone reality can come into being; and without this freedom, cunning is taken for intelligence. The ways of cunning are always complex and destructive. It is this self-protective cunning that makes for attachment; and when attachment causes pain, it is this same cunning that seeks detachment and finds pleasure in the pride and vanity of renunciation. The understanding of the ways of cunning, the ways of the self, is the beginning of intelligence.

Face the Fact and
See What Happens . . .

We have all had the experience of tremendous loneliness, where books, religion, everything is gone and we are tremendously, inwardly, lonely, empty. Most of us can't face that emptiness, that loneliness, and we run away from it. Dependence is one of the things we run to, depend on, because we can't stand being alone with ourselves. We must have the radio or books or talking, incessant chatter about this and that, about art and culture. So we come to that point when we know there is this extraordinary sense of self-isolation. We may have a very good job, work furiously, write books, but inwardly there is this tremendous vacuum. We want to fill that and dependence is one of the ways. We use dependence, amusement, church work, religions, drink, women, a dozen things to fill it up, cover it up. If we see that it is absolutely futile to try to cover it up, completely futile—not verbally, not with conviction and therefore agreement and determination—but if we see the total absurdity of it . . . then we are faced with a fact. It is not a question of how to be free from dependence; that's not a fact; that's only a reaction to a fact. . . . Why don't I face the fact and see what happens?

The problem now arises of the observer and the observed. The observer says, "I am empty; I don't like it," and runs away from it. The observer says, "I am different from the emptiness." But the observer is the emptiness; it is not emptiness seen by an observer. The observer is the observed. There is a tremendous revolution in thinking, in feeling, when that takes place.

Attachment Is Escape

Just try to be aware of your conditioning. You can only know it indirectly, in relation to something else. You cannot be aware of your conditioning as an abstraction, for then it is merely verbal, without much significance. We are only aware of conflict. Conflict exists when there is no integration between challenge and response. This conflict is the result of our conditioning. Conditioning is attachment: attachment to work, to tradition, to property, to people, to ideas, and so on. If there were no attachment, would there be conditioning? Of course not. So why are we attached? I am attached to my country because through identification with it I become somebody. I identify myself with my work, and the work becomes important. I am my family, my property; I am attached to them. The object of attachment offers me the means of escape from my own emptiness. Attachment is escape, and it is escape that strengthens conditioning.

To Be Alone

To be alone, which is not a philosophy of loneliness, is obviously to be in a state of revolution against the whole setup of society—not only this society, but the communist society, the fascist, every form of society as organized brutality, organized power. And that means an extraordinary perception of the effects of power. Sir, have you noticed those soldiers rehearsing? They are not human beings any more, they are machines, they are your sons and my sons, standing there in the sun. This is happening here, in America, in Russia, and everywhere—not only at the governmental level, but also at the monastic level, belonging to monasteries, to orders, to groups who employ astonishing power. And it is only the mind which does not belong that can be alone. And aloneness is not something to be cultivated. You see this? When you see all this, you are out, and no governor or president is going to invite you to dinner. Out of that aloneness there is humility. It is this aloneness that knows love—not power. The ambitious man, religious or ordinary, will never know what love is. So, if one sees all this, then one has this quality of total living and therefore total action. This comes through self-knowledge.

Craving Is Always Craving

To avoid suffering we cultivate detachment. Being fore-warned that attachment sooner or later entails sorrow, we want to become detached. Attachment is gratifying, but perceiving the pain in it, we want to be gratified in another manner, through detachment. Detachment is the same as attachment as long as it yields gratification. So what we are really seeking is gratification; we crave to be satisfied by whatever means.

We are dependent or attached because it gives us plea-sure, security, power, a sense of well-being, though in it there is sorrow and fear. We seek detachment also for pleasure, in order not to be hurt, not to be inwardly wounded. Our search is for pleasure, gratification. Without condemning or justifying we must try to understand this process, for unless we understand it there is no way out of our confusion and contradiction. Can craving ever be satisfied, or is it a bottomless pit? Whether we crave for the low or for the high, craving is always craving, a burning fire, and what can be consumed by it soon becomes ashes; but craving for gratification still remains, ever burning, ever consuming, and there is no end to it. Attachment and de-tachment are equally binding, and both must be transcended.

Intensity Free of All Attachment

In the state of passion without a cause, there is intensity free of all attachment; but when passion has a cause, there is attachment, and attachment is the beginning of sorrow. Most of us are attached; we cling to a person, to a country, to a belief, to an idea, and when the object of our attachment is taken away or otherwise loses its significance, we find ourselves empty, insufficient. This emptiness we try to fill by clinging to something else, which again becomes the object of our passion.

Relationship Is a Mirror

Surely, only in relationship the process of what I am unfolds, does it not? Relationship is a mirror in which I see myself as I am; but as most of us do not like what we are, we begin to discipline, either positively or negatively, what we perceive in the mirror of relationship. That is, I discover something in relationship, in the action of relationship, and I do not like it. So, I begin to modify what I do not like, what I perceive as being unpleasant. I want to change it—which means I already have a pattern of what I should be. The moment there is a pattern of what I should be, there is no comprehension of what I am. The moment I have a picture of what I want to be, or what I should be, or what I ought not to be—a standard according to which I want to change myself—then, surely, there is no comprehension of what I am at the moment of relationship.

I think it is really important to understand this, for I think this is where most of us go astray. We do not want to know what we actually are at a given moment in relationship. If we are concerned merely with self-improvement, there is no comprehension of ourselves, of *what is*.

The Function of Relationship

Relationship is inevitably painful, which is shown in our everyday existence. If in relationship there is no tension, it ceases to be relationship and merely becomes a comfortable sleep-state, an opiate—which most people want and prefer. Conflict is between this craving for comfort and the factual, between illusion and actuality. If you recognize the illusion then you can, by putting it aside, give your attention to the understanding of relationship. But if you seek security in relationship, it becomes an investment in comfort, in illusion—and the greatness of relationship is its very insecurity. By seeking security in relationship you are hindering its function, which brings its own peculiar actions and misfortunes.

Surely, the function of relationship is to reveal the state of one's whole being. Relationship is a process of self-revelation, of self-knowledge. This self-revelation is painful, demanding constant adjustment, pliability of thought-emotion. It is a painful struggle, with periods of enlightened peace . . .

But most of us avoid or put aside the tension in relationship, preferring the ease and comfort of satisfying dependency, an unchallenged security, a safe anchorage. Then family and other relationships become a refuge, the refuge of the thoughtless.

When insecurity creeps into dependency, as it inevitably does, then that particular relationship is cast aside and a new one taken on in the hope of finding lasting security; but there is no security in relationship, and dependency only breeds fear. Without understanding the process of security and fear, relationship becomes a binding hindrance, a way of ignorance. Then all existence is struggle and pain, and there is no way out of it save in right thinking, which comes through self-knowledge.

How Can There Be Real Love?

The image you have about a person, the image you have about your politicians, the prime minister, your god, your wife, your children—that image is being looked at. And that image has been created through your relationship, or through your fears, or through your hopes. The sexual and other pleasures you have had with your wife, your husband, the anger, the flattery, the comfort, and all the things that your family life brings—a deadly life it is—have created an image about your wife or husband. With that image you look. Similarly, your wife or husband has an image about you. So the relationship between you and your wife or husband, between you and the politician is really the relationship between these two images. Right? That is a fact. How can two images which are the result of thought, of pleasure and so on, have any affection or love?

So the relationship between two individuals, very close together or very far, is a relationship of images, symbols, memories. And in that, how can there be real love?

We Are That Which We Possess

To understand relationship, there must be a passive awareness, which does not destroy relationship. On the contrary, it makes relationship much more vital, much more significant. Then there is in that relationship a possibility of real affection; there is a warmth, a sense of nearness, which is not mere sentiment or sensation. And if we can so approach or be in that relationship to everything, then our problems will be easily solved—the problems of property, the problems of possession. Because, we are that which we possess. The man who possesses money is the money. The man who identifies himself with property is the property, or the house, or the furniture. Similarly with ideas, or with people; and when there is possessiveness, there is no relationship. But most of us possess because we have nothing else, if we do not possess. We are empty shells if we do not possess, if we do not fill our life with furniture, with music, with knowledge, with this or that. And that shell makes a lot of noise, and that noise we call living; and with that we are satisfied. And when there is a disruption, a breaking away of that, then there is sorrow because then you suddenly discover yourself as you are—an empty shell, without much meaning. So, to be aware of the whole content of relationship is action; and from that action there is a possibility of true relationship, a possibility of discovering its great depth, its great significance, and of knowing what love is.

 MARCH 18

Being Related

Without relationship, there is no existence: to be is to be related. . . . Most of us do not seem to realize this—that the world is my relationship with others, whether one or many. My problem is that of relationship. What I am, that I project, and obviously, if I do not understand myself, the whole of relationship is one of confusion in ever-widening circles. So, relationship becomes of extraordinary importance, not with the so-called mass, the crowd, but in the world of my family and friends, however small that may be—my relationship with my wife, my children, my neighbor. In a world of vast organizations, vast mobilizations of people, mass movements, we are afraid to act on a small scale; we are afraid to be little people clearing up our own patch. We say to ourselves, "What can I personally do? I must join a mass movement in order to reform." On the contrary, real revolution takes place not through mass movements but through the inward revaluation of relationship—that alone is real reformation, a radical, continuous revolution. We are afraid to begin on a small scale. Because the problem is so vast, we think we must meet it with large numbers of people, with a great organization, with mass movements. Surely, we must begin to tackle the problem on a small scale, and the small scale is the "me" and the "you." When I understand myself, I understand you, and out of that understanding comes love. Love is the missing factor; there is a lack of affection, of warmth in relationship; and because we lack that love, that tenderness, that generosity, that mercy in relationship, we escape into mass action, which produces further confusion, further misery. We fill our hearts with blueprints for world reform and do not look to that one resolving factor, which is love.

You and I Are the Problem, Not the World

The world is not something separate from you and me; the world, society, is the relationship that we establish or seek to establish between each other. So you and I are the problem, and not the world, because the world is the projection of ourselves, and to understand the world we must understand ourselves. That world is not separate from us; we are the world, and our problems are the world's problems.

 MARCH 20

There Is No Such Thing
As Living Alone

We want to run away from our loneliness, with its panicky fears, so we depend on another, we enrich ourselves with companionship, and so on. We are the prime movers, and others become pawns in our game; and when the pawn turns and demands something in return, we are shocked and grieved. If our own fortress is strong, without a weak spot in it, this battering from the outside is of little consequence to us. The peculiar tendencies that arise with advancing age must be understood and corrected while we are still capable of detached and tolerant self-observation and study; our fears must be observed and understood now. Our energies must be directed, not merely to the understanding of the outward pressures and demands for which we are responsible, but to the comprehension of ourselves, of our loneliness, our fears, demands, and frailties.

There is no such thing as living alone, for all living is relationship; but to live without direct relationship demands high intelligence, a swifter and greater awareness for self-discovery. A "lone" existence, without this keen and flowing awareness, strengthens the already dominant tendencies, thus causing unbalance, distortion. It is now that one has to become aware of the set and peculiar habits of thought-feeling which come with age, and by understanding them make away with them. Inward riches alone bring peace and joy.

Freedom from Fear

Is it possible for the mind to empty itself totally of fear? Fear of any kind breeds illusion; it makes the mind dull, shallow. Where there is fear there is obviously no freedom, and without freedom there is no love at all. And most of us have some form of fear; fear of darkness, fear of public opinion, fear of snakes, fear of physical pain, fear of old age, fear of death. We have literally dozens of fears. And is it possible to be completely free of fear?

We can see what fear does to each one of us. It makes one tell lies; it corrupts one in various ways; it makes the mind empty, shallow. There are dark corners in the mind which can never be investigated and exposed as long as one is afraid. Physical self-protection, the instinctive urge to keep away from the venomous snake, to draw back from the precipice, to avoid falling under the tramcar, and so on, is sane, normal, healthy. But I am asking about the psychological self-protectiveness which makes one afraid of disease, of death, of an enemy. When we seek fulfillment in any form, whether through painting, through music, through relationship, or what you will, there is always fear. So, what is important is to be aware of this whole process of oneself, to observe, to learn about it, and not ask how to get rid of fear. When you merely want to get rid of fear, you will find ways and means of escaping from it, and so there can never be freedom from fear.

Dealing with Fear

One is afraid of public opinion, afraid of not achieving, not fulfilling, afraid of not having the opportunity; and through it all there is this extraordinary sense of guilt—one has done a thing that one should not have done; the sense of guilt in the very act of doing; one is healthy and others are poor and unhealthy; one has food and others have no food. The more the mind is inquiring, penetrating, asking, the greater the sense of guilt, anxiety. . . . Fear is the urge that seeks a Master, a guru; fear is this coating of respectability, which everyone loves so dearly—to be respectable. Do you determine to be courageous to face events in life, or merely rationalize fear away, or find explanations that will give satisfaction to the mind that is caught in fear? How do you deal with it? Turn on the radio, read a book, go to a temple, cling to some form of dogma, belief?

Fear is the destructive energy in man. It withers the mind, it distorts thought, it leads to all kinds of extraordinarily clever and subtle theories, absurd superstitions, dogmas, and beliefs. If you see that fear is destructive, then how do you proceed to wipe the mind clean? You say that by probing into the cause of fear you would be free of fear. Is that so? Trying to uncover the cause and knowing the cause of fear does not eliminate fear.

The Door to Understanding

You cannot wipe away fear without understanding, without actually seeing into the nature of time, which means thought, which means word. From that arises the question: Is there a thought without word, is there a thinking without the word which is memory? Sir, without seeing the nature of the mind, the movement of the mind, the process of self-knowing, merely saying that I must be free of it, has very little meaning. You have to take fear in the context of the whole of the mind. To see, to go into all this, you need energy. Energy does not come through eating food—that is a part of physical necessity. But to see, in the sense I am using that word, requires an enormous energy; and that energy is dissipated when you are battling with words, when you are resisting, condemning, when you are full of opinions which are preventing you from looking, seeing—your energy is all gone in that. So in the consideration of this perception, this seeing, again you open the door.

Fear Makes Us Obey

Why do we do all this—obey, follow, copy? Why? Because we are frightened inwardly to be uncertain. We want to be certain—we want to be certain financially, we want to be certain morally—we want to be approved, we want to be in a safe position, we want never to be confronted with trouble, pain, suffering, we want to be enclosed. So, fear, consciously or unconsciously, makes us obey the Master, the leader, the priest, the government. Fear also controls us from doing something which may be harmful to others, because we will be punished. So behind all these actions, greeds, pursuits, lurks this desire for certainty, this desire to be assured. So, without resolving fear, without being free from fear, merely to obey or to be obeyed has little significance; what has meaning is to understand this fear from day to day and how fear shows itself in different ways. It is only when there is freedom from fear that there is that inward quality of understanding, that aloneness in which there is no accumulation of knowledge or of experience, and it is that alone which gives extraordinary clarity in the pursuit of the real.

Face-to-Face with the Fact

Are we afraid of a fact or of an idea *about* the fact? Are we afraid of the thing as it is, or are we afraid of what we *think* it is? Take death, for example. Are we afraid of the fact of death or of the idea of death? The fact is one thing and the idea about the fact is another. Am I afraid of the word *death* or of the fact itself? Because I am afraid of the word, of the idea, I never understand the fact, I never look at the fact, I am never in direct relation with the fact. It is only when I am in complete communion with the fact that there is no fear. If I am not in communion with the fact, then there is fear, and there is no communion with the fact so long as I have an idea, an opinion, a theory, *about* the fact; so I have to be very clear whether I am afraid of the word, the idea, or the fact. If I am face-to-face with the fact, there is nothing to understand about it: the fact is there, and I can deal with it. If I am afraid of the word, then I must understand the word, go into the whole process of what the word, the term, implies.

It is my opinion, my idea, my experience, my knowledge about the fact, that creates fear. So long as there is verbalization of the fact, giving the fact a name and therefore identifying or condemning it, so long as thought is judging the fact as an observer, there must be fear. Thought is the product of the past; it can only exist through verbalization, through symbols, through images. So long as thought is regarding or translating the fact, there must be fear. Thought is the product of the past; it can only exist through verbalization, through symbols, through images; so long as thought is regarding or translating the fact, there must be fear.

Contacting Fear

There is physical fear. You know, when you see a snake, a wild animal, instinctively there is fear; that is a normal, healthy, natural fear. It is not fear, it is a desire to protect oneself—that is normal. But the psychological protection of oneself—that is, the desire to be always certain—breeds fear. A mind that is seeking always to be certain is a dead mind, because there is no certainty in life, there is no permanency. . . . When you come directly into contact with fear, there is a response of the nerves and all the rest of it. Then, when the mind is no longer escaping through words or through activity of any kind, there is no division between the observer and the thing observed as fear. It is only the mind that is escaping that separates itself from fear. But when there is a direct contact with fear, there is no observer, there is no entity that says, "I am afraid." So, the moment you are directly in contact with life, with anything, there is no division—it is this division that breeds competition, ambition, fear.

So what is important is not "how to be free of fear?" If you seek a way, a method, a system to be rid of fear, you will be everlastingly caught in fear. But if you understand fear—which can only take place when you come directly in contact with it, as you are in contact with hunger, as you are directly in contact when you are threatened with losing your job—then you do something; only then will you find that all fear ceases—we mean all fear, not fear of this kind or of that kind.

Fear Is Nonacceptance of What Is

Fear finds various escapes. The common variety is identification, is it not?—identification with country, with society, with an idea. Haven't you noticed how you respond when you see a procession, a military procession or a religious procession, or when the country is in danger of being invaded? You then identify yourself with the country, with a being, with an ideology. There are other times when you identify yourself with your child, with your wife, with a particular form of action, or inaction. Identification is a process of self-forgetfulness. So long as I am conscious of the "me" I know there is pain, there is struggle, there is constant fear. But if I can identify myself with something greater, with something worthwhile, with beauty, with life, with truth, with belief, with knowledge, at least temporarily, there is an escape from the "me," is there not? If I talk about "my country" I forget myself temporarily, do I not? If I can say something about God, I forget myself. If I can identify myself with my family, with a group, with a particular party, with a certain ideology, then there is a temporary escape.

Do we now know what fear is? Is it not the non-acceptance of *what is?* We must understand the word *acceptance.* I am not using that word as meaning the effort made to accept. There is no question of accepting when I perceive *what is.* When I do not see clearly *what is,* then I bring in the process of acceptance. Therefore, fear is the nonacceptance of *what is.*

 MARCH 28

The Disorder That Time Creates

Time means moving from *what is* to "what should be." I am afraid, but one day I shall be free of fear; therefore, time is necessary to be free of fear—at least, that is what we think. To change from *what is* to "what should be" involves time. Now, time implies effort in that interval between *what is* and "what should be." I don't like fear, and I am going to make an effort to understand, to analyze, to dissect it, or I am going to discover the cause of it, or I am going to escape totally from it. All this implies effort—and effort is what we are used to. We are always in conflict between *what is* and "what should be." The "what I should be" is an idea, and the idea is fictitious, it is not "what I am," which is the fact; and the "what I am" can be changed only when I understand the disorder that time creates.

. . . So, is it possible for me to be rid of fear totally, completely, on the instant? If I allow fear to continue, I will create disorder all the time; therefore, one sees that time is an element of disorder, not a means to be ultimately free of fear. So there is no gradual process of getting rid of fear, just as there is no gradual process of getting rid of the poison of nationalism. If you have nationalism and you say that eventually there will be the brotherhood of man, in the interval there are wars, there are hatreds, there is misery, there is all this appalling division between man and man; therefore, time is creating disorder.

How Do I Look at Anger?

Obviously, I look at it as an observer being angry. I say, "I am angry." At the moment of anger there is no "I"; the "I" comes in immediately afterwards—which means time. Can I look at the fact without the factor of time, which is the thought, which is the word? This happens when there is the looking without the observer. See where it has led me. I now begin to perceive a way of looking—perceiving without the opinion, the conclusion, without condemning, judging. Therefore, I perceive that there can be "seeing" without thought, which is the word. So the mind is beyond the clutches of ideas, of the conflict of duality and all the rest of it. So, can I look at fear not as an isolated fact?

If you isolate a fact that has not opened the door to the whole universe of the mind, then let us go back to the fact and begin again by taking another fact so that you yourself will begin to see the extraordinary thing of the mind, so that you have the key, you can open the door, you can burst into that. . . .

. . . By considering one fear—the fear of death, the fear of the neighbor, the fear of your spouse dominating over you, you know the whole business of domination—will that open the door? That is all that matters—not how to be free of it—because the moment you open the door, fear is completely wiped away. The mind is the result of time, and time is the word—how extraordinary to think of it! Time is thought; it is thought that breeds fear, it is thought that breeds the fear of death; and it is time which is thought, that has in its hand the whole intricacies and the subtleties of fear.

The Root of All Fear

The craving to become causes fears; to be, to achieve, and so to depend engenders fear. The state of nonfear is not negation, it is not the opposite of fear nor is it courage. In understanding the cause of fear, there is its cessation, not the becoming courageous, for in all becoming there is the seed of fear. Dependence on things, on people, or on ideas breeds fear; dependence arises from ignorance, from the lack of self-knowledge, from inward poverty; fear causes uncertainty of mind-heart, preventing communication and understanding. Through self-awareness we begin to discover and so comprehend the cause of fear, not only the superficial but the deep causal and accumulative fears. Fear is both inborn and acquired; it is related to the past, and to free thought-feeling from it, the past must be comprehended through the present. The past is ever wanting to give birth to the present which becomes the identifying memory of the "me" and the "mine," the "I." The self is the root of all fear.

◈

APRIL

Desire

Sex

Marriage

Passion

◈

There Is Only Craving

There is no entity separate from craving; there is only craving, there is no one who craves. Craving takes on different masks at different times, depending on its interests. The memory of these varying interests meets the new, which brings about conflict, and so the chooser is born, establishing himself as an entity separate and distinct from craving. But the entity is not different from its qualities. The entity who tries to fill or run away from emptiness, incompleteness, loneliness, is not different from that which he is avoiding; he *is* it. He cannot run away from himself; all that he can do is to understand himself. He *is* his loneliness, his emptiness; and as long as he regards it as something separate from himself, he will be in illusion and endless conflict. When he directly experiences that he is his own loneliness, then only can there be freedom from fear. Fear exists only in relationship to an idea, and idea is the response of memory as thought. Thought is the result of experience; and though it can ponder over emptiness, have sensations with regard to it, it cannot know emptiness directly. The word *loneliness,* with its memories of pain and fear, prevents the experiencing of it afresh. The word is memory, and when the word is no longer significant, then the relationship between the experiencer and the experienced is wholly different; then that relationship is direct and not through a word, through memory; then the experiencer *is* the experience, which alone brings freedom from fear.

Understanding Desire

We have to understand desire; and it is very difficult to understand something which is so vital, so demanding, so urgent, because in the very fulfillment of desire passion is engendered, with the pleasure and the pain of it. And if one is to understand desire, obviously, there must be no choice. You cannot judge desire as being good or bad, noble or ignoble, or say, "I will keep this desire and deny that one." All that must be set aside if we are to find out the truth of desire—the beauty of it, the ugliness or whatever it may be.

Desire Has to Be Understood

Let us go on to consider desire. We know, do we not, the desire which contradicts itself, which is tortured, pulling in different directions; the pain, the turmoil, the anxiety of desire, and the disciplining, the controlling. And in the everlasting battle with it we twist it out of all shape and recognition; but it is there, constantly watching, waiting, pushing. Do what you will, sublimate it, escape from it, deny it or accept it, give it full rein—it is always there. And we know how the religious teachers and others have said that we should be desireless, cultivate detachment, be free from desire—which is really absurd, because desire has to be understood, not destroyed. If you destroy desire, you may destroy life itself. If you pervert desire, shape it, control it, dominate it, suppress it, you may be destroying something extraordinarily beautiful.

The Quality of Desire

. . . What happens if you do not condemn desire, do not judge it as being good or bad, but simply be aware of it? I wonder if you know what it means to be aware of something? Most of us are not aware because we have become so accustomed to condemning, judging, evaluating, identifying, choosing. Choice obviously prevents awareness because choice is always made as a result of conflict. To be aware when you enter a room, to see all the furniture, the carpet or its absence, and so on—just to see it, to be aware of it all without any sense of judgment—is very difficult. Have you ever tried to look at a person, a flower, at an idea, an emotion, without any choice, any judgment?

And if one does the same thing with desire, if one lives with it—not denying it or saying, "What shall I do with this desire? It is so ugly, so rampant, so violent," not giving it a name, a symbol, not covering it with a word—then, is it any longer the cause of turmoil? Is desire then something to be put away, destroyed? We want to destroy it because one desire tears against another, creating conflict, misery, and contradiction; and one can see how one tries to escape from this everlasting conflict. So can one be aware of the totality of desire? What I mean by totality is not just one desire or many desires, but the total quality of desire itself.

Why Shouldn't One Have Pleasure?

You see a beautiful sunset, a lovely tree, a river that has a wide, curving movement, or a beautiful face, and to look at it gives great pleasure, delight. What is wrong with that? It seems to me the confusion and the misery begin when that face, that river, that cloud, that mountain becomes a memory, and this memory then demands a greater continuity of pleasure; we want such things repeated. We all know this. I have had a certain pleasure, or you have had a certain delight in something, and we want it repeated. Whether it be sexual, artistic, intellectual, or something not quite of this character, we want it repeated—and I think that is where pleasure begins to darken the mind and create values which are false, not actual.

What matters is to understand pleasure, not try to get rid of it—that is too stupid. Nobody can get rid of pleasure. But to understand the nature and the structure of pleasure is essential; because if life is only pleasure, and if that is what one wants, then with pleasure go the misery, the confusion, the illusions, the false values which we create, and therefore there is no clarity.

A Healthy, Normal Reaction

. . . I have to find out why desire has such potency in my life. It may be right or it may not be right. I have to find out. I see that. Desire arises, which is a reaction, which is a healthy, normal reaction; otherwise, I would be dead. I see a beautiful thing and I say, "By Jove, I want that." If I didn't, I'd be dead. But in the constant pursuit of it there is pain. That's my problem— there is pain as well as pleasure. I see a beautiful woman, and she is beautiful; it would be most absurd to say, "No, she's not." This is a fact. But what gives continuity to the pleasure? Obviously it is thought, thinking about it. . . .

I think about it. It is no longer the direct relationship with the object, which is desire, but thought now increases that desire by thinking about it, by having images, pictures, ideas. . . .

Thought comes in and says, "Please, you must have it; that's growth; that is important; that is not important; this is vital for your life; this is not vital for your life."

But I can look at it and have a desire, and that's the end of it, without interference of thought.

Dying to Little Things

Have you ever tried dying to a pleasure voluntarily, not forcibly? Ordinarily when you die you don't want to; death comes and takes you away; it is not a voluntary act, except in suicide. But have you ever tried dying voluntarily, easily, felt that sense of the abandonment of pleasure? Obviously not! At present your ideals, your pleasures, your ambitions are the things which give so-called significance to them. Life is living, abundance, fullness, abandonment, not a sense of the "I" having significance. That is mere intellection. If you experiment with dying to little things—that is good enough. Just to die to little pleasures—with ease, with comfort, with a smile—is enough, for then you will see that your mind is capable of dying to many things, dying to all memories. Machines are taking over the functions of memory—the computers—but the human mind is something more than a merely mechanical habit of association and memory. But it cannot be that something else if it does not die to everything it knows.

Now to see the truth of all this, a young mind is essential, a mind that is not merely functioning in the field of time. The young mind dies to everything. Can you see the truth of that immediately, feel the truth of it instantly? You may not see the whole extraordinary significance of it, the immense subtlety, the beauty of that dying, the richness of it, but even to listen to it sows the seed, and the significance of these words takes root—not only at the superficial, conscious level, but right through all the unconscious.

Sex

Sex is a problem because it would seem that in that act there is complete absence of the self. In that moment you are happy, because there is the cessation of self-consciousness, of the "me"; and desiring more of it—more of the abnegation of the self in which there is complete happiness, without the past or the future—demanding that complete happiness through full fusion, integration, naturally it becomes all-important. Isn't that so? Because it is something that gives me unadulterated joy, complete self-forgetfulness, I want more and more of it. Now, why do I want more of it? Because, everywhere else I am in conflict, everywhere else, at all the different levels of existence, there is the strengthening of the self. Economically, socially, religiously, there is the constant thickening of self-consciousness, which is conflict. After all, you are self-conscious only when there is conflict. Self-consciousness is in its very nature the result of conflict. . . .

So, the problem is not sex, surely, but how to be free from the self. You have tasted that state of being in which the self is not, if only for a few seconds, if only for a day, or what you will; and where the self is, there is conflict, there is misery, there is strife. So, there is the constant longing for more of that self-free state.

 APRIL 8

The Ultimate Escape

What do we mean by the problem of sex? Is it the act, or is it a thought about the act? Surely, it is not the act. The sexual act is no problem to you any more than eating is a problem to you, but if you think about eating or anything else all day long because you have nothing else to think about, it becomes a problem to you. . . . Why do you build it up, which you are obviously doing? The cinemas, the magazines, the stories, the way women dress, everything is building up your thoughts of sex. And why does the mind build it up, why does the mind think about sex at all? Why, sirs and ladies? It is your problem. Why? Why has it become a central issue in your life? When there are so many things calling, demanding your attention, you give complete attention to the thought of sex. What happens, why are your minds so occupied with it? Because that is a way of ultimate escape, is it not? It is a way of complete self-forgetfulness. For the time being, at least for the moment, you can forget yourself—and there is no other way of forgetting yourself. Everything else you do in life gives emphasis to the "me," to the self. Your business, your religion, your gods, your leaders, your political and economic actions, your escapes, your social activities, your joining one party and rejecting another—all that is emphasizing and giving strength to the "me." . . . When there is only one thing in your life that is an avenue to ultimate escape, to complete forgetfulness of yourself if only for a few seconds, you cling to it because that is the only moment you are happy. . . .

So, sex becomes an extraordinarily difficult and complex problem as long as you do not understand the mind that thinks about the problem.

We Have Made Sex a Problem

Why is it that whatever we touch we turn into a problem? . . . Why has sex become a problem? Why do we submit to living with problems; why do we not put an end to them? Why do we not die to our problems instead of carrying them day after day, year after year? Surely, sex is a relevant question, which I shall answer presently, but there is the primary question: why do we make life into a problem? Working, sex, earning money, thinking, feeling, experiencing, you know, the whole business of living—why is it a problem? Is it not essentially because we always think from a particular point of view, from a fixed point of view? We are always thinking from a center towards the periphery, but the periphery is the center for most of us, and so anything we touch is superficial. But life is not superficial; it demands living completely, and because we are living only superficially, we know only superficial reaction. Whatever we do on the periphery must inevitably create a problem, and that is our life—we live in the superficial and we are content to live there with all the problems of the superficial. So, problems exist as long as we live in the superficial, on the periphery—the periphery being the "me" and its sensations, which can be externalized or made subjective, which can be identified with the universe, with the country, or with some other thing made up by the mind. So, as long as we live within the field of the mind there must be complications, there must be problems; and that is all we know.

What Do You Mean by Love?

Love is the unknowable. It can be realized only when the known is understood and transcended. Only when the mind is free of the known, then only there will be love. So, we must approach love negatively and not positively.

What is love to most of us? With us, when we love, in it there is possessiveness, dominance, or subservience. From this possession arises jealousy and fear of loss, and we legalize this possessive instinct. From possessiveness arise jealousy and the innumerable conflicts with which each one is familiar. Possessiveness, then, is not love. Nor is love sentimental. To be sentimental, to be emotional, excludes love. Sensitivity and emotions are merely sensations.

. . . Love alone can transform insanity, confusion, and strife. No system, no theory of the left or of the right can bring peace and happiness to man. Where there is love, there is no possessiveness, no envy; there is mercy and compassion, not in theory, but actually—for your wife and for your children, for your neighbor and for your servant. . . . Love alone can bring about mercy and beauty, order and peace. There is love with its blessing when "you" cease to be.

As Long As We Possess,
We Shall Never Love

We know love as sensation, do we not? When we say we love, we know jealousy, we know fear, we know anxiety. When you say you love someone, all that is implied: envy, the desire to possess, the desire to own, to dominate, the fear of loss, and so on. All this we call love, and we do not know love without fear, without envy, without possession; we merely verbalize that state of love which is without fear, we call it impersonal, pure, divine, or God knows what else; but the fact is that we are jealous, we are dominating, possessive. We shall know that state of love only when jealousy, envy, possessiveness, domination, come to an end; and as long as we possess, we shall never love. . . . When do you think about the person whom you love? You think about her when she is gone, when she is away, when she has left you. . . . So, you miss the person whom you say you love only when you are disturbed, when you are in suffering; and as long as you possess that person, you do not have to think about that person, because in possession there is no disturbance. . . .

Thinking comes when you are disturbed—and you are bound to be disturbed as long as your thinking is what you call *love*. Surely, love is not a thing of the mind; and because the things of the mind have filled our hearts, we have no love. The things of the mind are jealousy, envy, ambition, the desire to be somebody, to achieve success. These things of the mind fill your hearts, and then you say you love; but how can you love when you have all these confusing elements in you? When there is smoke, how can there be a pure flame?

Love Is Not a Duty

. . . When there is love, there is no duty. When you love your wife, you share everything with her—your property, your trouble, your anxiety, your joy. You do not dominate. You are not the man and she the woman to be used and thrown aside, a sort of breeding machine to carry on your name. When there is love, the word *duty* disappears. It is the man with no love in his heart who talks of rights and duties, and in this country duties and rights have taken the place of love. Regulations have become more important that the warmth of affection. When there is love, the problem is simple; when there is no love, the problem becomes complex. When a man loves his wife and his children, he can never possibly think in terms of *duty* and *rights*. Sirs, examine your own hearts and minds. I know you laugh it off—that is one of the tricks of the thoughtless, to laugh at something and push it aside. Your wife does not share your responsibility, your wife does not share your property, she does not have the half of everything that you have because you consider the woman less than yourself, something to be kept and to be used sexually at your convenience when your appetite demands it. So you have invented the words *rights* and *duty;* and when the woman rebels, you throw at her these words. It is a static society, a deteriorating society, that talks of duty and rights. If you really examine your hearts and minds, you will find that you have no love.

A Thing of the Mind

What we call our love is a thing of the mind. Look at yourselves, sirs and ladies, and you will see that what I am saying is obviously true; otherwise, our lives, our marriage, our relationships, would be entirely different, we would have a new society. We bind ourselves to another, not through fusion, but through contract, which is called love, marriage. Love does not fuse, adjust—it is neither personal nor impersonal, it is a state of being. The man who desires to fuse with something greater, to unite himself with another, is avoiding misery, confusion; but the mind is still in separation, which is disintegration. Love knows neither fusion nor diffusion, it is neither personal nor impersonal, it is a state of being which the mind cannot find; it can describe it, give it a term, a name, but the word, the description, is not love. It is only when the mind is quiet that it shall know love, and that state of quietness is not a thing to be cultivated.

In Considering Marriage

We are trying to understand the problem of marriage, in which is implied sexual relationship, love, companionship, communion. Obviously if there is no love, marriage becomes a disgrace, does it not? Then it becomes mere gratification. To love is one of the most difficult things, is it not? Love can come into being, can exist only when the self is absent. Without love, relationship is a pain; however gratifying, or however superficial, it leads to boredom, to routine, to habit with all its implications. Then, sexual problems become all important. In considering marriage, whether it is necessary or not, one must first comprehend love. Surely, love is chaste, without love you cannot be chaste; you may be a celibate, whether a man or a woman, but that is not being chaste, that is not being pure, if there is no love. If you have an ideal of chastity, that is if you want to become chaste, there is no love in it either because it is merely the desire to become something which you think is noble, which you think will help you to find reality; there is no love there at all. Licentiousness is not chaste, it leads only to degradation, to misery. So does the pursuit of an ideal. Both exclude love, both imply becoming something, indulging in something; and therefore you become important, and where you are important, love is not.

Love Is Incapable of Adjustment

Love is not a thing of the mind, is it? Love is not merely the sexual act, is it? Love is something which the mind cannot possibly conceive. Love is something which cannot be formulated. And without love, you become related; without love, you marry. Then, in that marriage, you "adjust yourselves" to each other. Lovely phrase! You adjust yourselves to each other, which is again an intellectual process, is it not? . . . This adjustment is obviously a mental process. All adjustments are. But, surely, love is incapable of adjustment. You know, sirs, don't you, that if you love another, there is no "adjustment." There is only complete fusion. Only when there is no love do we begin to adjust. And this adjustment is called marriage. Hence, marriage fails, because it is the very source of conflict, a battle between two people. It is an extraordinarily complex problem, like all problems, but more so because the appetites, the urges, are so strong. So, a mind which is merely adjusting itself can never be chaste. A mind which is seeking happiness through sex can never be chaste. Though you may momentarily have, in that act, self-abnegation, self-forgetfulness, the very pursuit of that happiness, which is of the mind, makes the mind unchaste. Chastity comes into being only where there is love.

To Love Is to Be Chaste

This problem of sex is not simple and it cannot be solved on its own level. To try to solve it purely biologically is absurd; and to approach it through religion or to try to solve it as though it were a mere matter of physical adjustment, of glandular action, or to hedge it in with taboos and condemnations is all too immature, childish, and stupid. It requires intelligence of the highest order. To understand ourselves in our relationship with another requires intelligence far more swift and subtle than to understand nature. But we seek to understand without intelligence; we want immediate action, an immediate solution, and the problem becomes more and more important. . . . Love is not mere thought; thoughts are only the external action of the brain. Love is much deeper, much more profound, and the profundity of life can be discovered only in love. Without love, life has no meaning—and that is the sad part of our existence. We grow old while still immature; our bodies become old, fat, and ugly, and we remain thoughtless. Though we read and talk about it, we have never known the perfume of life. Mere reading and verbalizing indicates an utter lack of the warmth of heart that enriches life; and without that quality of love, do what you will, join any society, bring about any law, you will not solve this problem. To love is to be chaste.

Mere intellect is not chastity. The man who tries to be chaste in thought is unchaste, because he has no love. Only the man who loves is chaste, pure, incorruptible.

Constant Thought
Is a Waste of Energy

Most of us spend our life in effort, in struggle; and the effort, the struggle, the striving, is a dissipation of that energy. Man, throughout the historical period of man, has said that to find that reality or God—whatever name he may give to it—you must be celibate; that is, you take a vow of chastity and suppress, control, battle with yourself endlessly all your life, to keep your vow. Look at the waste of energy! It is also a waste of energy to indulge. And it has far more significance when you suppress. The effort that has gone into suppression, into control, into this denial of your desire distorts your mind, and through that distortion you have a certain sense of austerity which becomes harsh. Please listen. Observe it in yourself and observe the people around you. And observe this waste of energy, the battle. Not the implications of sex, not the actual act, but the ideals, the images, the pleasure—the constant thought about them is a waste of energy. And most people waste their energy either through denial, or through a vow of chastity, or in thinking about it endlessly.

The Idealist Cannot Know Love

Those who are trying to be celibate in order to achieve God are unchaste for they are seeking a result or gain and so substituting the end, the result, for sex—which is fear. Their hearts are without love, and there can be no purity, and a pure heart alone can find reality. A disciplined heart, a suppressed heart, cannot know what love is. It cannot know love if it is caught in habit, in sensation—religious or physical, psychological or sensate. The idealist is an imitator and therefore he cannot know love. He cannot be generous, give himself over completely without the thought of himself. Only when the mind and heart are unburdened of fear, of the routine of sensational habits, when there is generosity and compassion, there is love. Such love is chaste.

Understanding Passion

Is it a religious life to punish oneself? Is mortification of the body or of the mind a sign of understanding? Is self-torture a way to reality? Is chastity denial? Do you think you can go far through renunciation? Do you really think there can be peace through conflict? Does not the means matter infinitely more than the end? The end may be, but the means is. The actual, the *what is*, must be understood and not smothered by determinations, ideals, and clever rationalizations. Sorrow is not the way of happiness. The thing called passion has to be understood and not suppressed or sublimated, and it is no good finding a substitute for it. Whatever you may do, any device that you invent, will only strengthen that which has not been loved and understood. To love what we call passion is to understand it. To love is to be in direct communion; and you cannot love something if you resent it, if you have ideas, conclusions about it. How can you love and understand passion if you have taken a vow against it? A vow is a form of resistance, and what you resist ultimately conquers you. Truth is not to be conquered; you cannot storm it; it will slip through your hands if you try to grasp it. Truth comes silently, without your knowing. What you know is not truth, it is only an idea, a symbol. The shadow is not the real.

Means and End Are One

For the attainment of liberation, nothing is necessary. You cannot attain it through bargaining, through sacrifice, through elimination; it is not a thing that you can buy. If you do these things, you will get a thing of the marketplace, therefore not real. Truth cannot be bought, there is no means to truth; if there is a means, the end would not be truth, because means and end are one, they are not separate. Chastity as a means to liberation, to truth, is a denial of truth. Chastity is not a coin with which you buy it. . . .

Why do we think chastity is essential? . . . What do we mean by sex? Not merely the act but thinking about it, feeling about it, anticipating it, escaping from it—that is our problem. Our problem is sensation, wanting more and more. Watch yourself, don't watch your neighbor. Why are your thoughts so occupied with sex? Chastity can exist only when there is love, and without love there is no chastity. Without love, chastity is merely lust in a different form. To become chaste is to become something else; it is like a man becoming powerful, succeeding as a prominent lawyer, politician, or whatever else—the change is on the same level. That is not chastity but merely the end result of a dream, the outcome of the continual resistance to a particular desire. . . . So, chastity ceases to be a problem where there is love. Then life is not a problem, life is to be lived completely in the fullness of love, and that revolution will bring about a new world.

Total Abandonment

Perhaps you have never experienced that state of mind in which there is total abandonment of everything, a complete letting go. And you cannot abandon everything without deep passion, can you? You cannot abandon everything intellectually or emotionally. There is total abandonment, surely, only when there is intense passion. Don't be alarmed by that word, because a man who is not passionate, who is not intense, can never understand or feel the quality of beauty. The mind that holds something in reserve, the mind that has a vested interest, the mind that clings to position, power, prestige, the mind that is respectable, which is a horror—such a mind can never abandon itself.

This Pure Flame of Passion

In most of us there is very little passion. We may be lustful, we may be longing for something, we may be wanting to escape from something, and all this does give one a certain intensity. But unless we awaken and feel our way into this flame of passion without a cause, we shall not be able to understand that which we call sorrow. To understand something you must have passion, the intensity of complete attention. Where there is the passion for something that produces contradiction, conflict, this pure flame of passion cannot be; and this pure flame of passion must exist in order to end sorrow, dissipate it completely.

Beauty Beyond Feeling

Without passion how can there be beauty? I do not mean the beauty of pictures, buildings, painted women, and all the rest of it. They have their own forms of beauty. A thing put together by man, like a cathedral, a temple, a picture, a poem, or a statue may or may not be beautiful. But there is a beauty which is beyond feeling and thought and which cannot be realized, understood, or known if there is not passion. So do not misunderstand the word passion. It is not an ugly word; it is not a thing you can buy in the market or talk about romantically. It has nothing whatever to do with emotion, feeling. It is not a respectable thing; it is a flame that destroys anything that is false. And we are always so afraid to allow that flame to devour the things that we hold dear, the things that we call important.

A Passion for Everything

For most of us, passion is employed only with regard to one thing, sex; or you suffer passionately and try to resolve that suffering. But I am using the word *passion* in the sense of a state of mind, a state of being, a state of your inward core, if there is such a thing, that feels very strongly, that is highly sensitive— sensitive alike to dirt, to squalor, to poverty, and to enormous riches and corruption, to the beauty of a tree, of a bird, to the flow of water, and to a pond that has the evening sky reflected upon it. To feel all this intensely, strongly, is necessary. Because without passion life becomes empty, shallow, and without much meaning. If you cannot see the beauty of a tree and love that tree, if you cannot care for it intensely, you are not living.

Love, I Assure You, Is Passion

You cannot be sensitive if you are not passionate. Do not be afraid of that word *passion*. Most religious books, most gurus, swamis, leaders, and all the rest of them say, "Don't have passion." But if you have no passion, how can you be sensitive to the ugly, to the beautiful, to the whispering leaves, to the sunset, to a smile, to a cry? How can you be sensitive without a sense of passion in which there is abandonment? Sirs, please listen to me, and do not ask how to acquire passion. I know you are all passionate enough in getting a good job, or hating some poor chap, or being jealous of someone; but I am talking of something entirely different—a passion that loves. Love is a state in which there is no "me"; love is a state in which there is no condemnation, no saying that sex is right or wrong, that this is good and something else is bad. Love is none of these contradictory things. Contradiction does not exist in love. And how can one love if one is not passionate? Without passion, how can one be sensitive? To be sensitive is to feel your neighbor sitting next to you; it is to see the ugliness of the town with its squalor, its filth, its poverty, and to see the beauty of the river, the sea, the sky. If you are not passionate, how can you be sensitive to all that? How can you feel a smile, a tear? Love, I assure you, is passion.

A Passionate Mind Is Inquiring

Obviously there must be passion, and the question is how to revive that passion. Do not let us misunderstand each other. I mean passion in every sense, not merely sexual passion, which is a very small thing. And most of us are satisfied with that because every other passion has been destroyed—in the office, in the factory, through following a certain job, routine, learning techniques—so there is no passion left; there is no creative sense of urgency and release. Therefore sex becomes important to us, and there we get lost in petty passion which becomes an enormous problem to the narrow, virtuous mind, or else it soon becomes a habit and dies. I am using the word passion as a total thing. A passionate man who feels strongly is not satisfied merely with some little job—whether it be the job of a prime minister, or of a cook, or what you will. A mind that is passionate is inquiring, searching, looking, asking, demanding, not merely trying to find for its discontent some object in which it can fulfill itself and go to sleep. A passionate mind is groping, seeking, breaking through, not accepting any tradition; it is not a decided mind, not a mind that has arrived, but it is a young mind that is ever arriving.

Petty Mind

A passionate mind is groping, seeking, breaking through, not accepting any tradition; it is not a decided mind, not a mind that has arrived, but it is a young mind that is ever arriving.

Now, how is such a mind to come into being? It must happen. Obviously, a petty mind cannot work at it. A petty mind trying to become passionate will merely reduce everything to its own pettiness. It must happen, and it can only happen when the mind sees its own pettiness and yet does not try to do anything about it. Am I making myself clear? Probably not. But as I said earlier, any restricted mind, however eager it is, will still be petty, and surely that is obvious. A small mind, though it can go to the moon, though it can acquire a technique, though it can cleverly argue and defend, is still a small mind. So when the small mind says, "I must be passionate in order to do something worthwhile," obviously its passion will be very petty, will it not?—like getting angry about some petty injustice or thinking that the whole world is changing because of some petty, little reform done in a potty, little village by a potty, little mind. If the little mind sees all that, then the very perception that it is small enough, then its whole activity, undergoes a change.

Lost Passion

The word is not the thing. The word *passion* is not passion. To feel that and to be caught in it without any volition or directive or purpose, to listen to this thing called desire, to listen to your own desires which you have, plenty of them, weak or strong—when you do that, you will see what a tremendous damage you do when you suppress desire, when you distort it, when you want to fulfill it, when you want to do something about it, when you have an opinion about it.

Most people have lost this passion. Probably one has had it once in one's youth—to become a rich man, to have fame, and to live a bourgeois or a respectable life; perhaps a vague muttering of that. And society—which is what you are—suppresses that. And so one has to adjust oneself to you who are dead, who are respectable, who have not even a spark of passion; and then one becomes a part of you, and thereby loses this passion.

Passion Without a Cause

In the state of passion without a cause there is intensity free of all attachment; but when passion has a cause, there is attachment, and attachment is the beginning of sorrow. Most of us are attached, we cling to a person, to a country, to a belief, to an idea, and when the object of our attachment is taken away or otherwise loses its significance, we find ourselves empty, insufficient. This emptiness we try to fill by clinging to something else, which again becomes the object of our passion.

Examine your own heart and mind. I am merely a mirror in which you are looking at yourself. If you don't want to look, that is quite all right; but if you do want to look, then look at yourself clearly, ruthlessly, with intensity—not in the hope of dissolving your miseries, your anxieties, your sense of guilt, but in order to understand this extraordinary passion which always leads to sorrow.

When passion has a cause it becomes lust. When there is a passion for something—for a person, for an idea, for some kind of fulfillment—then out of that passion there comes contradiction, conflict, effort. You strive to achieve or maintain a particular state, or to recapture one that has been and is gone. But the passion of which I am speaking does not give rise to contradiction, conflict. It is totally unrelated to a cause, and therefore it is not an effect.

◇

MAY

Intelligence

Feelings

Words

Conditioning

◇

A Mind Rich with Innocence

Truth, the real God—the real God, not the God that man has made—does not want a mind that has been destroyed, petty, shallow, narrow, limited. It needs a healthy mind to appreciate it; it needs a rich mind—rich, not with knowledge but with innocence—a mind upon which there has never been a scratch of experience, a mind that is free from time. The gods that you have invented for your own comforts accept torture; they accept a mind that is being made dull. But the real thing does not want it; it wants a total, complete human being whose heart is full, rich, clear, capable of intense feeling, capable of seeing the beauty of a tree, the smile of a child, and the agony of a woman who has never had a full meal.

You have to have this extraordinary feeling, this sensitivity to everything—to the animal, to the cat that walks across the wall, to the squalor, the dirt, the filth of human beings in poverty, in despair. You have to be sensitive—which is to feel intensely, not in any particular direction, which is not an emotion which comes and goes, but which is to be sensitive with your nerves, with your eyes, with your body, with your ears, with your voice. You have to be sensitive completely all the time. Unless you are so completely sensitive, there is no intelligence. Intelligence comes with sensitivity and observation.

What Role Has Emotion in Life?

How do emotions come into being? Very simple. They come into being through stimuli, through the nerves. You put a pin into me, I jump; you flatter me and I am delighted; you insult me and I don't like it. Through our senses emotions come into being. And most of us function through our emotion of pleasure; obviously, sir. You like to be recognized as a Hindu. Then you belong to a group, to a community, to a tradition, however old; and you like that, with the Gita, the Upanishads and the old traditions mountain high. And the Muslim likes his and so on. Our emotions have come into being through stimuli, through environment, and so on. It is fairly obvious.

What role has emotion in life? Is emotion life? You understand? Is pleasure love? Is desire love? If emotion is love, there is something that changes all the time. Right? Don't you know all that?

. . . So one has to realize that emotions, sentiment, enthusiasm, the feeling of being good, and all that, have nothing whatsoever to do with real affection, compassion. All sentiment, emotions, have to do with thought and therefore lead to pleasure and pain. Love has no pain, no sorrow, because it is not the outcome of pleasure or desire.

 MAY 2

Freeing Intelligence

The very first thing to do, if I may suggest it, is to find out why you are thinking in a certain way, and why you are feeling in a certain manner. Don't try to alter it, don't try to analyze your thoughts and your emotions; but become conscious of why you are thinking in a particular groove and from what motive you act. Although you can discover the motive through analysis, although you may find out something through analysis, it will not be real; it will be real only when you are intensely aware at the moment of the functioning of your thought and emotion; then you will see their extraordinary subtlety, their fine delicacy. So long as you have a "must" and a "must not," in this compulsion you will never discover that swift wandering of thought and emotion. And I am sure you have been brought up in the school of "must" and "must not" and hence you have destroyed thought and feeling. You have been bound and crippled by systems, methods, by your teachers. So leave all those "must" and "must nots." This does not mean that there shall be licentiousness, but become aware of a mind that is ever saying, "I must," and "I must not." Then as a flower blossoms forth of a morning, so intelligence happens, is there, functioning, creating comprehension.

Intellect vs. Intelligence

Training the intellect does not result in intelligence. Rather, intelligence comes into being when one acts in perfect harmony, both intellectually and emotionally. There is a vast distinction between intellect and intelligence. Intellect is merely thought functioning independently of emotion. When intellect, irrespective of emotion, is trained in any particular direction, one may have great intellect, but one does not have intelligence, because in intelligence there is the inherent capacity to feel as well as to reason; in intelligence both capacities are equally present, intensely and harmoniously.

. . . If you bring your emotions into business, you say, business cannot be well-managed or be honest. So you divide your mind into compartments: in one compartment you keep your religious interest, in another your emotions, in a third your business interest which has nothing to do with your intellectual and emotional life. Your business mind treats life merely as a means of getting money in order to live. So this chaotic existence, this division of your life continues. If you really used your intelligence in business, that is, if your emotions and your thoughts were acting harmoniously, your business might fail. It probably would. And you will probably let it fail when you really feel the absurdity, the cruelty, and the exploitation that is involved in this way of living.

Until you really approach all of life with your intelligence, instead of merely with your intellect, no system in the world will save man from the ceaseless toil for bread.

Sentiment and Emotion Breed Cruelty

One can see that neither emotion nor sentiment has any place at all where love is concerned. Sentimentality and emotion are merely reactions of like or dislike. I like you and I get terribly enthusiastic about you—I like this place, oh, it is lovely and all the rest, which implies that I don't like the other and so on. Thus sentiment and emotion breed cruelty. Have you ever looked at it? Identification with the rag called the national flag is an emotional and sentimental factor and for that factor you are willing to kill another—and that is called the love of your country, love of the neighbour . . . ? One can see that where sentiment and emotion come in, love is not. It is emotion and sentiment that breed the cruelty of like and dislike. And one can see also that where there is jealousy, there is no love, obviously. I am envious of you because you have a better position, better job, better house, you look nicer, more intelligent, more awake and I am jealous of you. I don't in fact say I am jealous of you, but I compete with you, which is a form of jealousy, envy. So envy and jealousy are not love and I wipe them out; I don't go on talking about how to wipe them out and in the meantime continue to be envious—I actually wipe them out as the rain washes the dust of many days off a leaf, I just wash them away.

We Must Die to All Our Emotions

What do we mean by emotion? Is it a sensation, a reaction, a response of the senses? Hate, devotion, the feeling of love or sympathy for another—they are all emotions. Some, like love and sympathy, we call positive, while others, like hate, we call negative and want to get rid of. Is love the opposite of hate? And is love an emotion, a sensation, a feeling that is stretched out through memory?

. . . So, what do we mean by love? Surely, love is not memory. That is very difficult for us to understand because for most of us, love is memory. When you say that you love your wife or your husband, what do you mean by that? Do you love that which gives you pleasure? Do you love that with which you have identified yourself and which you recognize as belonging to you? Please, these are facts; I am not inventing anything, so don't look horrified.

. . . It is the image, the symbol of "my wife" or "my husband" that we love, or think we love, not the living individual. I don't know my wife or my husband at all; and I can never know that person as long as knowing means recognition. For recognition is based on memory—memory of pleasure and pain, memory of the things I have lived for, agonized over, the things I possess and to which I am attached. How can I love when there is fear, sorrow, loneliness, the shadow of despair? How can an ambitious man love? And we are all very ambitious, however honourably.

So, really to find out what love is, we must die to the past, to all our emotions, the good and the bad—die effortlessly, as we would to a poisonous thing, because we understand it.

One Must Have Great Feelings

In the modern world where there are so many problems, one is apt to lose great feeling. I mean by that word *feeling*, not sentiment, not emotionalism, not mere excitement, but that quality of perception, the quality of hearing, listening, the quality of feeling, a bird singing on a tree, the movement of a leaf in the sun. To feel things greatly, deeply, penetratingly, is very difficult for most of us because we have so many problems. Whatever we seem to touch turns into a problem. And, apparently, there is no end to man's problems, and he seems utterly incapable of resolving them because the more the problems exist, the less the feelings become.

I mean by "feeling" the appreciation of the curve of a branch, the squalor, the dirt on the road, to be sensitive to the sorrow of another, to be in a state of ecstasy when we see a sunset. These are not sentiments, these are not mere emotions. Emotion and sentiment or sentimentality turn to cruelty, they can be used by society; and when there is sentiment, sensation, then one becomes a slave to society. But one must have great feelings. The feeling for beauty, the feeling for a word, the silence between two words, and the hearing of a sound clearly—all that generates feeling. And one must have strong feelings, because it is only the feelings that make the mind highly sensitive.

Observation Without Thought

There is no feeling without thought; and behind thought is pleasure; so those things go together: pleasure, the word, the thought, the feeling; they are not separated. Observation without thought, without feeling, without word is energy. Energy is dissipated by word, association, thought, pleasure, and time; therefore, there is no energy to look.

The Totality of Feeling

What is feeling? Feeling is like thought. Feeling is a sensation. I see a flower and I respond to that flower; I like it or dislike it. The like or the dislike is dictated by my thought, and the thought is the response of the background of memory. So, I say, "I like that flower," or "I do not like that flower"; "I like this feeling" or "I do not like that feeling." . . . Now, is love related to feeling? Feeling is sensation, obviously—sensation of like and dislike, of good and bad, of good taste and all the rest of it. Is that feeling related to love? . . . Have you watched your street, have you watched the way you live in your houses, the way you sit, the way you talk? And have you noticed all your saints whom you worship? For them passion is sex, and therefore they deny passion, therefore they deny beauty—deny in the sense of putting those aside. So, with sensation you have put away love because you say, "Sensation will make me a prisoner, I will be a slave to sex-desire; therefore I must cut it out." Therefore you have made sex into an immense problem. . . . When you have understood feeling completely, not partially, when you have really understood the totality of feeling, then you will know what love is. When you can see the beauty of a tree, when you can see the beauty of a smile, when you can see the sun setting behind the walls of your town—see totally—then you will know what love is.

If You Do Not Name That Feeling

When you observe a feeling, that feeling comes to an end. But even though the feeling comes to an end, if there is an observer, a spectator, a censor, a thinker who remains apart from the feeling, then there is still a contradiction. So it is very important to understand how we look at a feeling.

Take, for instance, a very common feeling: jealousy. We all know what it is to be jealous. Now, how do you look at your jealousy? When you look at that feeling, you are the observer of jealousy as something apart from yourself. You try to change jealousy, to modify it, or you try to explain why you are justified in being jealous, and so on and so forth. So there is a being, a censor, an entity apart from jealousy who observes it. For the moment jealousy may disappear, but it comes back again; and it comes back because you do not really see that jealousy is part of you.

. . . What I am saying is that the moment you give a name, a label to that feeling, you have brought it into the framework of the old; and the old is the observer, the separate entity who is made up of words, of ideas, of opinions about what is right and what is wrong. . . . But if you don't name that feeling—which demands tremendous awareness, a great deal of immediate understanding—then you will find that there is no observer, no thinker, no center from which you are judging, and that you are not different from the feeling. There is no "you" who feels it.

Emotions Lead Nowhere

Whether you are guided by your emotions or guided by your intellect, it leads to despair because it leads nowhere. But you realize that love is not pleasure, love is not desire.

You know what pleasure is, sir? When you look at something or when you have a feeling, to think about that feeling, to dwell constantly upon that feeling gives you pleasure, and that pleasure you want and you repeat that pleasure over and over again. When a man is very ambitious or a little ambitious, that gives him pleasure. When a man is seeking power, position, prestige in the name of the country, in the name of an idea, and all the rest of it, that gives him pleasure. He has no love at all, and therefore he creates mischief in the world. He brings about war within and without.

So one has to realize that emotions, sentiment, enthusiasm, the feeling of being good, and all that have nothing whatsoever to do with real affection, compassion. All sentiment, emotions have to do with thought and therefore lead to pleasure and pain. Love has no pain, no sorrow, because it is not the outcome of pleasure or desire.

Memory Negates Love

Is it possible to love without thinking? What do you mean by thinking? Thinking is a response to memories of pain or pleasure. There is no thinking without the residue which incomplete experience leaves. Love is different from emotion and feeling. Love cannot be brought into the field of thought; whereas feeling and emotion can be brought. Love is a flame without smoke, ever fresh, creative, joyous. Such love is dangerous to society, to relationship. So, thought steps in, modifies, guides it, legalizes it, puts it out of danger; then one can live with it. Do you not know that when you love someone, you love the whole of mankind? Do you not know how dangerous it is to love man? Then, there is no barrier, no nationality; then, there is no craving for power and position, and things assume their values. Such a man is a danger to society.

For the being of love, the process of memory must come to an end. Memory comes into being only when experience is not fully, completely understood. Memory is only the residue of experience; it is the result of a challenge which is not fully comprehended. Life is a process of challenge and response. Challenge is always new but the response is ever old. This response, which is conditioning, which is the result of the past, must be understood and not disciplined or condemned away. It means living each day anew, fully and completely. This complete living is possible only when there is love, when your heart is full, not with the words nor with the things made by the mind. Only where there is love, memory ceases; then every movement is a rebirth.

Do Not Name a Feeling

What happens when you do not name? You look at an emotion, at a sensation, more directly and therefore have quite a different relationship to it, just as you have to a flower when you do not name it. You are forced to look at it anew. When you do not name a group of people, you are compelled to look at each individual face and not treat them all as a mass. Therefore you are much more alert, much more observing, more understanding; you have a deeper sense of pity, love; but if you treat them all as the mass, it is over.

If you do not label, you have to regard every feeling as it arises. When you label, is the feeling different from the label? Or does the label awaken the feeling?. . .

If I do not name a feeling, that is to say if thought is not functioning merely because of words or if I do not think in terms of words, images, or symbols, which most of us do—then what happens? Surely the mind then is not merely the observer. When the mind is not thinking in terms of words, symbols, images, there is no thinker separate from the thought, which is the word. Then the mind is quiet, is it not?—not made quiet, it is quiet. When the mind is really quiet, then the feelings that arise can be dealt with immediately. It is only when we give names to feelings and thereby strengthen them that the feelings have continuity; they are stored up in the center, from which we give further labels, either to strengthen or to communicate them.

Remain with a Feeling
and See What Happens

You never remain with any feeling, pure and simple, but always surround it with the paraphernalia of words. The word distorts it; thought, whirling round it, throws it into shadow, overpowers it with mountainous fears and longings. You never remain with a feeling, and with nothing else: with hate, or with that strange feeling of beauty. When the feeling of hate arises, you say how bad it is; there is the compulsion, the struggle to overcome it, the turmoil of thought about it. . . .

Try remaining with the feeling of hate, with the feeling of envy, jealousy, with the venom of ambition; for after all, that's what you have in daily life, though you may want to live with love, or with the word *love*. Since you have the feeling of hate, of wanting to hurt somebody with a gesture or a burning word, see if you can stay with that feeling. Can you? Have you ever tried? Try to remain with a feeling, and see what happens. You will find it amazingly difficult. Your mind will not leave the feeling alone; it comes rushing in with its remembrances, its associations, its do's and don'ts, its everlasting chatter. Pick up a piece of shell. Can you look at it, wonder at its delicate beauty, without saying how pretty it is, or what animal made it? Can you look without the movement of the mind? Can you live with the feeling behind the word, without the feeling that the word builds up? If you can, then you will discover an extraordinary thing, a movement beyond the measure of time, a spring that knows no summer.

Understanding Words

I do not know if you have ever thought out or gone into this whole process of verbalizing, giving a name. If you have done so, it is really a most astonishing thing and a very stimulating and interesting thing. When we give a name to anything we experience, see, or feel, the word becomes extraordinarily significant; and word is time. Time is space, and the word is the center of it. All thinking is verbalization; you think in words. And can the mind be free of the word? Don't say, "How am I to be free?" That has no meaning. But put that question to yourself and see how slavish you are to words like India, Gita, communism, Christian, Russian, American, English, the caste below you and the caste above you. The word *love,* the word *God,* the word *meditation*—what extraordinary significance we have given to these words and how slavish we are to them.

Memory Clouds Perception

Are you speculating, or are you actually experiencing as we are going along? You do not know what a religious mind is, do you? From what you have said, you don't know what it means; you may have just a flutter or a glimpse of it, just as you see the clear, lovely blue sky when the cloud is broken through; but the moment you have perceived the blue sky, you have a memory of it, you want more of it and therefore you are lost in it; the more you want the word for storing it as an experience, the more you are lost in it.

Words Create Limitations

Is there a thinking without the word? When the mind is not cluttered up with words, then thinking is not thinking as we know; but it is an activity without the word, without the symbol; therefore it has no frontier—the word is the frontier.

The word creates the limitation, the boundary. And a mind that is not functioning in words has no limitation; it has no frontiers; it is not bound. . . . Take the word *love* and see what it awakens in you, watch yourself; the moment I mention that word, you are beginning to smile and you sit up, you feel. So the word *love* awakens all kinds of ideas, all kinds of divisions such as carnal, spiritual, profane, infinite, and all the rest of it. But find out what love is. Surely, sir, to find out what love is the mind must be free of that word and the significance of that word.

Going Beyond Words

To understand one another, I think it is necessary that we should not be caught in words; because, a word like *God,* for example, may have a particular meaning for you, while for me it may represent a totally different formulation, or no formulation at all. So it is almost impossible to communicate with each other unless both of us have the intention of understanding and going beyond mere words. The word *freedom* generally implies being free from something, does it not? It ordinarily means being free from greed, from envy, from nationalism, from anger, from this or that. Whereas, freedom may have quite another meaning, which is a sense of being free; and I think it is very important to understand this meaning.

. . . After all, the mind is made up of words, amongst other things. Now, can the mind be free of the word *envy?* Experiment with this and you will see that words like *God, truth, hate, envy,* have a profound effect on the mind. And can the mind be both neurologically and psychologically free of these words? If it is not free of them, it is incapable of facing the fact of envy. When the mind can look directly at the fact which it calls "envy," then the fact itself acts much more swiftly than the mind's endeavor to do something about the fact. As long as the mind is thinking of getting rid of envy through the ideal of non-envy, and so on, it is distracted, it is not facing the fact; and the very word *envy* is a distraction from the fact. The process of recognition is through the word; and the moment I recognize the feeling through the word, I give continuity to that feeling.

Extraordinary Seeing

So we are asking, as at the beginning, can the mind come to that extraordinary seeing, not from the periphery, from the outside, from the boundary, but come upon it without any seeking? And to come upon it without seeking is the only way to find it. Because in coming upon it unknowingly, there is no effort, no seeking, no experience; and there is the total denial of all the normal practices to come into that center, to that flowering. So the mind is highly sharpened, highly awake, and is no longer dependent upon any experience to keep itself awake.

When one asks oneself, one may ask verbally; for most people, naturally, it must be verbal. And one has to realize that the word is not the thing—like the word *tree* is not the tree, is not the actual fact. The actual fact is when one touches it, not through the word, but when one actually comes into contact with it. Then it is an actuality —which means the word has lost its power to mesmerize people. For example, the word *God* is so loaded and it has mesmerized people so much that they will accept or deny, and function like a squirrel in a cage! So the word and the symbol must be set aside.

Perception of Truth Is Immediate

The verbal state has been carefully built up through centuries, in relation between the individual and society; so the word, the verbal state is a social state as well as an individual state. To communicate as we are doing, I need memory, I need words, I must know English, and you must know English; it has been acquired through centuries upon centuries. The word is not only being developed in social relationships, but also as a re-action in that social relationship to the individual; the word is necessary. The question is, it has taken so long, centuries upon centuries, to build up the symbolical, the verbal state, and can that be wiped away immediately? . . . Through time are we going to get rid of the verbal imprisonment of the mind, which has been built up for centuries? Or must it break immediately? Now, you may say, "It must take time, I can't do it immediately." This means that you must have many days, this means a continuity of what has been, though it is modified in the process, till you reach a stage where there is no further to go. Can you do that? Because we are afraid, we are lazy, we are indolent, we say, "Why bother about all this? It is too difficult"; or "I do not know what to do"—so you postpone, postpone, postpone. But you have to see the truth of the continuation and the modification of the word. The perception of the truth of anything is immediate—not in time. Can the mind break through instantly, on the very questioning? Can the mind see the barrier of the word, understand the significance of the word in a flash and be in that state when the mind is no longer caught in time? You must have experienced this; only it is a very rare thing for most of us.

 MAY 20

Subtle Truth

You have the flash of understanding, that extraordinary rapidity of insight, when the mind is very still, when thought is absent, when the mind is not burdened with its own noise. So, the understanding of anything—of a modern picture, of a child, of your wife, of your neighbor, or the understanding of truth, which is in all things—can only come when the mind is very still. But such stillness cannot be cultivated because if you cultivate a still mind, it is not a still mind, it is a dead mind.

. . . The more you are interested in something, the more your intention to understand, the more simple, clear, free the mind is. Then verbalization ceases. After all, thought is word, and it is the word that interferes. It is the screen of words, which is memory, that intervenes between the challenge and the response. It is the word that is responding to the challenge, which we call intellection. So, the mind that is chattering, that is verbalizing, cannot understand truth—truth in relationship, not an abstract truth. There is no abstract truth. But truth is very subtle. It is the subtle that is difficult to follow. It is not abstract. It comes so swiftly, so darkly, it cannot be held by the mind. Like a thief in the night, it comes darkly, not when you are prepared to receive it. Your reception is merely an invitation of greed. So a mind that is caught in the net of words cannot understand truth.

All Thought Is Partial

You and I realize that we are conditioned. If you say, as some people do, that conditioning is inevitable, then there is no problem; you are a slave, and that is the end of it. But if you begin to ask yourself whether it is at all possible to break down this limitation, this conditioning, then there is a problem; so you will have to inquire into the whole process of thinking, will you not? If you merely say, "I must be aware of my conditioning, I must think about it, analyze it in order to understand and destroy it," then you are exercising force. Your thinking, your analyzing is still the result of your background, so through your thought you obviously cannot break down the conditioning of which it is a part.

Just see the problem first, don't ask what is the answer, the solution. The fact is that we are conditioned, and that all thought to understand this conditioning will always be partial; therefore there is never a total comprehension, and only in total comprehension of the whole process of thinking is there freedom. The difficulty is that we are always functioning within the field of the mind, which is the instrument of thought, reasonable or unreasonable; and as we have seen, thought is always partial.

Freedom from the Self

To free the mind from all conditioning, you must see the totality of it without thought. This is not a conundrum; experiment with it and you will see. Do you ever see anything without thought? Have you ever listened, looked, without bringing in this whole process of reaction? You will say that it is impossible to see without thought; you will say no mind can be unconditioned. When you say that, you have already blocked yourself by thought, for the fact is you do not know.

So can I look, can the mind be aware of its conditioning? I think it can. Please experiment. Can you be aware that you are a Hindu, a Socialist, a communist, this or that, just be aware without saying that it is right or wrong? Because it is such a difficult task just to see, we say it is impossible. I say it is only when you are aware of this totality of your being without any reaction that the conditioning goes, totally, deeply—which is really the freedom from the self.

Awareness May
Burn Away the Problems

All thinking obviously is conditioned; there is no such thing as free thinking. Thinking can never be free, it is the outcome of our conditioning, of our background, of our culture, of our climate, of our social, economic, political background. The very books that you read and the very practices that you do are all established in the background, and any thinking must be the result of that background. So if we can be aware—and we can go presently into what it signifies, what it means, to be aware—perhaps we shall be able to uncondition the mind without the process of will, without the determination to uncondition the mind. Because the moment you determine, there is an entity who wishes, an entity who says, "I must uncondition my mind." That entity itself is the outcome of our desire to achieve a certain result, so a conflict is already there. So, is it possible to be aware of our conditioning, just to be aware?—in which there is no conflict at all. That very awareness, if allowed, may perhaps burn away the problems.

There Is No Noble
or Better Conditioning

Does not the urge of the mind to free itself from its conditioning set going another pattern of resistance and conditioning? Having become aware of the pattern or mold in which you have grown up, you want to be free from it; but will not this desire to be free condition the mind again in a different manner? The old pattern insists that you conform to authority, and now you are developing a new one which maintains that you must not conform; so you have two patterns, one in conflict with the other. As long as there is this inner contradiction, further conditioning takes place.

. . . There is the urge that makes for conformity, and the urge to be free. However dissimilar these two urges may seem to be, are they not fundamentally similar? And if they are fundamentally similar, then your pursuit of freedom is vain, for you will only move from one pattern to another, endlessly. There is no noble or better conditioning, and it is this desire that has to be understood.

Freedom from Conditioning

The desire to free oneself from conditioning only furthers conditioning. But if, instead of trying to suppress desire, one understands the whole process of desire, in that very understanding there comes freedom from conditioning. Freedom from conditioning is not a direct result. Do you understand? If I set about deliberately to free myself from my conditioning, that desire creates its own conditioning. I may destroy one form of conditioning, but I am caught in another. Whereas, if there is an understanding of desire itself, which includes the desire to be free, then that very understanding destroys all conditioning. Freedom from conditioning is a byproduct; it is not important. The important thing is to understand what it is that creates conditioning.

Simple Awareness

Surely any form of accumulation, either of knowledge or experience, any form of ideal, any projection of the mind, any determined practice to shape the mind—what it should be and should not be—all this is obviously crippling the process of investigation and discovery. . . .

So I think our inquiry must be not for the solution of our immediate problems but rather to find out whether the mind—the conscious as well as the deep unconscious mind in which is stored all the tradition, the memories, the inheritance of racial knowledge—whether all of it can be put aside. I think it can be done only if the mind is capable of being aware without any sense of demand, without any pressure—just to be aware. I think it is one of the most difficult things—to be so aware—because we are caught in the immediate problem and in its immediate solution, and so our lives are very superficial. Though one may go to all the analysts, read all the books, acquire much knowledge, attend churches, pray, meditate, practice various disciplines; nevertheless, our lives are obviously very superficial because we do not know how to penetrate deeply. I think the understanding, the way of penetration, how to go very, very deeply, lies through awareness—just to be aware of our thoughts and feelings, without condemnation, without comparison, just to observe. You will see, if you will experiment, how extraordinarily difficult it is, because our whole training is to condemn, to approve, to compare.

No Part of the Mind Is Unconditioned

Your mind is conditioned right through: there is no part of you which is unconditioned. That is a fact, whether you like it or not. You may say there is a part of you—the watcher, the supersoul, the atma—which is not conditioned; but because you think about it, it is within the field of thought; therefore, it is conditioned. You can invent lots of theories about it, but the fact is that your mind is conditioned right through, the conscious as well as the unconscious, and any effort it makes to free itself is also conditioned. So what is the mind to do? Or rather, what is the state of the mind when it knows that it is conditioned and realizes that any effort it makes to uncondition itself is still conditioned?

Now, when you say, "I know I am conditioned," do you really know it, or is that merely a verbal statement? Do you know it with the same potency with which you see a cobra? When you see a snake and know it to be a cobra, there is immediate, unpremeditated action; and when you say, "I know I am conditioned," has it the same vital significance as your perception of the cobra? Or is it merely a superficial acknowledgment of the fact, and not the realization of the fact? When I realize the fact that I am conditioned, there is immediate action. I don't have to make an effort to unconditioned myself. The very fact that I am conditioned, and the realization of that fact, brings an immediate clarification. The difficulty lies in not realizing it in the sense of understanding all its implications, seeing that all thought, however subtle, however cunning, however sophisticated or philosophical, is conditioned.

The Burden of the Unconscious

Inwardly, unconsciously, there is the tremendous weight of the past pushing you in a certain direction. . . .

Now, how is one to wipe all that away? How is the unconscious to be cleansed immediately of the past? The analysts think that the unconscious can be partially or even completely cleansed through analysis—through investigation, exploration, confession, the interpretation of dreams, and so on—so that at least you become a "normal" human being, able to adjust yourself to the present environment. But in analysis there is always the analyzer and the analyzed, an observer who is interpreting the thing observed, which is a duality, a source of conflict.

So I see that mere analysis of the unconscious will not lead anywhere. It may help me to be a little less neurotic, a little kinder to my wife, to my neighbor, or some superficial thing like that; but that is not what we are talking about. I see that the analytical process—which involves time, interpretation, the movement of thought as the observer analyzing the thing observed—cannot free the unconscious; therefore I reject the analytical process completely. The moment I perceive the fact that analysis cannot under any circumstances clear away the burden of the unconscious, I am out of analysis. I no longer analyze. So what has taken place? Because there is no longer an analyzer separated from the thing that he analyzes, he *is* that thing. He is not an entity apart from it. Then one finds that the unconscious is of very little importance.

The Interval Between Thoughts

Now, I say it is definitely possible for the mind to be free from all conditioning—not that you should accept my authority. If you accept it on authority, you will never discover, it will be another substitution and that will have no significance. . . .

The understanding of the whole process of conditioning does not come to you through analysis or introspection, because the moment you have the analyzer, that very analyzer himself is part of the background and therefore his analysis is of no significance. . . .

How is it possible for the mind to be free? To be free, the mind must not only see and understand its pendulum-like swing between the past and the future but also be aware of the interval between thoughts. . . .

If you watch very carefully, you will see that though the response, the movement of thought, seems so swift, there are gaps, there are intervals between thoughts. Between two thoughts is a period of silence that is not related to the thought process. If you observe you will see that that period of silence, that interval, is not of time; and the discovery of that interval, the full experiencing of that interval, liberates you from conditioning—or rather it does not liberate "you" but there is liberation from conditioning. . . . It is only when the mind is not giving continuity to thought, when it is still with a stillness that is not induced, that is without any causation—it is only then that there can be freedom from the background.

Observe How Habits Are Formed

Without freedom from the past there is no freedom at all, because the mind is never new, fresh, innocent. It is only the fresh, innocent mind that is free. Freedom has nothing to do with age, it has nothing to do with experience; and it seems to me that the very essence of freedom lies in understanding the whole mechanism of habit, both conscious and unconscious. It is not a question of ending habit, but of seeing totally the structure of habit. You have to observe how habits are formed and how, by denying or resisting one habit, another habit is created. What matters is to be totally conscious of habit; for then, as you will see for yourself there is no longer the formation of habit. To resist habit, to fight it, to deny it, only gives continuity to habit. When you fight a particular habit you give life to that habit, and then the very fighting of it becomes a further habit. But if you are simply aware of the whole structure of habit without resistance, then you will find there is freedom from habit, and in that freedom a new thing takes place.

It is only the dull, sleepy mind that creates and clings to habit. A mind that is attentive from moment to moment—attentive to what it is saying, attentive to the movement of its hands, of its thoughts, of its feelings—will discover that the formation of further habits has come to an end. This is very important to understand, because as long as the mind is breaking down one habit, and in that very process creating another, it can obviously never be free; and it is only the free mind that can perceive something beyond itself.

◈

JUNE

Energy

Attention

Choiceless Awareness

Violence

◈

Energy Creates Its Own Discipline

To seek reality requires immense energy; and if man is not doing that, he dissipates his energy in ways that create mischief, and therefore society has to control him. Now, is it possible to liberate energy in seeking God or truth and, in the process of discovering what is true, to be a citizen who understands the fundamental issues of life and whom society cannot destroy?

You see, man is energy, and if man does not seek truth, this energy becomes destructive; therefore society controls and shapes the individual, which smothers this energy. . . And perhaps you have noticed another interesting and very simple fact: that the moment you really want to do something, you have the energy to do it. . . . That very energy becomes the means of controlling itself, so you don't need outside discipline. In the search for reality, energy creates its own discipline. The man who is seeking reality spontaneously becomes the right kind of citizen, which is not according to the pattern of any particular society or government.

Duality Creates Conflict

Conflict of any kind—physically, psychologically, intellectually—is a waste of energy. Please, it is extraordinarily difficult to understand and to be free of this because most of us are brought up to struggle, to make effort. When we are at school, that is the first thing that we are taught—to make an effort. And that struggle, that effort is carried throughout life—that is, to be good you must struggle, you must fight evil, you must resist, control. So, educationally, sociologically, religiously, human beings are taught to struggle. You are told that to find God you must work, discipline, do practice, twist and torture your soul, your mind, your body, deny, suppress; that you must not look; that you must fight, fight, fight at that so-called spiritual level—which is not the spiritual level at all. Then, socially each one is out for himself, for his family.

. . . So, all around, we are wasting energy. And that waste of energy in essence is conflict: the conflict between "I should" and "I should not," "I must" and "I must not." Once having created duality, conflict is inevitable. So one has to understand this whole process of duality—not that there is not man and woman, green and red, light and darkness, tall and short; all those are facts. But in the effort that goes into this division between the fact and the idea, there is the waste of energy.

The Pattern of an Idea

If you say, "How am I to save energy?" then you have created a pattern of an idea—how to save it—and then conduct your life according to that pattern; therefore, there begins again a contradiction. Whereas if you perceive for yourself where your energies are being wasted, you will see that the principal force causing the waste is conflict—which is having a problem and never resolving it, living with a deadly memory of something gone, living in tradition. One has to understand the nature of the dissipation of energy, and the understanding of the dissipation of energy is not according to Shankara, Buddha, or some saint, but the actual observation of one's daily conflict in life. So the principal waste of energy is conflict—which doesn't mean that you sit back and be lazy. Conflict will always exist as long as the idea is more important than the fact.

Where There Is Contradiction
There Is Conflict

You see that most of us are in conflict, live a life of contradiction, not only outwardly, but also inwardly. Contradiction implies effort. . . . Where there is effort, there is wastage—there is a waste of energy. Where there is contradiction, there is conflict. Where there is conflict, there is effort to get over that conflict—which is another form of resistance. And where you resist, there is also a certain form of energy engendered—you know that when you resist something, that very resistance creates energy. . . .

All action is based on this friction that I must and I must not. And this form of resistance, this form of conflict, does breed energy; but that energy, if you observe very closely, is very destructive; it is not creative. . . . Most people are in contradiction. And if they have a gift, a talent to write or to paint or to do this or that, the tension of that contradiction gives them the energy to express, to create, to write, to be. The more the tension, the greater the conflict, the greater is the output, and that is what we call creation. But it is not at all creation. It is the result of conflict. To face the fact that you are in conflict, that you are in contradiction, will bring that quality of energy that is not the outcome of resistance.

Creative Energy

Now the question is: Is there an energy which is not within the field of thought, which is not the result of self-contradictory, compulsive energy, of self-fulfillment as frustration? You understand the question? I hope I am making myself clear. Because, unless we find the quality of that energy which is not merely the product of thought that bit by bit creates the energy but also is mechanical, action is destructive, whether we do social reform, write excellent books, be very clever in business, or create nationalistic divisions and take part in other political activities, and so on. Now, the question is whether there is such an energy, not theoretically—because when we are confronted with facts, to introduce theories is infantile, immature. It is like the case of a man who has cancer and is to be operated upon; it is no good discussing what kinds of instruments are to be used and all the rest of it; you have to face the fact that he is to be operated upon. So, similarly, a mind has to penetrate or be in such a state when the mind is not a slave to thought. After all, all thought in time is invention; all the gadgets, jets, the refrigerators, the rockets, the exploration into the atom, space, they are all the result of knowledge, thought. All these are not creation; invention is not creation; capacity is not creation; thought can never be creative because thought is always conditioned and can never be free. It is only that energy which is not the product of thought that is creative.

The Highest Form of Energy

An idea about energy is entirely different from the fact of energy itself. We have formulas or concepts of how to bring about a quality of energy that is of the highest quality. But the formula is entirely different from the renovating, renewing quality of energy itself.

. . . The highest form of this energy, the apogee, is the state of mind when it has no idea, no thought, no sense of a direction or motive—that is pure energy. And that quality of energy cannot be sought after. You can't say, "Well, tell me how to get it, the modus operandi, the way." There is no way to it. To find out for ourselves the nature of this energy, we must begin to understand the daily energy that is wasted—the energy when we talk, when we hear a bird, a voice, when we see the river, the vast sky and the villagers, dirty, ill-kept, ill, half-starved, and the tree that withdraws of an evening from all the light of day. The very observation of everything is energy. And this energy we derive through food, through the sun's rays. This physical, daily energy that one has, obviously can be augmented, increased, by the right kind of food, and so on. That is necessary, obviously. But that same energy which becomes the energy of the psyche— that is, thought—the moment that energy has any contradiction in itself, that energy is a waste of energy.

The Art of Listening
Is the Art of Release

Somebody is telling you something, you listen. The very act of listening is the act of release. When you see the fact, the very perception of that fact is the release of that fact. The very listening, the very seeing of something as a fact, has an extraordinary effect without the effort of thought.

. . . Let us take one thing—say ambition. We have gone sufficiently into what it does, what its effects are. A mind that is ambitious can never know what it is to sympathize, to have pity, to love. An ambitious mind is a cruel mind—whether spiritually or outwardly or inwardly. You have heard it. You hear it; when you hear that, you translate it and say, "How can I live in this world which is built on ambition?" Therefore, you have not listened. You have responded, you have reacted to a statement, to a fact; therefore, you are not looking at the fact. You are merely translating the fact or giving an opinion about the fact or responding to the fact; therefore, you are not looking at the fact. . . . If one listens—in the sense without any evaluation, reaction, judgment—surely then, the fact creates that energy which destroys, wipes away, sweeps away ambition which creates conflict.

Attention Without Resistance

You know what space is. There is space in this room. The distance between here and your hostel, between the bridge and your home, between this bank of the river and the other— all that is space. Now, is there also space in your mind? Or is it so crowded that there is no space in it at all? If your mind has space, then in that space there is silence—and from that silence everything else comes, for then you can listen, you can pay attention without resistance. That is why it is very important to have space in the mind. If the mind is not overcrowded, not ceaselessly occupied, then it can listen to that dog barking, to the sound of a train crossing the distant bridge, and also be fully aware of what is being said by a person talking here. Then the mind is a living thing, it is not dead.

Attention Free of Effort

Is there attention without anything absorbing the mind? Is there attention without concentrating upon an object? Is there attention without any form of motive, influence, compulsion? Can the mind give full attention without any sense of exclusion? Surely it can, and that is the only state of attention; the others are mere indulgence, or tricks of the mind. If you can give full attention without being absorbed in something, and without any sense of exclusion, then you will find out what it is to meditate; because in that attention there is no effort, no division, no struggle, no search for a result. So meditation is a process of freeing the mind from systems, and of giving attention without either being absorbed or making an effort to concentrate.

An Attention That Is Not Exclusive

I think there is a difference between attention that is given to an object and attention without object. We can concentrate on a particular idea, belief, object—which is an exclusive process; and there is also an attention, an awareness, which is not exclusive. Similarly, there is a discontent which has no motive, which is not the outcome of some frustration, which cannot be canalized, which cannot accept any fulfillment. Perhaps I may not be using the right word for it, but I think that that extraordinary discontent is the essential. Without that, every other form of discontent merely becomes a way to satisfaction.

Attention Is Limitless,
Without Frontiers

In the cultivation of the mind, our emphasis should not be on concentration, but on attention. Concentration is a process of forcing the mind to narrow down to a point, whereas attention is without frontiers. In that process the mind is always limited by a frontier or boundary, but when our concern is to understand the totality of the mind, mere concentration becomes a hindrance. Attention is limitless, without the frontiers of knowledge. Knowledge comes through concentration, and any extension of knowledge is still within its own frontiers. In the state of attention the mind can and does use knowledge, which of necessity is the result of concentration; but the part is never the whole, and adding together the many parts does not make for the perception of the whole. Knowledge, which is the additive process of concentration does not bring about the understanding of the immeasurable. The total is never within the brackets of a concentrated mind.

So attention is of primary importance, but it does not come through the effort of concentration. Attention is a state in which the mind is ever learning without a center around which knowledge gathers as accumulated experience. A mind that is concentrated upon itself uses knowledge as a means of its own expansion; and such activity becomes self-contradictory and antisocial.

Complete Attention

What do we mean by attention? Is there attention when I am forcing my mind to attend? When I say to myself, "I must pay attention, I must control my mind and push aside all other thoughts," would you call that attention? Surely that is not attention. What happens when the mind forces itself to pay attention? It creates a resistance to prevent other thoughts from seeping in; it is concerned with resistance, with pushing away; therefore it is incapable of attention. That is true, is it not?

To understand something totally you must give your complete attention to it. But you will soon find out how extraordinarily difficult that is, because your mind is used to being distracted, so you say, "By Jove, it is good to pay attention, but how am I to do it?" That is, you are back again with the desire to get something, so you will never pay complete attention. . . . When you see a tree or a bird, for example, to pay complete attention is not to say, "That is an oak," or, "That is a parrot," and walk by. In giving it a name you have already ceased to pay attention. . . . Whereas, if you are wholly aware, totally attentive when you look at something, then you will find that a complete transformation takes place, and that total attention is the good. There is no other, and you cannot get total attention by practice. With practice you get concentration, that is, you build up walls of resistance, and within those walls of resistance is the concentrator, but that is not attention, it is exclusion.

Elimination of Fear
Is the Beginning of Attention

How is the state of attention to be brought about? It cannot be cultivated through persuasion, comparison, reward, or punishment, all of which are forms of coercion. The elimination of fear is the beginning of attention. Fear must exist as long as there is an urge to be or to become, which is the pursuit of success, with all its frustrations and tortuous contradictions. You can teach concentration, but attention cannot be taught, just as you cannot possibly teach freedom from fear, and in understanding these causes there is the elimination of fear. So attention arises spontaneously when around the student there is an atmosphere of well-being, when he has the feeling of being secure, of being at ease, and is aware of the disinterested action that comes with love. Love does not compare, and so the envy and torture of "becoming" cease.

There Is No Place at Which to Arrive

Can humility be practiced? Surely, to be conscious that you are humble is not to be humble. You want to know that you have arrived. This indicates, does it not, that you are listening in order to achieve a particular state, a place where you will never be disturbed, where you will find everlasting happiness, permanent bliss? But as I said previously, there is no arriving, there is only the movement of learning—and that is the beauty of life. If you have arrived, there is nothing more. And all of you have arrived, or you want to arrive, not only in your business, but in everything you do; so you are dissatisfied, frustrated, miserable. Sirs, there is no place at which to arrive, there is just this movement of learning, which becomes painful only when there is accumulation. A mind that listens with complete attention will never look for a result because it is constantly unfolding; like a river, it is always in movement. Such a mind is totally unconscious of its own activity, in the sense that there is no perpetuation of a self, of a "me," which is seeking to achieve an end.

Knowledge Is Not Awareness

Awareness is that state of mind which observes something without any condemnation or acceptance, which merely faces the thing as it is. When you look at a flower nonbotanically, then you see the totality of the flower; but if your mind is completely taken up with the botanical knowledge of what the flower is, you are not totally looking at the flower. Though you may have knowledge of the flower, if that knowledge takes the whole ground of your mind, the whole field of your mind, then you are not looking totally at the flower.

So, to look at a fact is to be aware. In that awareness, there is no choice, no condemnation, no like or dislike. But most of us are incapable of doing this because traditionally, occupationally, in every way, we are not capable of facing the fact without the background. We have to be aware of the background. We have to be aware of our conditioning, and that conditioning shows itself when we observe a fact; and as you are concerned with the observation of the fact and not with the background, the background is pushed aside. When the main interest is to understand the fact only, and when you see that the background prevents you from understanding the fact, then the vital interest in the fact wipes away the background.

Introspection Is Incomplete

In awareness there is only the present—that is, being aware, you see the past process of influence which controls the present and modifies the future. Awareness is an integral process, not a process of division. For example, if I ask the question, "Do I believe in God?"—in the very process of asking, I can observe, if I am aware, what it is that is making me ask that question; if I am aware I can perceive what have been and what are the forces at work that are compelling me to ask that question. Then I am aware of various forms of fear—those of my ancestors who have created a certain idea of God and have handed it down to me, and combining their idea with my present reactions, I have modified or changed the concept of God. If I am aware, I perceive this entire process of the past, its effect in the present and in the future, integrally, as a whole.

If one is aware, one sees how through fear one's concept of God arose; or perhaps there was a person who had an original experience of reality or of God and communicated it to another who in his greediness made it his own, and gave impetus to the process of imitation. Awareness is the process of completeness, and introspection is incomplete. The result of introspection is morbid, painful, whereas awareness is enthusiasm and joy.

Seeing the Whole

How do you look at a tree? Do you see the whole of the tree? If you don't see it as a whole, you don't see the tree at all. You may pass it by and say, "There is a tree, how nice it is!" or say, "It is a mango tree," or "I do not know what those trees are; they may be tamarind trees." But when you stand and look—I am talking actually, factually—you never see the totality of it; and if you don't see the totality of the tree, you do not see the tree. In the same way is *awareness*. If you don't see the operations of your mind totally in that sense—as you see the tree—you are not aware. The tree is made up of the roots, the trunk, the branches, the big ones and the little ones and the very delicate one that goes up there; and the leaf, the dead leaf, the withered leaf and the green leaf, the leaf that is eaten, the leaf that is ugly, the leaf that is dropping, the fruit, the flower—all that you see as a whole when you see the tree. In the same way, in that state of *seeing* the operations of your mind, in that state of awareness, there is your sense of condemnation, approval, denial, struggle, futility, the despair, the hope, the frustration; awareness covers all that, not just one part. So, are you aware of your mind in that very simple sense, as seeing a whole picture—not one corner of the picture and saying, "Who painted that picture?"

Awareness Cannot Be Disciplined

If awareness is practiced, made into a habit, then it becomes tedious and painful. Awareness cannot be disciplined. That which is practiced is no longer awareness, for in practice is implied the creation of habit, the exertion of effort and will. Effort is distortion. There is not only the awareness of the outer—of the flight of birds, of shadows, of the restless sea, the trees and the wind, the beggar and the luxurious cars that pass by—but also there is the awareness of the psychological process, the inward tension and conflict. You do not condemn a bird in flight: you observe it, you see the beauty of it. But, when you consider your own inward strife, you condemn it or justify it. You are incapable of observing this inward conflict without choice or justification.

To be aware of your thought and feeling without identification and denial is not tedious and painful; but in search of a result, an end to be gained, conflict is increased and the tedium of strife begins.

Let a Thought Flower

Awareness is that state of mind which takes in everything—the crows flying across the sky, the flowers on the trees, the people sitting in front, the colors they are wearing—being extensively aware, which needs watching, observing, taking in the shape of the leaf, the shape of the trunk, the shape of the head of another, what he is doing. To be extensively aware and from there acting—that is to be aware of the totality of one's own being. To have a mere sectional capacity, a fragmentation of capacity or capacity fragmented, and to pursue that capacity and derive experience through that capacity which is limited—that makes the quality of the mind mediocre, limited, narrow. But an awareness of the totality of one's own being, understood through the awareness of every thought and every feeling, and never limiting it, letting every thought and every feeling flower, and therefore being aware—that is entirely different from action or concentration that is merely capacity and therefore limited.

To let a thought flower or a feeling flower requires attention—not concentration. I mean by the flowering of a thought giving freedom to it to see what happens, what is taking place in your thought, in your feeling. Anything that flowers must have freedom, must have light; it cannot be restricted. You cannot put any value on it, you cannot say, "That is right, that is wrong; this should be, and that should not be"—thereby, you limit the flowering of thought. And it can only flower in this awareness. Therefore, if you go into it very deeply, you will find that this flowering of thought is the ending of thought.

Passive Awareness

In awareness there is no becoming, there is no end to be gained. There is silent observation without choice and condemnation, from which there comes understanding. In this process when thought and feeling unfold themselves, which is only possible when there is neither acquisition nor acceptance, then there comes an extensional awareness, all the hidden layers and their significance are revealed. This awareness reveals that creative emptiness which cannot be imagined or formulated. This extensional awareness and the creative emptiness are a total process and are not different stages. When you silently observe a problem without condemnation, justification, there comes passive awareness. In this passive awareness, the problem is understood and dissolved. In awareness there is heightened sensitivity, in which there is the highest form of negative thinking. When the mind is formulating, producing, there can be no creation. It is only when the mind is still and empty, when it is not creating a problem—in that alert passivity there is creation. Creation can only take place in negation, which is not the opposite of the positive. Being nothing is not the antithesis of being something. A problem comes into being only when there is a search for result. When the search for result ceases, then only is there no problem.

What Is Thoroughly Understood
Will Not Repeat Itself

In self-awareness there is no need for confession, for self-awareness creates the mirror in which all things are reflected without distortion. Every thought-feeling is thrown, as it were, on the screen of awareness to be observed, studied and understood; but this flow of understanding is blocked when there is condemnation or acceptance, judgment or identification. The more the screen is watched and understood—not as a duty or enforced practice, but because pain and sorrow have created the insatiable interest that brings its own discipline—the greater the intensity of awareness, and this in turn brings heightened understanding.

. . . You can follow a thing if it moves slowly; a rapid machine must be made to slow down if one is to study its movements. Similarly, thoughts-feelings can be studied and understood only if the mind is capable of proceeding slowly; but once it has awakened this capacity, it can move at a high velocity, which makes it extremely calm. When revolving at high speed the several blades of a fan appear to be a solid sheet of metal. Our difficulty is to make the mind revolve slowly so that each thought-feeling can be followed and understood. What is deeply and thoroughly understood will not repeat itself.

Violence

What takes place when you give complete attention to the thing that we call violence?—violence being not only what separates human beings, through belief, conditioning, and so on, but also what comes into being when we are seeking personal security, or the security of individuality through a pattern of society. Can you look at that violence with complete attention? And when you look at that violence with complete attention, what takes place? When you give complete attention to anything—your learning of history or mathematics, looking at your wife or your husband—what takes place? I do not know if you have gone into it—probably most of us have never given complete attention to anything—but when you do, what takes place? Sirs, what is attention? Surely when you are giving complete attention there is care, and you cannot care if you have no affection, no love. And when you give attention in which there is love, is there violence? You are following? Formally I have condemned violence, I have escaped from it, I have justified it, I have said it is natural. All these things are inattention. But when I give attention to what I have called violence—and in that attention there is care, affection, love—where is there space for violence?

Is It Possible to End Violence?

When you talk about violence, what do you mean by it? It is really quite an interesting question, if you go into it deeply, to inquire whether a human being, living in this world, can totally cease to be violent. Societies, religious communities, have tried not to kill animals. Some have even said, "If you don't want to kill animals, what about the vegetables?" You can carry it to such an extent that you would cease to exist. Where do you draw the line? Is there an arbitrary line according to your ideal, to your fancy, to your norm, to your temperament, to your conditioning, and you say, "I'll go up to there but not beyond"? Is there a difference between individual anger, with violent action on the part of the individual, and the organized hatred of a society which breeds and builds up an army to destroy another society? Where, at what level, and what fragment of violence are you discussing, or do you want to discuss whether man can be free of total violence, not a particular fragment which he calls violence? . . .

We know what violence is without expressing in words, in phrases, in action. As a human being in whom the animal is still very strong, in spite of centuries of so-called civilization, where shall I begin? Shall I begin at the periphery, which is society, or at the center, which is myself? You tell me not to be violent, because it is ugly. You explain to me all the reasons, and I see that violence is a terrible thing in human beings, outwardly and inwardly. Is it possible to end this violence?

The Central Cause of Conflict

Do not think by merely wishing for peace you will have peace, when in your daily life of relationship you are aggressive, acquisitive, seeking psychological security here or in the hereafter. You have to understand the central cause of conflict and sorrow and then dissolve it and not merely look to the outside for peace. But you see, most of us are indolent. We are too lazy to take hold of ourselves and understand ourselves, and being lazy, which is really a form of conceit, we think others will solve this problem for us and give us peace, or that we should destroy the apparently few people that are causing wars. When the individual is in conflict within himself he must inevitably create conflict without, and only he can bring about peace within himself and so in the world, for he is the world.

Realize You Are Violent

The animal is violent. Human beings who are the result of the animal, are also violent; it is part of their being to be violent, to be angry, to be jealous, to be envious, to seek power, position, prestige and all the rest of it, to dominate, to be aggressive. Man is violent—this is shown by thousands of wars—and he has developed an ideology which he calls nonviolence. . . . And when there is actual violence as a war between this country and the next country, everybody is involved in it. They love it. Now, when you are actually violent and you have an ideal of nonviolence, you have a conflict. You are always trying to become nonviolent—which is a part of the conflict. You discipline yourself in order not to be violent—which, again, is a conflict, friction. So when you are violent and have the ideal of nonviolence, you are essentially violent. To realize that you are violent is the first thing to do—not try to become nonviolent. To see violence as it is, not try to translate it, not to discipline it, not to overcome it, not to suppress it, but to see it as though you are seeing it for the first time—that is to look at it without any thought. I have explained already what we mean by looking at a tree with innocence—which is to look at it without the image. In the same way, you have to look at violence without the image that is involved in the word itself. To look at it without any movement of thought is to look at it as though you are looking at it for the first time, and therefore looking at it with innocence.

Freedom from Violence

So can you see the fact of violence—the fact not only outside of you but also inside you—and not have any time interval between listening and acting? This means by the very act of listening you are free from violence. You are totally free from violence because you have not admitted time, an ideology through which you can get rid of violence. This requires very deep meditation, not just a verbal agreement or disagreement. We never listen to anything; our minds, our brain cells are so conditioned to an ideology about violence that we never look at the fact of violence. We look at the fact of violence through an ideology, and the looking at violence through an ideology creates a time interval. And when you admit time, there is no end to violence; you go on showing violence, preaching nonviolence.

The Major Cause of Violence

The major cause of violence, I think, is that each one of us is inwardly, psychologically, seeking security. In each one of us the urge for psychological security—that inward sense of being safe—projects the demand, the outward demand, for security. Inwardly each one of us wants to be secure, sure, certain. That is why we have all these marriage laws; in order that we may possess a woman, or a man, and so be secure in our relationship. If that relationship is attacked we become violent, which is the psychological demand, the inward demand, to be certain of our relationship to everything. But there is no such thing as certainty, security, in any relationship. Inwardly, psychologically, we should like to be secure, but there is no such thing as permanent security. . . .

So all these are the contributory causes of the violence that is prevalent, rampaging, throughout the world. I think anybody who has observed, even if only a little, what is going on in the world, and especially in this unfortunate country, can also, without a great deal of intellectual study, observe and find out in himself those things which, projected outwardly, are the causes of this extraordinary brutality, callousness, indifference, violence.

The Fact Is We Are Violent

We all see the importance of the cessation of violence. And how am I, as an individual, to be free of violence—not just superficially but totally, completely, inwardly? If the ideal of nonviolence will not free the mind from violence, then will the analysis of the cause of violence help to dissolve violence?

After all, this is one of our major problems, is it not? The whole world is caught up in violence, in wars; the very structure of our acquisitive society is essentially violent. And if you and I as individuals are to be free from violence—totally, inwardly free, not merely superficially or verbally—then how is one to set about it without becoming self-centered?

You understand the problem, do you not? If my concern is to free the mind from violence and I practice discipline in order to control violence and change it into nonviolence, surely that brings about self-centered thought and activity, because my mind is focused all the time on getting rid of one thing and acquiring something else. And yet I see the importance of the mind being totally free from violence. So what am I to do? Surely, it is not a question of how one is not to be violent. The fact is that we are violent, and to ask "How am I not to be violent?" merely creates the ideal, which seems to me to be utterly futile. But if one is capable of looking at violence and understanding it, then perhaps there is a possibility of resolving it totally.

To Destroy Hate

We see the world of hate taking its harvest at the present. This world of hate has been created by our fathers and their forefathers and by us. Thus, ignorance stretches indefinitely into the past. It has not come into being by itself. It is the outcome of human ignorance, a historical process, isn't it? We as individuals have cooperated with our ancestors, who, with their forefathers, set going this process of hate, fear, greed, and so on. Now, as individuals, we partake of this world of hate so long as we, individually, indulge in it.

The world, then, is an extension of yourself. If you as an individual desire to destroy hate, then you as an individual must cease hating. To destroy hate, you must dissociate yourself from hate in all its gross and subtle forms, and so long as you are caught up in it you are part of that world of ignorance and fear. Then the world is an extension of yourself, yourself duplicated and multiplied. The world does not exist apart from the individual. It may exist as an idea, as a state, as a social organization, but to carry out that idea, to make that social or religious organization function, there must be the individual. His ignorance, his greed, and his fear maintain the structure of ignorance, greed, and hate. If the individual changes, can he affect the world, the world of hate, greed, and so on? . . . The world is an extension of yourself so long as you are thoughtless, caught up in ignorance, hate, greed, but when you are earnest, thoughtful, and aware, there is not only a dissociation from those ugly causes that create pain and sorrow, but also in that understanding there is a completeness, a wholeness.

That Thing Which You Fight
You Become

Surely that thing which you fight you become. . . . If I am angry and you meet me with anger what is the result? More anger. You have become that which I am. If I am evil and you fight me with evil means then you also become evil, however righteous you may feel. If I am brutal and you use brutal methods to overcome me, then you become brutal like me. And this we have done for thousands of years. Surely there is a different approach than to meet hate by hate? If I use violent methods to quell anger in myself then I am using wrong means for a right end, and thereby the right end ceases to be. In this there is no understanding; there is no transcending anger. Anger is to be studied tolerantly and understood; it is not to be overcome through violent means. Anger may be the result of many causes, and without comprehending them there is no escape from anger.

We have created the enemy, the bandit, and becoming ourselves the enemy in no way brings about an end to enmity. We have to understand the cause of enmity and cease to feed it by our thought, feeling, and action. This is an arduous task demanding constant self-awareness and intelligent pliability, for what we are the society, the state, is. The enemy and the friend are the outcome of our thought and action. We are responsible for creating enmity and so it is more important to be aware of our own thought and action than to be concerned with the foe and the friend, for right thinking puts an end to division. Love transcends the friend and the enemy.

❖

JULY

Happiness

Grief

Hurt

Sorrow

❖

Happiness vs. Gratification

What is it that most of us are seeking? What is it that each one of us wants? Especially in this restless world, where everybody is trying to find some kind of peace, some kind of happiness, a refuge, surely it is important to find out, isn't it, what it is that we are trying to seek, what it is that we are trying to discover? Probably most of us are seeking some kind of happiness, some kind of peace; in a world that is ridden with turmoil, wars, contention, strife, we want a refuge where there can be some peace. I think that is what most of us want. So we pursue, go from one leader to another, from one religious organization to another, from one teacher to another.

Now, is it that we are seeking happiness or is it that we are seeking gratification of some kind from which we hope to derive happiness? There is a difference between happiness and gratification. Can you seek happiness? Perhaps you can find gratification but surely you cannot find happiness. Happiness is derivative; it is a by-product of something else. So, before we give our minds and hearts to something that demands a great deal of earnestness, attention, thought, care, we must find out, must we not, what it is that we are seeking; whether it is happiness, or gratification?

One Must Go Deep to Know Joy

Very few of us enjoy anything. We have very little joy in seeing the sunset, or the full moon, or a beautiful person, or a lovely tree, or a bird in flight, or a dance. We do not really enjoy anything. We look at it, we are superficially amused or excited by it, we have a sensation that we call joy. But enjoyment is something far deeper, which must be understood and gone into. . . .

As we grow older, though we want to enjoy things, the best has gone out of us; we want to enjoy other kinds of sensations—passions, lust, power, position. These are all the normal things of life, though they are superficial; they are not to be condemned, not to be justified, but to be understood and given their right place. If you condemn them as being worthless, as being sensational, stupid, or unspiritual, you destroy the whole process of living . . .

To know joy one must go much deeper. Joy is not mere sensation. It requires extraordinary refinement of the mind, but not the refinement of the self that gathers more and more to itself. Such a self, such a man, can never understand this state of joy in which the enjoyer is not. One has to understand this extraordinary thing; otherwise, life becomes very small, petty, superficial—being born, learning a few things, suffering, bearing children, having responsibilities, earning money, having a little intellectual amusement and then to die.

Happiness Cannot Be Pursued

What do you mean by happiness? Some will say happiness consists of getting what you want. You want a car, and you get it, and you are happy. I want a sari or clothes; I want to go to Europe and if I can, I am happy. I want to be the . . . greatest politician, and if I get it, I am happy; if I cannot get it, I am unhappy. So, what you call happiness is getting what you want, achievement or success, becoming noble, getting anything that you want. As long as you want something and you can get it, you feel perfectly happy; you are not frustrated, but if you cannot get what you want, then unhappiness begins. All of us are concerned with this, not only the rich and the poor. The rich and the poor all want to get something for themselves, for their family, for society; and if they are prevented, stopped, they will be unhappy. We are not discussing, we are not saying that the poor should not have what they want. That is not the problem. We are trying to find out what is happiness and whether happiness is something of which you are conscious. The moment you are conscious that you are happy, that you have much, is that happiness? The moment you are conscious that you are happy, it is not happiness, is it? So you cannot go after happiness. The moment you are conscious that you are humble, you are not humble. So happiness is not a thing to be pursued; it comes. But if you seek it, it will evade you.

Happiness Is Not Sensation

Mind can never find happiness. Happiness is not a thing to be pursued and found, as sensation. Sensation can be found again and again, for it is ever being lost; but happiness cannot be found. Remembered happiness is only a sensation, a reaction for or against the present. What is over is not happiness; the experience of happiness that is over is sensation, for remembrance is the past and the past is sensation. Happiness is not sensation. . . .

What you know is the past, not the present; and the past is sensation, reaction, memory. You remember that you were happy; and can the past tell what happiness is? It can recall but it cannot be. Recognition is not happiness; to know what it is to be happy is not happiness. Recognition is the response of memory; and can the mind, the complex of memories, experiences, ever be happy? The very recognition prevents the experiencing.

When you are aware that you are happy, is there happiness? When there is happiness, are you aware of it? Consciousness comes only with conflict, the conflict of remembrance of the more. Happiness is not the remembrance of the more. Where there is conflict, happiness is not. Conflict is where the mind is. Thought at all levels is the response of memory, and so thought invariably breeds conflict. Thought is sensation, and sensation is not happiness. Sensations are ever seeking gratifications. The end is sensation, but happiness is not an end; it cannot be sought out.

Can Happiness
Be Found Through Anything?

We seek happiness through things, through relationship, through thoughts, ideas. So things, relationship, and ideas
become all-important and not happiness. When we seek happiness through something, then the thing becomes of greater value
than happiness itself. When stated in this manner, the problem
sounds simple and it is simple. We seek happiness in property,
in family, in name; then property, family, idea become all-important, for then happiness is sought through a means, and then the
means destroys the end. Can happiness be found through any
means, through anything made by the hand or by the mind?
Things, relationship, and ideas are so transparently impermanent, we are ever made unhappy by them. . . . Things are impermanent, they wear out and are lost; relationship is constant
friction and death awaits; ideas and beliefs have no stability, no
permanency. We seek happiness in them and yet do not realize
their impermanency. So sorrow becomes our constant companion and overcoming it our problem.

To find out the true meaning of happiness, we must ex-
plore the river of self-knowledge. Self-knowledge is not an end
in itself. Is there a source to a stream? Every drop of water from
the beginning to the end makes the river. To imagine that we will
find happiness at the source is to be mistaken. It is to be found
where you are on the river of self-knowledge.

Happiness That Is Not of the Mind

We may move from one refinement to another, from one subtlety to another, from one enjoyment to another; but at the center of it all, there is "the me"—"the me" that is enjoying, that wants more happiness, "the me" that searches, looks for, longs for happiness, "the me" that struggles, "the me" that becomes more and more refined, but never likes to come to an end. It is only when "the me" in all subtle forms comes to an end that there is a state of bliss that cannot be sought after, an ecstasy, a real joy without pain, without corruption. . . .

When the mind goes beyond the thought of the "me," the experiencer, the observer, the thinker, then there is a possibility of a happiness that is incorruptible. That happiness cannot be permanent, in the sense in which we use that word. But our mind is seeking permanent happiness, something that will last, that will continue. That very desire for continuity is corruption. . . .

If we can understand the process of life without condemning, without saying it is right or wrong, then, I think, there comes a creative happiness that is not "yours" or "mine." That creative happiness is like sunshine. If you want to keep the sunshine to yourself, it is no longer the clear, warm, life-giving sun. Similarly, if you want happiness because you are suffering, or because you have lost somebody, or because you have not been successful, then that is merely a reaction. But when the mind can go beyond, then there is a happiness that is not of the mind.

Understanding Suffering

Why do we inquire, "what is happiness"? Is that the right approach? Is that the right probing? We are not happy. If we were happy, our world would be entirely different; our civilization, our culture would be wholly, radically different. We are unhappy human beings, petty, miserable, struggling, vain, surrounding ourselves with useless, futile things, satisfied with petty ambitions, with money, and position. We are unhappy beings, though we may have knowledge, though we may have money, rich houses, plenty of children, cars, experience. We are unhappy, suffering, human beings, and because we are suffering, we want happiness, and so we are led away by those who promise this happiness—social, economic, or spiritual. . . .

What is the good of my asking if there is happiness when I am suffering? Can I understand suffering? That is my problem, not how to be happy. I am happy when I am not suffering, but the moment I am conscious of it, it is not happiness. . . . So I must understand what is suffering. Can I understand what is suffering when a part of my mind is running away seeking happiness, seeking a way out of this misery? So must I not, if I am to understand suffering, be completely one with it, not reject it, not justify it, not condemn it, not compare it, but completely be with it and understand it?

The truth of what is happiness will come if I know how to listen. I must know how to listen to suffering; if I can listen to suffering I can listen to happiness, because that is what I am.

Suffering Is Suffering,
Not Yours or Mine

Is your suffering as an individual different from my suffering, or from the suffering of a man in Asia, in America, or in Russia? The circumstances, the incidents may vary, but in essence another man's suffering is the same as mine and yours, isn't it? Suffering is suffering, surely, not yours or mine. Pleasure is not your pleasure, or my pleasure—it is pleasure. When you are hungry, it is not your hunger only, it is the hunger of the whole of Asia too. When you are driven by ambition, when you are ruthless, it is the same ruthlessness that drives the politician, the man in power, whether he is in Asia, in America, or in Russia.

You see, that is what we object to. We don't see that we are all one humanity, caught in different spheres of life, in different areas. When you love somebody, it is not your love. If it is, it becomes tyrannical, possessive, jealous, anxious, brutal. Similarly, suffering is suffering; it is not yours or mine. I am not just making it impersonal, I am not making it something abstract. When one suffers, one suffers. When a man has no food, no clothing, no shelter, he is suffering, whether he lives in Asia, or in the West. The people who are now being killed or wounded—the Vietnamese and the Americans—are suffering. To understand this suffering—which is neither yours nor mine, which is not impersonal or abstract, but actual and which we all have—requires a great deal of penetration, insight. And the ending of this suffering will naturally bring about peace, not only within, but outside.

Understand Suffering

Why am I or why are you callous to another man's suffering? Why are we indifferent to the coolie who is carrying a heavy load, to the woman who is carrying a baby? Why are we so callous? To understand that, we must understand why suffering makes us dull. Surely, it is suffering that makes us callous; because we don't understand suffering, we become indifferent to it. If I understand suffering, then I become sensitive to suffering, awake to everything, not only to myself, but to the people about me, to my wife, to my children, to an animal, to a beggar. But we don't want to understand suffering, and the escape from suffering makes us dull, and therefore we are callous. Sir, the point is that suffering, when not understood, dulls the mind and heart; and we do not understand suffering because we want to escape from it, through the guru, through a savior, through mantras, through reincarnation, through ideas, through drink and every other kind of addiction—anything to escape *what is*. . . .

Now, the understanding of suffering does not lie in finding out what the cause is. Any man can know the cause of suffering; his own thoughtlessness, his stupidity, his narrowness, his brutality, and so on. But if I look at the suffering itself without wanting an answer, then what happens? Then, as I am not escaping, I begin to understand suffering; my mind is watchfully alert, keen, which means I become sensitive, and being sensitive, I am aware of other people's suffering.

Acquiring Beliefs to Ward Off Pain

Physical pain is a nervous response, but psychological pain arises when I hold on to things that give me satisfaction, for then I am afraid of anyone or anything that may take them away from me. The psychological accumulations prevent psychological pain as long as they are undisturbed; that is, I am a bundle of accumulations, experiences, which prevent any serious form of disturbance—and I do not want to be disturbed. Therefore, I am afraid of anyone who disturbs them. Thus my fear is of the known; I am afraid of the accumulations, physical or psychological, that I have gathered as a means of warding off pain or preventing sorrow. But sorrow is in the very process of accumulating to ward off psychological pain. Knowledge also helps to prevent pain. As medical knowledge helps to prevent physical pain, so beliefs help to prevent psychological pain, and that is why I am afraid of losing my beliefs, though I have no perfect knowledge or concrete proof of the reality of such beliefs. I may reject some of the traditional beliefs that have been foisted on me because my own experience gives me strength, confidence, understanding; but such beliefs and the knowledge that I have acquired are basically the same—a means of warding off pain.

Integrated Understanding

What do we mean by "grief"? Is it something apart from you? Is it something outside of you, inwardly or outwardly, which you are observing, which you are experiencing? Are you merely the observer experiencing? Or, is it something different? Surely that is an important point, is it not? When I say "I suffer," what do I mean by it? Am I different from the suffering? Surely that is the question, is it not? Let us find out.

There is sorrow—I am not loved, my son dies, what you will. There is one part of me that is demanding why, demanding the explanation, the reasons, the causes. The other part of me is in agony for various reasons. And there is also another part of me that wants to be free from the sorrow, which wants to go beyond it. We are all these things, are we not? So, if one part of me is rejecting, resisting sorrow, another part of me is seeking an explanation, is caught up in theories, and another part of me is escaping from the fact—how then can I understand it totally? It is only when I am capable of integrated understanding that there is a possibility of freedom from sorrow. But if I am torn in different directions, then I do not see the truth of it. . . .

Now, please listen carefully; and you will see that when there is a fact, a truth, there is understanding of it only when I can experience the whole thing without division—and not when there is the separation of the "me" observing suffering. That is the truth.

You Are the Suffering

When there is no *observer* who is suffering, is the suffering different from you? You *are* the suffering, are you not? You are not apart from the pain—you *are* the pain. What happens? There is no labeling, there is no giving it a name and thereby brushing it aside—you are merely that pain, that feeling, that sense of agony. When you are that, what happens? When you do not name it, when there is no fear with regard to it, is the center related to it? If the center is related to it, then it is afraid of it. Then it must act and do something about it. But if the center *is* that, then what do you do? There is nothing to be done, is there? If you are that and you are not accepting it, not labeling it, not pushing it aside—if you *are* that thing, what happens? Do you say you suffer then? Surely, a fundamental transformation has taken place. Then there is no longer "I suffer" because there is no center to suffer, and the center suffers because we have never examined what the center is. We just live from word to word, from reaction to reaction.

Is Suffering Essential?

There are so many varieties and complications and degrees of suffering. We all know that. You know it very well, and we carry this burden right through life, practically from the moment we are born until the moment we collapse into the grave. . . .

If we say that it is inevitable, then there is no answer; if you accept it, then you have stopped inquiring into it. You have closed the door to further inquiry; if you escape from it, you have also closed the door. You may escape into man or woman, into drink, amusement, into various forms of power, position, prestige, and the internal chatter of nothingness. Then your escapes become all-important; the objects to which you fly assume colossal importance. So you have shut the door on sorrow also, and that is what most of us do. . . . Now, can we stop escape of every kind and come back to suffering? . . . That means not seeking a solution for suffering. There is physical suffering—a toothache, stomachache, an operation, accidents, various forms of physical sufferings that have their own answer. There is also the fear of future pain that would cause suffering. Suffering is closely related to fear, and without comprehension of these two major factors in life, we shall never comprehend what it is to be compassionate, to love. So a mind that is concerned with the comprehension of what is compassion, love, and all the rest of it must surely understand what is fear and what is sorrow.

Conscious Sorrow
and Unconscious Sorrow

Sorrow is . . . grief, uncertainty, the feeling of complete loneliness. There is the sorrow of death, the sorrow of not being able to fulfill oneself, the sorrow of not being recognized, the sorrow of loving and not being loved in return. There are innumerable forms of sorrow, and it seems to me that without understanding sorrow, there is no end to conflict, to misery, to the everyday travail of corruption and deterioration. . . .

There is conscious sorrow, and there is also unconscious sorrow, the sorrow that seems to have no basis, no immediate cause. Most of us know conscious sorrow, and we also know how to deal with it. Either we run away from it through religious belief or we rationalize it, or we take some kind of drug, whether intellectual or physical; or we bemuse ourselves with words, with amusements, with superficial entertainment. We do all this, and yet we cannot get away from conscious sorrow.

Then there is the unconscious sorrow that we have inherited through the centuries. Man has always sought to overcome this extraordinary thing called sorrow, grief, misery; but even when we are superficially happy and have everything we want, deep down in the unconscious there are still the roots of sorrow. So when we talk about the ending of sorrow, we mean the ending of all sorrow, both conscious and unconscious.

To end sorrow one must have a very clear, very simple mind. Simplicity is not a mere idea. To be simple demands a great deal of intelligence and sensitivity.

Hurt Feelings

How should we act in order not to trouble others? Is that what you want to know? I am afraid then we should not be acting at all. If you live completely, your actions may cause trouble; but what is more important: finding out what is true, or not disturbing others? This seems so simple that it hardly needs to be answered. Why do you want to respect other people's feelings and points of view? Are you afraid of having your own feelings hurt, your point of view being changed? If people have opinions that differ from yours, you can find out if they are true only by questioning them, by coming into active contact with them. And if you find that those opinions and feelings are not true, your discovery may cause disturbance to those who cherish them. Then what should you do? Should you comply with them, or compromise with them in order not to hurt your friends?

Self-Image Leads to Pain

Why divide problems as major and minor? Is not everything a problem? Why make them little or big problems, essential or unessential problems? If we could understand one problem, go into it very deeply however small or big it is, then we would uncover all problems. This is not a rhetorical answer. Take any problem: anger, jealousy, envy, hatred—we know them all very well. If you go into anger very deeply, not just brush it aside, then what is involved? Why is one angry? Because one is hurt, someone has said an unkind thing; and when someone says a flattering thing you are pleased. Why are you hurt? Self-importance, is it not? And why is there self-importance?

Because one has an idea, a symbol of oneself, an image of oneself, what one should be, what one is or what one should not be. Why does one create an image about oneself? Because one has never studied what one is, actually. We think we should be this or that, the ideal, the hero, the example. What awakens anger is that our ideal, the idea we have of ourselves, is attacked. And our idea about ourselves is our escape from the fact of what we are. But when you are observing the actual fact of what you are, no one can hurt you. Then, if one is a liar and is told that one is a liar it does not mean that one is hurt; it is a fact. But when you are pretending you are not a liar and are told that you are, then you get angry, violent. So we are always living in an ideational world, a world of myth, and never in the world of actuality. To observe *what is*, to see it, actually be familiar with it, there must be no judgment, no evaluation, no opinion, no fear.

Perverted Pleasure

There is such a thing as sadism. Do you know what that word means? An author called the Marquis de Sade once wrote a book about a man who enjoyed hurting people and seeing them suffer. From that comes the word *sadism*, which means deriving pleasure from the suffering of others. For certain people there is a peculiar satisfaction in seeing others suffer. Watch yourself and see if you have this feeling. It may not be obvious, but if it is there you will find that it expresses itself in the impulse to laugh when somebody falls. You want those who are high to be pulled down; you criticize, gossip thoughtlessly about others, all of which is an expression of insensitivity, a form of wanting to hurt people. One may injure another deliberately, with vengeance, or one may do it unconsciously with a word, with a gesture with a look; but in either case the urge is to hurt somebody, and there are very few who radically set aside this perverted form of pleasure.

Real Education

The mind creates through experience, tradition, memory. Can the mind be free from storing up, though it is experiencing? You understand the difference? What is required is not the cultivation of memory but the freedom from the accumulative process of the mind.

You hurt me, which is an experience; and I store up that hurt; and that becomes my tradition; and from that tradition, I look at you, I react from that tradition. That is the everyday process of my mind and your mind. Now, is it possible that, though you hurt me, the accumulative process does not take place? The two processes are entirely different.

If you say harsh words to me, it hurts me; but if that hurt is not given importance, it does not become the background from which I act; so it is possible that I meet you afresh. That is real education, in the deep sense of the word. Because, then, though I see the conditioning effects of experience, the mind is not conditioned.

Cessation of Anger

We have all, I am sure, tried to subdue anger but somehow that does not seem to dissolve it. Is there a different approach to dissipate anger? . . . Anger may spring from physical or psychological causes. One is angry, perhaps, because one is thwarted, one's defensive reactions are being broken down, or one's security, which has been carefully built up, is being threatened, and so on. We are all familiar with anger. How is one to understand and dissolve anger? If you consider that your beliefs, concepts, and opinions are of the greatest importance, then you are bound to react violently when questioned. Instead of clinging to beliefs and opinions, if you begin to question whether they are essential to one's comprehension of life, then through the understanding of its causes there is the cessation of anger. Thus one begins to dissolve one's own resistances, which cause conflict and pain. This again requires earnestness. We are used to controlling ourselves for sociological or religious reasons or for convenience, but to uproot anger requires deep awareness. . . .

You say you are angrey when you hear of injustice. Is it because you love humanity, because you are compassionate? Do compassion and anger dwell together? Can there be justice when there is anger, hatred? You are perhaps angry at the thought of general injustice, cruelty, but your anger does not alter injustice or cruelty; it can only do harm. To bring about order, you yourself have to be thoughtful, compassionate. Action born of hatred can only create further hatred. There can be no righteousness where there is anger. Righteousness and anger cannot dwell together.

Forgiveness Is Not True Compassion

What is it to be compassionate? Please find out for yourself, feel it out, whether a mind that is hurt, that can be hurt, can ever forgive. Can a mind that is capable of being hurt ever forgive? And can such a mind, which is capable of being hurt, which is cultivating virtue, which is conscious of generosity, can such a mind be compassionate? Compassion, as love, is something which is not of the mind. The mind is not conscious of itself as being compassionate, as loving. But the moment you forgive consciously, the mind is strengthening its own center in its own hurt. So the mind which consciously forgives can never forgive; it does not know forgiveness; it forgives in order not to be further hurt.

So it is very important to find out why the mind actually remembers, stores away. Because the mind is everlastingly seeking to aggrandize itself, to become big, to be something. When the mind is willing not to be anything, to be nothing, completely nothing, then in that state there is compassion. In that state there is neither forgiveness nor the state of hurt; but to understand that, one has to understand the conscious development of the "me. . . ."

So, as long as there is the conscious cultivation of any particular influence, any particular virtue, there can be no love, there can be no compassion, because love and compassion are not the result of conscious effort.

Where There Is the Possibility
of Pain There Is No Love

The questioner wants to know how he can act freely and without self-repression when he knows his action must hurt those he loves. You know, to love is to be free—both parties are free. Where there is the possibility of pain, where there is the possibility of suffering in love, it is not love, it is merely a subtle form of possession, of acquisitiveness. If you love, really love someone, there is no possibility of giving him pain when you do something that you think is right. It is only when you want that person to do what you desire or he wants you to do what he desires, that there is pain. That is, you like to be possessed; you feel safe, secure, comfortable; though you know that comfort is but transient, you take shelter in that comfort, in that transience. So each struggle for comfort, for encouragement, really but betrays the lack of inward richness; and therefore an action separate, apart from the other individual naturally creates disturbance, pain and suffering; and one individual has to suppress what he really feels in order to adjust himself to the other. In other words, this constant repression, brought about by so-called love, destroys the two individuals. In that love there is no freedom; it is merely a subtle bondage.

The Nature of the Trap

Sorrow is the result of a shock, it is the temporary shaking up of a mind that has settled down, that has accepted the routine of life. Something happens—a death, the loss of a job, the questioning of a cherished belief—and the mind is disturbed. But what does a disturbed mind do? It finds a way to be undisturbed again; it takes refuge in another belief, in a more secure job, in a new relationship. Again the wave of life comes along and shatters its safeguards, but the mind soon finds still further defenses; and so it goes on. This is not the way of intelligence, is it?

No form of external or inward compulsion will help, will it? All compulsion, however subtle, is the outcome of ignorance; it is born of the desire for reward or the fear of punishment. To understand the whole nature of the trap is to be free of it; no person, no system, no belief can set you free. The truth of this is the only liberating factor—but you have to see it for yourself, and not merely be persuaded. You have to take the voyage on an uncharted sea.

The End of Sorrow

If you walk down the road, you will see the splendor of nature, the extraordinary beauty of the green fields and the open skies; and you will hear the laughter of children. But in spite of all that, there is a sense of sorrow. There is the anguish of a woman bearing a child; there is sorrow in death; there is sorrow when you are looking forward to something, and it does not happen; there is sorrow when a nation runs down, goes to seed; and there is the sorrow of corruption, not only in the collective, but also in the individual. There is sorrow in your own house, if you look deeply—the sorrow of not being able to fulfill, the sorrow of your own pettiness or incapacity, and various unconscious sorrows.

There is also laughter in life. Laughter is a lovely thing—to laugh without reason, to have joy in one's heart without cause, to love without seeking anything in return. But such laughter rarely happens to us. We are burdened with sorrow; our life is a process of misery and strife, a continuous disintegration, and we almost never know what it is to love with our whole being. . . .

We want to find a solution, a means, a method by which to resolve this burden of life, and so we never actually look at sorrow. We try to escape through myths, through images, through speculation; we hope to find some way to avoid this weight, to stay ahead of the wave of sorrow.

. . . Sorrow has an ending, but it does not come about through any system or method. There is no sorrow when there is perception of *what is*.

Meeting Sorrow

How do you meet sorrow? I'm afraid that most of us meet it very superficially. Our education, our training, our knowledge, the sociological influences to which we are exposed, all make us superficial. A superficial mind is one that escapes to the church, to some conclusion, to some concept, to some belief or idea. Those are all a refuge for the superficial mind that is in sorrow. And if you cannot find a refuge, you build a wall around yourself and become cynical, hard, indifferent, or you escape through some facile, neurotic reaction. All such defenses against suffering prevent further inquiry. . . .

Please watch your own mind; observe how you explain your sorrows away, lose yourself in work, in ideas, or cling to a belief in God, or in a future life. And if no explanation, no belief has been satisfactory, you escape through drink, through sex, or by becoming cynical, hard, bitter, brittle. . . . Generation after generation it has been passed on by parents to their children, and the superficial mind never takes the bandage off that wound; it does not really know, it is not really acquainted with sorrow. It merely has an idea about sorrow. It has a picture, a symbol of sorrow, but it never meets sorrow—it meets only the word *sorrow*.

Evading Sorrow

Most of us have sorrow in different forms—in relationship, in the death of someone, in not fulfilling oneself and withering away to nothing, or in trying to achieve, trying to become something, and meeting with total failure. And there is the whole problem of sorrow on the physical side—illness, blindness, incapacitation, paralysis, and so on. Everywhere there is this extraordinary thing called sorrow—with death waiting round the corner. And we do not know how to meet sorrow, so either we worship it, or rationalize it, or try to run away from it. Go to any Christian church and you will find that sorrow is worshipped; it is made into something extraordinary, holy, and it is said that only through sorrow, through the crucified Christ, can you find God. In the East they have their own forms of evasion, other ways of avoiding sorrow, and it seems to me an extraordinary thing that so very few, whether in the East or in the West, are really free of sorrow.

It would be a marvelous thing if in the process of your listening—unemotionally, not sentimentally—to what is being said . . . you could really understand sorrow and be totally free of it; because then there would be no self-deception, no illusions, no anxieties, no fear, and the brain could function clearly, sharply, logically. And then, perhaps, one would know what love is.

Follow the Movement of Suffering

What is suffering? . . . What does it mean? What is it that is suffering? Not why there is suffering, not what is the cause of suffering, but what is actually happening? I do not know if you see the difference. Then I am simply aware of suffering, not as apart from me, not as an observer watching suffering—it is part of me, that is, the whole of me is suffering. Then I am able to follow its movement, see where it leads. Surely if I do that, it opens up, does it not? Then I see that I have laid emphasis on the "me"—not on the person whom I love. He only acted to cover me from my misery, from my loneliness, from my misfortune. As I am not something, I hoped he would be that. That has gone; I am left, I am lost, I am lonely. Without him, I am nothing. So I cry. It is not that he is gone but that I am left. I am alone.

. . . There are innumerable people to help me to escape—thousands of so-called religious people, with their beliefs and dogmas, hopes and fantasies—"It is karma, it is God's will"—you know, all giving me a way out. But if I can stay with it and not put it away from me, not try to circumscribe or deny it, then what happens? What is the state of my mind when it is thus following the movement of suffering?

Spontaneous Comprehension

We never say, "Let me see what that thing is that suffers." You cannot see by enforcement, by discipline. You must look with interest, with spontaneous comprehension. Then you will see that the thing we call suffering, pain, the thing that we avoid, and the discipline, have all gone. As long as I have no relationship to the thing as outside me, the problem is not; the moment I establish a relationship with it outside me, the problem is. As long as I treat suffering as something outside—I suffer because I lost my brother, because I have no money, because of this or that—I establish a relationship to it and that relationship is fictitious. But if I am that thing, if I see the fact, then the whole thing is transformed, it all has a different meaning. Then there is full attention, integrated attention and that which is completely regarded is understood and dissolved, and so there is no fear and therefore the word *sorrow* is non-existent.

The Center of Suffering

When you see a most lovely thing, a beautiful mountain, a beautiful sunset, a ravishing smile, a ravishing face, that fact stuns you, and you are silent; hasn't it ever happened to you? Then you hug the world in your arms. But that is something from outside which comes to your mind, and I am talking of the mind that is not stunned but which wants to look, to observe. Now, can you observe without all this upsurging of conditioning? To a person in sorrow, I explain in words; sorrow is inevitable, sorrow is the result of fulfillment. When all explanations have completely stopped, then only can you look—which means you are not looking from the center. When you look from a center, your faculties of observation are limited. If I hold to a post and want to be there, there is a strain, there is pain. When I look from the center into suffering, there is suffering. It is the incapacity to observe that creates pain. I cannot observe if I think, function, see from a center—as when I say, "I must have no pain, I must find out why I suffer, I must escape." When I observe from a center, whether the center is a conclusion, an idea, hope, despair, or anything else, that observation is very restricted, very narrow, very small, and that engenders sorrow.

An Immensity Beyond All Measure

What happens when you lose someone by death? The immediate reaction is a sense of paralysis, and when you come out of that state of shock, there is what we call sorrow. Now, what does that word *sorrow* mean? The companionship, the happy words, the walks, the many pleasant things you did and hoped to do together—all this is taken away in a second, and you are left empty, naked, lonely. That is what you are objecting to, that is what the mind rebels against: being suddenly left to itself, utterly lonely, empty, without any support. Now, what matters is to live with that emptiness, just to live with it without any reaction, without rationalizing it, without running away from it to mediums, to the theory of reincarnation, and all that stupid nonsense—to live with it with your whole being. And if you go into it step-by-step you will find that there is an ending of sorrow—a real ending, not just a verbal ending, not the superficial ending that comes through escape, through identification with a concept, or commitment to an idea. Then you will find there is nothing to protect, because the mind is completely empty and is no longer reacting in the sense of trying to fill that emptiness; and when all sorrow has thus come to an end, you will have started on another journey—a journey that has no ending and no beginning. There is an immensity that is beyond all measure, but you cannot possibly enter into that world without the total ending of sorrow.

Live with Sorrow

We all have sorrow. Don't you have sorrow in one form or another? And do you want to know about it? If you do, you can analyze it and explain why you suffer. You can read books on the subject, or go to the church, and you will soon know something about sorrow. But I am not talking about that; I am talking about the ending of sorrow. Knowledge does not end sorrow. The ending of sorrow begins with the facing of psychological facts within oneself and being totally aware of all the implications of those facts from moment to moment. This means never escaping from the fact that one is in sorrow, never rationalizing it, never offering an opinion about it, but living with that fact completely.

You know, to live with the beauty of those mountains and not get accustomed to it is very difficult. . . . You have beheld those mountains, heard the stream, and seen the shadows creep across the valley, day after day; and have you not noticed how easily you get used to it all? You say, "Yes, it is quite beautiful," and you pass by. To live with beauty, or to live with an ugly thing, and not become habituated to it requires enormous energy—an awareness that does not allow your mind to grow dull. In the same way, sorrow dulls the mind if you merely get used to it—and most of us do get used to it. But you need not get used to sorrow. You can live with sorrow, understand it, go into it—but not in order to know about it.

You know that sorrow is there; it is a fact, and there is nothing more to know. You have to live.

Be In Communion with Sorrow

Most of us are not in communion with anything. We are not directly in communion with our friends, with our wives, with our children. . . .

So to understand sorrow, surely you must love it, must you not? That is, you must be in direct communion with it. If you would understand something—your neighbor, your wife, or any relationship—if you would understand something completely, you must be near it. You must come to it without any objection, prejudice, condemnation, or repulsion; you must look at it, must you not? If I would understand you, I must have no prejudices about you. I must be capable of looking at you, not through barriers, screens of my prejudices and conditionings. I must be in communion with you, which means I must love you. Similarly, if I would understand sorrow, I must love it, I must be in communion with it. I cannot do so because I am running away from it through explanations, through theories, through hopes, through postponements, which are all the process of verbalization. So words prevent me from being in communion with sorrow. Words prevent me—words of explanations, rationalizations, which are still words, which are the mental process—from being directly in communion with sorrow. It is only when I am in communion with sorrow that I understand it.

◈

AUGUST

Truth

Reality

Observer and the Observed

What is

◈

Full Heart, Empty Mind

There is no path to truth, it must come to you. Truth can come to you only when your mind and heart are simple, clear, and there is love in your heart; not if your heart is filled with the things of the mind. When there is love in your heart, you do not talk about organizing for brotherhood; you do not talk about belief, you do not talk about division or the powers that create division, you need not seek reconciliation. Then you are simply a human being without a label, without a country. This means that you must strip yourself of all those things and allow truth to come into being; and it can come only when the mind is empty, when the mind ceases to create. Then it will come without your invitation. Then it will come as swiftly as the wind and unbeknown. It comes obscurely, not when you are watching, wanting. It is there as sudden as sunlight, as pure as the night; but to receive it, the heart must be full and the mind empty. Now you have the mind full and your heart empty.

Truth Is a State of Being

There is no path to truth, and there are not two truths. Truth is not of the past or of the present, it is timeless; and the man who quotes the truth of the Buddha, of Shankara, of the Christ, or who merely repeats what I am saying, will not find truth, because repetition is not truth. Repetition is a lie. Truth is a state of being which arises when the mind—which seeks to divide, to be exclusive, which can think only in terms of results, of achievement—has come to an end. Only then will there be truth. The mind that is making effort, disciplining itself in order to achieve an end, cannot know truth, because the end is its own projection, and the pursuit of that projection, however noble, is a form of self-worship. Such a being is worshipping himself, and therefore he cannot know truth. Truth is to be known only when we understand the whole process of the mind, that is, when there is no strife.

Truth Has No Abiding Place

Truth is a fact, and the fact can be understood only when the various things that have been placed between the mind and the fact are removed. The fact is your relationship to property, to your wife, to human beings, to nature, to ideas; and as long as you do not understand the fact of relationship, your seeking God merely increases the confusion because it is a substitution, an escape, and therefore it has no meaning. As long as you dominate your wife or she dominates you, as long as you possess and are possessed, you cannot know love; as long as you are suppressing, substituting, as long as you are ambitious, you cannot know truth.

He alone shall know truth who is not seeking, who is not striving, who is not trying to achieve a result. . . . Truth is not continuous, it has no abiding place, it can be seen only from moment to moment. Truth is always new, therefore timeless. What was truth yesterday is not truth today, what is truth today is not truth tomorrow. Truth has no continuity. It is the mind that wants to make the experience which it calls truth continuous, and such a mind shall not know truth. Truth is always new; it is to see the same smile, and see that smile newly, to see the same person, and see that person anew, to see the waving palms anew, to meet life anew.

There Is No Guide to Truth

Is God to be found by seeking him out? Can you search after the unknowable? To find, you must know what you are seeking. If you seek to find, what you find will be a self-projection; it will be what you desire, and the creation of desire is not truth. To seek truth is to deny it. Truth has no fixed abode; there is no path, no guide to it, and the word is not truth. Is truth to be found in a particular setting, in a special climate, among certain people? Is it here and not there? Is that one the guide to truth, and not another? Is there a guide at all? When truth is sought, what is found can only come out of ignorance, for the search itself is born of ignorance. You cannot search out reality; you must cease for reality to be.

Truth Is Found Moment to Moment

Truth cannot be accumulated. What is accumulated is always being destroyed; it withers away. Truth can never wither because it can only be found from moment to moment in every thought, in every relationship, in every word, in every gesture, in a smile, in tears. And if you and I can find that and live it—the very living is the finding of it—then we shall not become propagandists; we shall be creative human beings—not perfect human beings, but creative human beings, which is vastly different.

The True Revolutionary

Truth is not for those who are respectable, nor for those who desire self-extension, self-fulfillment. Truth is not for those who are seeking security, permanency; for the permanency they seek is merely the opposite of impermanency. Being caught in the net of time, they seek that which is permanent, but the permanent they seek is not the real because what they seek is the product of their thought. Therefore, a man who would discover reality must cease to seek—which does not mean that he must be contented with *what is*. On the contrary, a man who is intent upon the discovery of truth must be inwardly a complete revolutionary. He cannot belong to any class, to any nation, to any group or ideology, to any organized religion; for truth is not in the temple or the church, truth is not to be found in the things made by the hand or by the mind. Truth comes into being only when the things of the mind and of the hand are put aside, and that putting aside of the things of the mind and of the hand is not a matter of time. Truth comes to him who is free of time, who is not using time as a means of self-extension. Time means memory of yesterday, memory of your family, of your race, of your particular character, of the accumulation of your experience that makes up the "me" and the "mine."

See the Truth in the False

You may superficially agree when you hear it said that nationalism, with all its emotionalism and vested interest, leads to exploitation and the setting of man against man; but to really free your mind from the pettiness of nationalism is another matter. To be free, not only from nationalism but also from all the conclusions of organized religions and political systems, is essential if the mind is to be young, fresh, innocent, that is, in a state of revolution; and it is only such a mind that can create a new world—not the politicians, who are dead, nor the priests, who are caught in their own religious systems.

So, fortunately or unfortunately for yourself, you have heard something that is true; and if you merely hear it and are not actively disturbed so that your mind begins to free itself from all the things that are making it narrow and crooked, then the truth you have heard will become a poison. Surely, truth becomes a poison if it is heard and does not act in the mind, like the festering of a wound. But to discover for oneself what is true and what is false, and to see the truth in the false, is to let that truth operate and bring forth its own action.

Understand the Actual

It is really not complex, though it may be arduous. You see, we don't start with the actual, with the fact, with what we are thinking, doing, desiring; we start with assumptions, or with ideals, which are not actualities, and so we are led astray. To start with facts, and not with assumptions, we need close attention; and every form of thinking not originating from the actual is a distraction. That's why it is so important to understand what is actually taking place both within and around one.

If you are a Christian, your visions follow a certain pattern; if you are a Hindu, a Buddhist, or a Muslim, they follow a different pattern. You see Christ or Krishna, according to your conditioning; your education, the culture in which you have been brought up, determines your visions. Which is the actuality: the vision, or the mind that has been shaped in a certain mold? The vision is the projection of the particular tradition which happens to form the background of the mind. This conditioning, not the vision which it projects, is the actuality, the fact. To understand the fact is simple; but it is made difficult by our likes and dislikes, by our condemnation of the fact, by the opinions or judgments we have about the fact. To be free of these various forms of evaluation is to understand the actual, the *what is*.

Translation of
the Facts Prevents Seeing

A mind that gives an opinion about a fact is a narrow, limited, destructive mind. . . . You can translate the fact in one way, and I can translate it in another way. The translation of the fact is a curse that prevents us from seeing the actual fact and doing something about the fact. When you and I discuss our opinions about the fact, nothing is done about the fact; you can add perhaps more to the fact, see more nuances, implications, significance about the fact, and I may see less significance in the facts. But the fact cannot be interpreted; I cannot offer an opinion about the fact. It is so, and it is very difficult for a mind to accept the fact. We are always translating, we are always giving different meanings to it, according to our prejudices, conditionings, hopes, fears and all the rest of it. If you and I could see the fact without offering an opinion, interpreting, giving a significance, then the fact becomes much more alive—not more alive—the fact is there alone, nothing else matters; then the fact has its own energy that drives you in the right direction.

There Is Only
One Fact: Impermanence

We are trying to find out if there is, or is not, a permanent state—not what we would like, but the actual fact, the truth of the matter. Everything about us, within as well as without—our relationships, our thoughts, our feelings—is impermanent, in a constant state of flux. Being aware of this, the mind craves permanency, a perpetual state of peace, of love, of goodness, a security that neither time nor events can destroy; therefore it creates the soul, the Atman, and the visions of a permanent paradise. But this permanency is born of impermanency, and so it has within it the seeds of the impermanent. There is only one fact: impermanence.

Hankering After the Unknowable

You want me to tell you what reality is. Can the indescribable be put into words? Can you measure something immeasurable? Can you catch the wind in your fist? If you do, is that the wind? If you measure that which is immeasurable, is that the real? If you formulate it, is it the real? Surely not, for the moment you describe something which is indescribable, it ceases to be the real. The moment you translate the unknowable into the known, it ceases to be the unknowable. Yet that is what we are hankering after. All the time we want to *know*, because then we shall be able to continue, then we shall be able, we think, to capture ultimate happiness, permanency. We want to know because we are not happy, because we are striving miserably, because we are worn out, degraded. Yet instead of realizing the simple fact—that we *are* degraded, that we *are* dull, weary, in turmoil—we want to move away from what is the known into the unknown, which again becomes the known and therefore we can never find the real.

Is Suffering Merely
a Word or an Actuality?

Is suffering merely a word, or an actuality? If it is an actuality and not just a word, then the word has no meaning now, so there is merely the feeling of intense pain. With regard to what? With regard to an image, to an experience, to something that you have or have not. If you have it, you call it pleasure; if you haven't, it is pain. Therefore pain, sorrow, is in relationship *to* something. Is that something merely verbalization, or an actuality?—as fear cannot exist by itself but only in relationship *to* something: to an individual, to an incident, to a feeling. Now, you are fully aware of the suffering. Is that suffering apart from you and therefore you are merely the observer who perceives the suffering, or is that suffering *you*?

You and Nothingness Are One

You are nothing. You may have your name and title, your property and bank account, you may have power and be famous; but in spite of all these safeguards, you are as nothing. You may be totally unaware of this emptiness, this nothingness, or you may simply not want to be aware of it; but it is there, do what you will to avoid it. You may try to escape from it in devious ways, through personal or collective violence, through individual or collective worship, through knowledge or amusement; but whether you are asleep or awake, it is always there. You can come upon your relationship to this nothingness and its fear only by being choicelessly aware of the escapes. You are not related to it as a separate, individual entity; you are not the observer watching it; without you, the thinker, the observer, it is not. You and nothingness are one; you and nothingness are a joint phenomenon, not two separate processes. If you, the thinker, are afraid of it and approach it as something contrary and opposed to you, then any action you may take towards it must inevitably lead to illusion and so to further conflict and misery. When there is the discovery, the experiencing of that nothingness as you, then fear—which exists only when the thinker is separate from his thoughts and so tries to establish a relationship with them—completely drops away.

How Do We End Fear?

We are discussing something that needs your attention, not your agreement or disagreement. We are looking at life most rigorously, objectively, clearly—not according to your sentiment, your fancy, what you like or don't like. It's what we like and don't like that has created this misery. All that we are saying is this: "How do we end fear?" That's one of our great problems, because if a human being can't end it he lives in darkness everlastingly, not everlastingly in the Christian sense but in the ordinary sense; one life is good enough. For me, as a human being, there must be a way out and not by creating a hope in some future. Can I as a human being end fear, totally; not little bits of it? Probably you've never put this question to yourself, and probably you've not put the question because you don't know how to get out of it. But if you did put that question most seriously, with the intention of finding out not how to end it, but with the intention of finding out the nature and the structure of fear, the moment you have found out, fear itself comes to an end; you don't have to do anything about it.

When we are aware of it and come into contact with it directly, the observer is the observed. There is no difference between the observer and the thing observed. When fear is observed without the observer, there is action, but not the action of the observer acting upon fear.

The Duality of Thinker and Thought

As you watch anything—a tree, your wife, your children, your neighbor, the stars of a night, the light on the water, the bird in the sky, anything—there is always the observer—the censor, the thinker, the experiencer, the seeker—and the thing he is observing; the observer and the observed; the thinker and the thought. So, there is always a division. It is this division that is time. That division is the very essence of conflict. And when there is conflict, there is contradiction. There is "the observer and the observed"—that is a contradiction; there is a separation. And hence where there is contradiction, there is conflict. And when there is conflict, there is always the urgency to get beyond it, to conquer it, to overcome it, to escape from it, to do something about it, and all that activity involves time. . . . As long as there is this division, time will go on, and time is sorrow.

And a man who will understand the end of sorrow must understand this, must find, must go beyond this duality between the thinker and the thought, the experiencer and the experienced. That is, when there is a division between the observer and the observed, there is time, and therefore there is no ending of sorrow. Then, what is one to do? You understand the question? I see, within myself, the observer is always watching, judging, censoring, accepting, rejecting, disciplining, controlling, shaping. That observer, that thinker, is the result of thought, obviously. Thought is first; not the observer, not the thinker. If there was no thinking at all, there would be no observer, no thinker; then there would only be complete, total attention.

Thought Creates the Thinker

Thought is verbalized sensation; thought is the response of memory, the word, the experience, the image. Thought is transient, changing, impermanent, and it is seeking permanency. So thought creates the thinker, who then becomes the permanent; he assumes the role of the censor, the guide, the controller, the molder of thought. This illusory permanent entity is the product of thought, of the transient. This entity is thought; without thought he is not. The thinker is made up of qualities; his qualities cannot be separated from himself. The controller is the controlled, he is merely playing a deceptive game with himself. Till the false is seen as the false, truth is not.

A Wall of Impregnable Thought

How can there be a fusion of the thinker with his thoughts? Not through the action of will, nor through discipline, nor through any form of effort, control, or concentration, nor through any other means. The use of a means implies an agent who is acting, does it not? As long as there is an actor, there will be a division. The fusion takes place only when the mind is utterly still without trying to be still. There is this stillness, not when the thinker comes to an end, but only when thought itself has come to an end. There must be freedom from the response of conditioning, which is thought. Each problem is solved only when idea, conclusion, is not; conclusions, idea, thought, are the agitations of the mind. How can there be understanding when the mind is agitated? Earnestness must be tempered with the swift play of spontaneity. You will find, if you have heard all that has been said, that truth will come in moments when you are not expecting it. If I may say so, be open, sensitive, be fully aware of *what is* from moment to moment. Don't build around yourself a wall of impregnable thought. The bliss of truth comes when the mind is not occupied with its own activities and struggles.

When the Observer Is the Observed

Space is necessary. Without space there is no freedom. We are talking psychologically. . . . It is only when one is in contact, when there is no space between the observer and the observed that one is in total relationship—with a tree for instance. One is not identified with the tree, the flower, a woman, a man, or whatever it is, but when there is this complete absence of space as the observer and the observed, then there is vast space. In that space there is no conflict; in that space there is freedom.

Freedom is not a reaction. You cannot say, " Well, I am free." The moment you say you are free you are not free, because you are conscious of yourself as being free from something, and therefore you have the same situation as an observer observing a tree. He has created a space, and in that space he breeds conflict. To understand this requires not intellectual agreement or disagreement, or saying, "I don't understand," but rather it requires coming directly into contact with *what is.* It means seeing that all your actions, every moment of action is of the observer and the observed, and within that space there is pleasure, pain and suffering, the desire to fulfill, to become famous. Within that space there is no contact with anything. Contact, relationship has a quite different meaning when the observer is no longer apart from the observed. There is this extraordinary space, and there is freedom.

Is There an
Observer Watching Loneliness?

My mind observes loneliness, and avoids it, runs away from it. But if I do not run away from it, is there a division, is there a separation, is there an observer watching loneliness? Or, is there only a state of loneliness, my mind itself being empty, lonely? Not that there is an observer who knows that there is loneliness. I think this is important to grasp, swiftly, not verbalizing too much. We say now, "I am envious, and I want to get rid of envy," so there is an observer and the observed; the observer wishes to get rid of that which he observes. But is the observer not the same as the observed? It is the mind itself that has created the envy, and so the mind cannot do anything about envy. So, my mind observes loneliness; the thinker is aware that he is lonely. But by remaining with it, being fully in contact, which is, not to run away from it, not to translate and all the rest of it, then, is there a difference between the observer and the observed? Or is there only one state, which is, the mind itself is lonely, empty? Not that the mind observes itself as being empty, but mind itself is empty. Then, can the mind, being aware that it itself is empty, and that whatever its endeavor, any movement away from that emptiness is merely an escape, a dependence; can the mind put away all dependence and be what it is, completely empty, completely lonely? And if it is in that state, is there not freedom from all dependence, from all attachment?

What Is Accumulated Is Not Truth

As long as there is the experiencer remembering the experience, truth is not. Truth is not something to be remembered, stored up, recorded, and then brought out. What is accumulated is not truth. The desire to experience creates the experiencer, who then accumulates and remembers. Desire makes for the separation of the thinker from his thought; the desire to become, to experience, to be more or to be less, makes for division between the experiencer and the experience. Awareness of the ways of desire is self-knowledge. Self-knowledge is the beginning of meditation.

Immediate Action

If you are in contact with anything, with your wife, with your children, with the sky, with the clouds, with any fact, the moment thought interferes with it you lose contact. Thought springs from memory. Memory is the image, and from there you look and therefore there is a separation between the observer and the observed.

You have to understand this very deeply. It is this separation of the observer from the observed that makes the observer want more experience, more sensations, and so he is everlastingly pursuing, seeking. It has to be completely and totally understood that as long as there is an observer, the one that is seeking experience, the censor, the entity that evaluates, judges, condemns, there is no immediate contact with *what is*. When you have pain, physical pain, there is direct perception; there is not the observer who is feeling the pain; there is only pain. Because there is no observer there is immediate action. There is not the idea and then action, but there is only action when there is pain, because there is a direct physical contact. The pain is you; there is pain. As long as this is not completely understood, realized, explored, and felt deeply, as long as it is not wholly grasped, not intellectually, not verbally, that the observer is the observed, all life becomes conflict, a contradiction between opposing desires, the "what should be" and the "what is." You can do this only if you are aware whether you are looking at it as an observer, when you look at a flower or a cloud or anything.

Reality Is in What Is

Instead of asking who has realized or what God is, why not give your whole attention and awareness to *what is?* Then you will find the unknown, or rather it will come to you. If you understand what is the known, you will experience that extraordinary silence that is not induced, not enforced, that creative emptiness in which alone reality can enter. It cannot come to that which is *becoming,* which is striving; it can only come to that which is *being,* which understands *what is.* Then you will see that reality is not in the distance; the unknown is not far off; it is in *what is.* As the answer to a problem is in the problem, so reality is in *what is;* if we can understand it, then we shall know truth.

Face the Fact

I'm in sorrow. Psychologically, I'm terribly disturbed; and I have an idea about it: what I should do, what I should not do, how it should be changed. That idea, that formula, that concept prevents me from looking at the fact of *what is*. Ideation and the formula are escapes from *what is*. There is immediate action when there is great danger. Then you have no idea. You don't formulate an idea and then act according to that idea.

The mind has become lazy, indolent, through a formula which has given it a means of escape from action with regard to *what is*. Seeing for ourselves the whole structure of what has been said, not because it has been pointed out to us, is it possible to face the fact: the fact that we are violent, as an example? We are violent human beings, and we have chosen violence as the way of life—war and all the rest of it. Though we talk everlastingly, especially in the East, of nonviolence, we are not nonviolent people; we are violent people. The idea of nonviolence is an idea, which can be used politically. That's a different meaning, but it is an idea, and not a fact. Because the human being is incapable of meeting the fact of violence, he has invented the ideal of nonviolence, which prevents him from dealing with the fact.

After all, the fact is that I'm violent; I'm angry. What is the need of an idea? It is not the idea of being angry; it's the actual fact of being angry that is important, like the actual fact of being hungry. There's no idea about being hungry. The idea then comes as to what you should eat, and then according to the dictates of pleasure, you eat. There is only action with regard to *what is* when there is no idea of what should be done about that which confronts you, which is *what is*.

Freedom from What Is

Being virtuous comes through the understanding of *what is*, whereas becoming virtuous is postponement, the covering up of *what is* with what you would like to be. Therefore, in becoming virtuous you are avoiding action directly upon *what is*. This process of avoiding *what is* through the cultivation of the ideal is considered virtuous; but if you look at it closely and directly you will see that it is nothing of the kind. It is merely a postponement of coming face to face with *what is*. Virtue is not the becoming of what is not; virtue is the understanding of *what is* and therefore the freedom from *what is*. Virtue is essential in a society that is rapidly disintegrating.

Observing Thought

I must love the very thing I am studying. If you want to understand a child, you must love and not condemn him. You must play with him, watch his movements, his idiosyncrasies, his ways of behavior; but if you merely condemn, resist, or blame him, there is no comprehension of the child. Similarly, to understand *what is,* one must observe what one thinks, feels, and does from moment to moment. That is the actual.

Escape Breeds Conflict

Why are we ambitious? Why do we want to succeed, to be somebody? Why do we struggle to be superior? Why all this effort to assert oneself, whether directly, or through an ideology or the state? Is not this self-assertion the main cause of our conflict and confusion? Without ambition, would we perish? Can we not physically survive without being ambitious?

Why are we clever and ambitious? Is not ambition an urge to avoid *what is*? Is not this cleverness really stupid, which is what we are? Why are we so frightened of *what is*? What is the good of running away if whatever we are is always there? We may succeed in escaping, but what we are is still there, breeding conflict and misery. Why are we so frightened of our loneliness, or our emptiness? Any activity away from *what is* is bound to bring sorrow and antagonism. Conflict is the denial of *what is* or the running away from *what is*; there is no conflict other than that. Our conflict becomes more and more complex and insoluble because we do not face *what is*. There is no complexity in *what is*, but only in the many escapes that we seek.

Discontent Has No Answer

What is it that we are discontented with? Surely with *what is*. The *what is* may be the social order, the *what is* may be the relationship, the *what is* may be what we are, the thing we are essentially—which is, the ugly, the wandering thoughts, the ambitions, the frustrations, the innumerable fears; that is what we are. In going away from that, we think we shall find an answer to our discontent. So we are always seeking a way, a means to change the *what is*—that is what our mind is concerned with. If I am discontent and if I want to find a way, the means to contentment, my mind is occupied with the means, the way and the practicing of the way in order to arrive at contentment. So I am no longer concerned with discontent, with the embers, the flame that is burning, which we call discontent. We do not find out what is behind that discontent. We are only concerned with going away from that flame, from that burning anxiety. . . .

This is enormously difficult because our mind is never satisfied, never content in the examination of *what is*. It always wants to transform *what is* into something else—which is the process of condemnation, justification, or comparison. If you observe your own mind you will see that when it comes face to face with *what is*, then it condemns, then it compares it with "what it should be," or it justifies it and so on, and thereby pushes away *what is*, setting aside the thing that is causing the disturbance, the pain, the anxiety.

Effort Is Distraction from What Is

We must understand the problem of striving. If we can understand the significance of effort, then we can translate it into action in our daily life. Does not effort mean a struggle to change *what is* into what it is not, or what it should be, or what it should become? We are constantly escaping from *what is,* to transform or modify it. He who is truly content is he who understands *what is,* who gives the right significance to *what is.* True contentment lies not in few or many possessions, but in understanding the whole significance of *what is.* Only in passive awareness is the meaning of *what is* understood. I am not, at the moment, talking of the physical struggle with the earth, with construction or a technical problem, but of psychological striving. The psychological struggles and problems always overshadow the physiological. You may build a careful social structure, but as long as the psychological darkness and strife are not understood, they invariably overturn the carefully built structure.

Effort is distraction from *what is.* In the acceptance of *what is,* striving ceases. There is no acceptance when there is the desire to transform or modify *what is.* Striving, an indication of destruction, must exist so long as there is a desire to change *what is.*

A Contentment Not of the Mind

Is not discontent essential, not to be smothered away, but to be encouraged, inquired into, probed, so that with the understanding of *what is* there comes contentment? That contentment is not the contentment that is produced by a system of thought; but it is that contentment which comes with the understanding of *what is*. That contentment is not the product of the mind—the mind that is disturbed, agitated, incomplete, when it is seeking peace, when it is seeking a way away from *what is*. And so the mind, through justification, comparison, judgment, tries to alter *what is*, and thereby hopes to arrive at a state when it will not be disturbed, when it will be peaceful, when there will be quietness. And when the mind is disturbed by social conditions, by poverty, starvation, degradation, by the appalling misery, seeing all that, it wants to alter it; it gets entangled in the way of altering, in the system of altering. But if the mind is capable of looking at *what is* without comparison, without judgment, without the desire to alter it into something else, then you will see that there comes a kind of contentment which is not of the mind.

The contentment which is the product of the mind is an escape. It is sterile. It is dead. But there is contentment which is not of the mind, which comes into being when there is the understanding of *what is,* in which there is profound revolution that affects society and individual relationship.

Keep Discontent Alive

Is not discontent essential in our life, to any question, to any inquiry, to probing, to finding out what is the real, what is truth, what is essential in life? I may have this flaming discontent in college; and then I get a good job and this discontent vanishes. I am satisfied, I struggle to maintain my family, I have to earn a livelihood and so my discontent is calmed, destroyed, and I become a mediocre entity satisfied with things of life, and I am not discontent. But the flame has to be maintained from the beginning to the end, so that there is true inquiry, true probing into the problem of what discontent is. Because the mind seeks very easily a drug to make it content with virtues, with qualities, with ideas, with actions, it establishes a routine and gets caught up in it. We are quite familiar with that, but our problem is not how to calm discontent, but how to keep it smoldering, alive, vital. All our religious books, all our gurus, all political systems pacify the mind, quieten the mind, influence the mind to subside, to put aside discontent and wallow in some form of contentment. . . . Is it not essential to be discontented in order to find what is true?

To Understand What Is

We are in conflict with each other and our world is being destroyed. There is crisis after crisis, war after war; there is starvation, misery; there are the enormously rich clothed in their respectability, and there are the poor. To solve these problems, what is necessary is not a new system of thought, not a new economic revolution, but to understand *what is*—the discontent, the constant probing of *what is*—which will bring about a revolution which is more far-reaching than the revolution of ideas. And it is this revolution that is so necessary to bring about a different culture, a different religion, a different relationship between man and man.

◈

SEPTEMBER

Intellect

Thought

Knowledge

Mind

◈

We Think We Are Intellectual

Most of us have developed intellectual capacities—so-called intellectual capacities, which are not really intellectual capacities at all—we read so many books, filled with what other people have said, their many theories and ideas. We think we are very intellectual if we can quote innumerable books by innumerable authors, if we have read many different varieties of books, and have the capacity to correlate and to explain. But none of us, or very few, have original, intellectual conception. Having cultivated the intellect—so-called—every other capacity, every other feeling, has been lost and we have the problem of how to bring about a balance in our lives so as to have not only the highest intellectual capacity and be able to reason objectively, to see things exactly as they are—not to endlessly offer opinions about theories and codes, but to think for ourselves, to see for ourselves very closely the false and the true. And this, it seems to me, is one of our difficulties: the incapacity to see, not only outward things, but also such inward life that one has, if one has any at all.

All Thought Is Distraction

A mind that is competitive, held in the conflict of becoming, thinking in terms of comparison, is not capable of discovering the real. Thought-feeling which is intensely aware is in the process of constant self-discovery—which discovery, being true, is liberating and creative. Such self-discovery brings about freedom from acquisitiveness and from the complex life of the intellect. It is this complex life of the intellect that finds gratification in addictions: destructive curiosity, speculation, mere knowledge, capacity, gossip, and so on; and these hindrances prevent simplicity of life. An addiction, a specialization gives sharpness to the mind, a means of focusing thought, but it is not the flowering of thought-feeling into reality.

The freedom from distraction is more difficult as we do not fully understand the process of thinking-feeling, which in itself has become the means of distraction. Being ever incomplete, capable of speculative curiosity and formulation, it has the power to create its own hindrances, illusions, which prevent the awareness of the real. So it becomes its own distraction, its own enemy. As the mind is capable of creating illusion, this power must be understood before it can be wholly free from its own self-created distractions. Mind must be utterly still, silent, for all thought becomes a distraction.

Unity of Mind and Heart

Training the intellect does not result in intelligence. Rather, intelligence comes into being when one acts in perfect harmony, both intellectually and emotionally. There is a vast distinction between intellect and intelligence. Intellect is merely thought functioning independently of emotion. When intellect, irrespective of emotion, is trained in any particular direction, one may have great intellect, but one does not have intelligence, because in intelligence there is the inherent capacity to feel as well as to reason; in intelligence both capacities are equally present, intensely and harmoniously.

Now modern education is developing the intellect, offering more and more explanations of life, more and more theories, without the harmonious quality of affection. Therefore we have developed cunning minds to escape from conflict; hence we are satisfied with explanations that scientists and philosophers give us. The mind—the intellect—is satisfied with these innumerable explanations, but intelligence is not, for to understand there must be complete unity of mind and heart in action.

Intellect Corrupts Feeling

You know, there is the intellect, and there is pure feeling—the pure feeling of loving something, of having great, generous emotions. The intellect reasons, calculates, weighs, balances. It asks, "Is it worthwhile? Will it give me benefit?" On the other hand, there is pure feeling—the extraordinary feeling for the sky, for your neighbor, for your wife or husband, for your child, for the world, for the beauty of a tree, and so on. When these two come together, there is death. Do you understand? When pure feeling is corrupted by the intellect, there is mediocrity. That is what most of us are doing. Our lives are mediocre because we are always calculating, asking ourselves whether it is worthwhile, what profit we will get, not only in the world of money, but also in the so-called spiritual world—"If I do this, will I get that?"

Intellect Will Not Solve Our Problems

Most of us are so unconcerned with this extraordinary universe about us; we never even see the waving of the leaf in the wind; we never watch a blade of grass, touch it with our hand and know the quality of its being. This is not just being poetic, so please do not go off into a speculative, emotional state. I say it is essential to have that deep feeling for life and not be caught in intellectual ramifications, discussions, passing examinations, quoting and brushing something new aside by saying it has already been said. Intellect is not the way. Intellect will not solve our problems; the intellect will not give us that nourishment which is imperishable. The intellect can reason, discuss, analyze, come to a conclusion from inferences, and so on, but intellect is limited, for intellect is the result of our conditioning. But sensitivity is not. Sensitivity has no conditioning; it takes you right out of the field of fears and anxieties. . . . We spend our days and years in cultivating the intellect, in arguing, discussing, fighting, struggling to be something, and so on. And yet this extraordinarily wonderful world, this earth that is so rich—not the Bombay earth, the Punjab earth, the Russian earth, or the American earth—this earth is ours, yours and mine, and that is not sentimental nonsense; it is a fact. But unfortunately we have divided it up through our pettiness, through our provincialism. And we know why we have done it—for our security, for better jobs and more jobs. That is the political game that is being played throughout the world, and so we forget to be human beings, to live happily on this earth that is ours, and to make something of it.

The Flash of Understanding

I do not know if you have noticed that there is understanding when the mind is very quiet, even for a second; there is the flash of understanding when the verbalization of thought is not. Just experiment with it and you will see for yourself that you have the flash of understanding, that extraordinary rapidity of insight, when the mind is very still, when thought is absent, when the mind is not burdened with its own noise. So, the understanding of anything—of a modern picture, of a child, of your wife, of your neighbor, or the understanding of truth, which is in all things—can only come when the mind is very still. But such stillness cannot be cultivated because if you cultivate a still mind, it is not a still mind, it is a dead mind.

The more you are interested in something, the more your intention to understand, the more simple, clear, free the mind is. Then verbalization ceases. After all, thought is word, and it is the word that interferes. It is the screen of words, which is memory, that intervenes between the challenge and the response. It is the word that is responding to the challenge, which we call intellection. So, the mind that is chattering, that is verbalizing, cannot understand truth—truth in relationship, not an abstract truth. There is no abstract truth. But truth is very subtle. . . .

Like a thief in the night, it comes darkly, not when you are prepared to receive it.

The Unguarded Intellect

You can know yourself only when you are unaware, when you are not calculating, not protecting, not constantly watching to guide, to transform, to subdue, to control; when you see yourself unexpectedly, that is, when the mind has no preconceptions with regard to itself, when the mind is open, unprepared to meet the unknown.

If your mind is prepared, surely you cannot know the unknown, for you are the unknown. If you say to yourself, "I am God," or "I am nothing but a mass of social influences or a bundle of qualities"—if you have any preconception of yourself, you cannot comprehend the unknown, that which is spontaneous.

So spontaneity can come only when the intellect is unguarded, when it is not protecting itself, when it is no longer afraid for itself; and this can happen only from within. That is, the spontaneous must be the new, the unknown, the incalculable, the creative, that which must be expressed, loved, in which the will as the process of intellect, controlling, directing, has no part. Observe your own emotional states and you will see that the moments of great joy, great ecstasy, are unpremeditated; they happen, mysteriously, darkly, unknowingly.

Memory Has No Life in Itself

What do we mean by thought? When do you think? Obviously, thought is the result of a response, neurological or psychological, is it not? It is the immediate response of the senses to a sensation, or it is psychological, the response of stored-up memory. There is the immediate response of the nerves to a sensation, and there is the psychological response of stored-up memory, the influence of race, group, guru, family, tradition, and so on—all of which you call thought. So, the thought process is the response of memory, is it not? You would have no thoughts if you had no memory, and the response of memory to a certain experience brings the thought process into action.

What, then, is memory? If you observe your own memory and how you gather memory, you will notice that it is either factual, technical, having to do with information, with engineering, mathematics, physics, and all the rest of it—or, it is the residue of an unfinished, uncompleted experience, is it not? Watch your own memory and you will see. When you finish an experience, complete it, there is no memory of that experience in the sense of a psychological residue. There is a residue only when an experience is not fully understood, and there is no understanding of experience because we look at each experience through past memories, and therefore we never meet the new as the new, but always through the screen of the old. Therefore, it is clear that our response to experience is conditioned, always limited.

Consciousness Is of the Past

If you watch very carefully you will see that it is not a constant but that there is an interval between two thoughts; though it may be but an infinitesimal fraction of a second, there is an interval that has significance in the swinging backwards and forwards of the pendulum. We see the fact that our thinking is conditioned by the past, which is projected into the future; the moment you admit the past, you must also admit the future, because there are not two such states as the past and the future but one state which includes both the conscious and the unconscious, both the collective past and the individual past. The collective and the individual past, in response to the present, give out certain responses that create the individual consciousness; therefore consciousness is of the past and that is the whole background of our existence. The moment you have the past, you inevitably have the future, because the future is merely the continuity of the modified past, but it is still the past, so our problem is how to bring about a transformation in this process of the past without creating another conditioning, another past.

Why Is One Thoughtless?

The thinker thinks his thoughts through habit, through repetition, through copying, which brings ignorance and sorrow. Is not habit thoughtlessness? Awareness creates order, but it never creates habit. Settled tendencies only bring about thoughtlessness. Why is one thoughtless? Because to think is painful, it creates disturbances, it brings opposition, it may cause one's actions to go contrary to the established pattern. To think-feel extensionally, to become choicelessly aware may lead to unknown depths, and the mind rebels against the unknown; so it moves from the known to the known, from habit to habit, from pattern to pattern. Such a mind never abandons the known to discover the unknown. Realizing the pain of thought, the thinker becomes thoughtless through copying, through habit; being afraid to think, he creates patterns of thoughtlessness. As the thinker is afraid, his actions are born of fear, and then he regards his actions and tries to change them. The thinker is afraid of his own creations; but the deed is the doer, so the thinker is afraid of himself. The thinker is fear itself; the thinker is the cause of ignorance, of sorrow. The thinker may divide himself into many categories of thought, but the thought is still the thinker. The thinker and his efforts to be, to become, are the very cause of conflict and confusion.

The Thinker Is the Thought

Is it not necessary to understand the thinker, the doer, the actor, since his thought, his deed, his action cannot be separated from him? The thinker is the thought, the doer is the deed, the actor is the action. In his thought the thinker is revealed. The thinker through his actions creates his own misery, his ignorance, his strife. The painter paints this picture of passing happiness, of sorrow, of confusion. Why does he produce this painful picture? Surely, this is the problem that must be studied, understood and dissolved. Why does the thinker think his thoughts, from which flow all his actions? This is the rock wall against which you have been battering your head, is it not? If the thinker can transcend himself, then all conflict will cease: and to transcend he must know himself. What is known and understood, what is fulfilled and completed does not repeat itself. It is repetition that gives continuity to the thinker.

There Is No Freedom of Thought

I do not know if it is clear to each one of us that we live in a state of contradiction. We talk about peace, and prepare for war. We talk about nonviolence, and are fundamentally violent. We talk about being good, and we are not. We talk about love, and we are full of ambition, competitiveness, ruthless efficiency. So there is contradiction. The action that springs from that contradiction only brings about frustration and further contradiction. . . .

You see, sirs, all thought is partial, it can never be total. Thought is the response of memory, and memory is always partial because memory is the result of experience, so thought is the reaction of a mind that is conditioned by experience. All thinking, all experience, all knowledge is inevitably partial; therefore, thought cannot solve the many problems that we have. You may try to reason logically, sanely, about these many problems, but if you observe your own mind you will see that your thinking is conditioned by your circumstances, by the culture in which you were born, by the food you eat, by the climate you live in, by the newspapers you read, by the pressures and influences of your daily life. . . .

So we must understand very clearly that our thinking is the response of memory, and memory is mechanistic. Knowledge is ever incomplete, and all thinking born of knowledge is limited, partial, never free. So there is no freedom of thought. But we can begin to discover a freedom which is not a process of thought, and in which the mind is simply aware of all its conflicts and of all the influences impinging upon it.

Thinking Without the Thinker

The monkey in the tree feels hungry, and then the urge arises to take a fruit or a nut. Action comes first, and then the idea that you had better store it up. To put it in different words, does action come first, or the actor? Is there an actor without action? Do you understand? This is what we are always asking ourselves: Who is it that sees? Who is the watcher? Is the thinker apart from his thoughts, the observer apart from the observed, the experiencer apart from the experience, the actor apart from the action? . . . But if you really examine the process, very carefully, closely and intelligently, you will see that there is always action first, and that action with an end in view creates the actor. Do you follow? If action has an end in view, the gaining of that end brings about the actor. If you think very clearly and without prejudice, without conformity, without trying to convince somebody, without an end in view, in that very thinking there is no thinker—there is only the thinking. It is only when you seek an end in your thinking that *you* become important, and not thought. Perhaps some of you have observed this. It is really an important thing to find out, because from that we shall know how to act. If the thinker comes first, then the thinker is more important than thought, and all the philosophies, customs, and activities of the present civilization are based on this assumption; but if thought comes first then thought is more important than the thinker.

Immediate Perception

To me there is only perception—which is to see something as false or true immediately. This immediate perception of what is false and what is true is the essential factor—not the intellect, with its reasoning based upon its cunning, its knowledge, its commitments. It must sometimes have happened to you that you have seen the truth of something immediately—such as the truth that you cannot belong to anything. That is perception: seeing the truth of something immediately, without analysis, without reasoning, without all the things that the intellect creates in order to postpone perception. It is entirely different from intuition, which is a word that we use with glibness and ease. . . .

To me there is only this direct perception—not reasoning, not calculation, not analysis. You must have the capacity to analyze; you must have a good, sharp mind in order to reason; but a mind that is limited to reason and analysis is incapable of perceiving what is truth. . . .

If you commune with yourself, you will know why you belong, why you have committed yourself; and if you push further, you will see the slavery, the cutting down of freedom, the lack of human dignity which that commitment entails. When you perceive all this instantaneously, you are free; you don't have to make an effort to be free. That is why perception is essential.

Moment-to-Moment Understanding

The fundamental understanding of oneself does not come through knowledge or through the accumulation of experiences, which is merely the cultivation of memory. The understanding of oneself is from moment to moment; if we merely accumulate knowledge of the self, that very knowledge prevents further understanding, because accumulated knowledge and experience become the center through which thought focuses and has its being.

Understand the
Process of Your Thinking

Suppose you had never read a book, religious or psychological, and you had to find the meaning, the significance of life. How would you set about it? Suppose there were no Masters, no religious organizations, no Buddha, no Christ, and you had to begin from the beginning. How would you set about it? First, you would have to understand your process of thinking, would you not?—and not project yourself, your thoughts, into the future and create a God who pleases you; that would be too childish. So first you would have to understand the process of your thinking. That is the only way to discover anything new, is it not?

When we say that learning or knowledge is an impediment, a hindrance, we are not including technical knowledge—how to drive a car, how to run machinery—or the efficiency that such knowledge brings. We have in mind quite a different thing: that sense of creative happiness that no amount of knowledge or learning will bring. To be creative in the truest sense of that word is to be free of the past from moment to moment, because it is the past that is continually shadowing the present. Merely to cling to information, to the experiences of others, to what someone has said, however great, and try to approximate your action to that—all that is knowledge, is it not? But to discover anything new you must start on your own; you must start on a journey completely denuded, especially of knowledge, because it is very easy, through knowledge and belief, to have experiences; but these experiences are merely the products of self-projection and therefore utterly unreal, false.

Knowledge Is Not Wisdom

In our search for knowledge, in our acquisitive desires, we are losing love, we are blunting the feeling for beauty, the sensitivity to cruelty; we are becoming more and more specialized and less and less integrated. Wisdom cannot be replaced by knowledge, and no amount of explanation, no accumulation of facts, will free man from suffering. Knowledge is necessary, science has its place; but if the mind and heart are suffocated by knowledge, and if the cause of suffering is explained away, life becomes vain and meaningless. . . .

Information, the knowledge of facts, though ever increasing, is by its very nature limited. Wisdom is infinite, it includes knowledge and the way of action; but we take hold of a branch and think it is the whole tree. Through the knowledge of the part, we can never realize the joy of the whole. Intellect can never lead to the whole, for it is only a segment, a part.

We have separated intellect from feeling, and have developed intellect at the expense of feeling. We are like a three-legged object with one leg much longer than the others, and we have no balance. We are trained to be intellectual; our education cultivates the intellect to be sharp, cunning, acquisitive, and so it plays the most important role in our life. Intelligence is much greater than intellect, for it is the integration of reason and love; but there can be intelligence only when there is self-knowledge, the deep understanding of the total process of oneself.

The Function of the Intellect

I do not know if you have considered the nature of the intellect. The intellect and its activities are all right at a certain level, are they not? But when the intellect interferes with that pure feeling, then mediocrity sets in. To know the function of the intellect, and to be aware of that pure feeling, without letting the two mingle and destroy each other, requires a very clear, sharp awareness. . . .

So the function of the intellect is always, is it not, to inquire, to analyze, to search out; but because we want to be secure inwardly, psychologically, because we are afraid, anxious about life, we come to some form of conclusion to which we are committed. From one commitment we proceed to another, and I say that such a mind, such an intellect, being slave to a conclusion, has ceased to think, to inquire.

Be an Outsider

I do not know if you have observed what an enormous part the intellect plays in our life. The newspapers, the magazines, everything about us is cultivating reason. Not that I am against reason. On the contrary, one must have the capacity to reason very clearly, sharply. But if you observe you find that the intellect is everlastingly analyzing why we belong or do not belong, why one must be an outsider to find reality, and so on. We have learned the process of analyzing ourselves. So there is the intellect with its capacity to inquire, to analyze, to reason and come to conclusions; and there is feeling, pure feeling, which is always being interrupted, colored by the intellect. And when the intellect interferes with pure feeling, out of this interference grows a mediocre mind. On the one hand we have intellect, with its capacity to reason based upon its likes and dislikes, upon its conditioning, upon its experience and knowledge; and on the other, we have feeling, which is corrupted by society, by fear. And will these two reveal what is true? Or is there only perception, and nothing else?

A Mind That Is Learning

What do we mean by learning? Is there learning when you are merely accumulating knowledge, gathering information? That is one kind of learning, is it not? As a student of engineering, you study mathematics, and so on; you are learning, informing yourself about the subject. You are accumulating knowledge in order to use that knowledge in practical ways. Your learning is accumulative, additive. Now, when the mind is merely taking on, adding, acquiring, is it learning? Or is learning something entirely different? I say the additive process that we now call learning is not learning at all. It is merely a cultivation of memory, which becomes mechanical; and a mind that functions mechanically, like a machine, is not capable of learning. A machine is never capable of learning, except in the additive sense. Learning is something quite different, as I shall try to show you.

A mind that is learning never says, "I know," because knowledge is always partial, whereas learning is complete all the time. Learning does not mean starting with a certain amount of knowledge, and adding to it further knowledge. That is not learning at all; it is a purely mechanistic process. To me, learning is something entirely different. I am learning about myself from moment to moment, and the myself is extraordinarily vital; it is living, moving; it has no beginning and no end. When I say, "I know myself," learning has come to an end in accumulated knowledge. Learning is never cumulative; it is a movement of knowing which has no beginning and no end.

Knowledge Assumes Authority

There is no movement of learning when there is the acquisition of knowledge; the two are incompatible, they are contradictory. The movement of learning implies a state in which the mind has no previous experience stored up as knowledge. Knowledge is acquired, whereas learning is a constant movement which is not an additive or acquisitive process; therefore, the movement of learning implies a state in which the mind has no authority. All knowledge assumes authority, and a mind that is entrenched in the authority of knowledge cannot possibly learn. The mind can learn only when the additive process has completely ceased.

It is rather difficult for most of us to differentiate between learning and acquiring knowledge. Through experience, through reading, through listening, the mind accumulates knowledge; it is an acquisitive process, a process of adding to what is already known, and from this background of knowledge we function. Now, what we generally call learning is this very same process of acquiring new information and adding it to the store of knowledge we already have. . . . But I am talking about something entirely different. By learning I do not mean adding to what you already know. You can learn only when there is no attachment to the past as knowledge, that is, when you see something new and do not translate it in terms of the known.

The mind that is learning is an innocent mind, whereas the mind that is merely acquiring knowledge is old, stagnant, corrupted by the past. An innocent mind perceives instantly; it is learning all the time without accumulating, and such a mind alone is mature.

The Brain Produces the Mind

. . . What is the mind? When I put that question, please don't wait for a reply from me. Look at your own mind; observe the ways of your own thought. What I describe is only an indication; it is not the reality. The reality you must experience for yourself. The word, the description, the symbol, is not the actual thing. The word *door* is obviously not the door. The word *love* is not the feeling, the extraordinary quality that the word indicates. So do not let us confuse the word, the name, the symbol, with the fact. If you merely remain on the verbal level and discuss what the mind is, you are lost, for then you will never feel the quality of this astonishing thing called the mind.

So, what is the mind? Obviously, the mind is our total awareness or consciousness; it is the total way of our existence, the whole process of our thinking. The mind is the result of the brain. The brain produces the mind. Without the brain there is no mind, but the mind is separate from the brain. It is the child of the brain. If the brain is limited, damaged, the mind is also damaged. The brain, which records every sensation, every feeling of pleasure or pain, the brain with all its tissues, with all its responses, creates what we call the mind, although the mind is independent of the brain.

You don't have to accept this. You can experiment with it and see for yourself.

The Anchored Mind

We carry on like machines with our tiresome daily routine. How eagerly the mind accepts a pattern of existence, and how tenaciously it clings to it! As by a driven nail, the mind is held together by idea, and around the idea it lives and has its being. The mind is never free, pliable, for it is always anchored; it moves within the radius, narrow or wide, of its own center. From its center it dare not wander; and when it does, it is lost in fear. Fear is not of the unknown, but of the loss of the known. The unknown does not incite fear, but dependence on the known does. Fear is always with desire, the desire for the more or for the less. The mind, with its incessant weaving of patterns, is the maker of time; and with time there is fear, hope, and death.

The Mind Is the Result of Time

The mind is being influenced all the time to think along a certain line. It used to be that only the organized religions were after your mind, but now governments have largely taken over that job. They want to shape and control your mind. On the surface the mind can resist their control. . . . Superficially you have some say in the matter, but below the surface, in the deep unconscious, there is the whole weight of time, of tradition, urging you in a particular direction. The conscious mind may to some extent control and guide itself, but in the unconscious your ambitions, your unsolved problems, your compulsions, superstitions, fears, are waiting, throbbing, urging. . . .

This whole field of the mind is the result of time; it is the result of conflicts and adjustments, of a whole series of acceptances without full comprehension. Therefore, we live in a state of contradiction; our life is a process of endless struggle. We are unhappy, and we want to be happy. Being violent, we practice the ideal of nonviolence. So there is a conflict going on—the mind is a battlefield. We want to be secure, knowing inwardly, deeply, that there is no such thing as security at all. The truth is that we do not want to face the fact that there is no security; therefore, we are always pursuing security, with the resultant fear of not being secure.

Living Is the Greatest Revolution

Mind is held in a pattern; its very existence is the frame within which it works and moves. The pattern is of the past or the future, it is despair and hope, confusion and Utopia, the what has been and the what should be. With this we are all familiar. You want to break the old pattern and substitute a "new" one, the new being the modified old. . . . You want to produce a new world. It is impossible. You may deceive yourself and others, but unless the old pattern is broken completely there cannot be a radical transformation. You may play around with it, but you are not the hope of the world. The breaking of the pattern, both the old and the so-called new, is of the utmost importance if order is to come out of this chaos. That is why it is essential to understand the ways of the mind. . . .

Is it possible for the mind to be without a pattern, to be free of this backward and forward swing of desire? It is definitely possible. Such action is living in the now. To live is to be without hope, without the care of tomorrow; it is not hopelessness or indifference. But we are not living, we are always pursuing death, the past or the future. Living is the greatest revolution. Living has no pattern, but death has: the past or the future, the what has been or the Utopia. You are living for the Utopia, and so you are inviting death and not life.

Inward Revolution

What is true can only be found from moment to moment, it is not a continuity, but the mind which wants to discover it, being itself the product of time, can only function in the field of time; therefore it is incapable of finding what is true.

To know the mind, the mind must know itself, for there is no "I" apart from the mind. There are no qualities separate from the mind, just as the qualities of the diamond are not separate from the diamond itself. To understand the mind you cannot interpret it according to somebody else's idea, but you must observe how your own total mind works. When you know the whole process of it—how it reasons, its desires, motives, ambitions, pursuits, its envy, greed, and fear—then the mind can go beyond itself, and when it does there is the discovery of something totally new. That quality of newness gives an extraordinary passion, a tremendous enthusiasm that brings about a deep inward revolution: and it is this inward revolution which alone can transform the world, not any political or economic system.

There Is Only Consciousness

There is in fact only one state, not two states such as the conscious and the unconscious; there is only a state of being, which is consciousness, though you may divide it as the conscious and the unconscious. But that consciousness is always of the past, never of the present; you are conscious only of things that are over. You are conscious of what I am trying to convey the second afterwards, are you not? You understand it a moment later. You are never conscious or aware of the now. Watch your own hearts and minds and you will see that consciousness is functioning between the past and the future and that the present is merely a passage of the past to the future. . . .

If you watch your own mind at work, you will see that the movement to the past and to the future is a process in which the present is not. Either the past is a means of escape from the present, which may be unpleasant, or the future is a hope away from the present. So the mind is occupied with the past or with the future and sloughs off the present. . . . It either condemns and rejects the fact or accepts and identifies itself with the fact. Such a mind is obviously not capable of seeing any fact as a fact. That is, our state of consciousness, which is conditioned by the past and our thought, is the conditioned response to the challenge of a fact; the more you respond according to the conditioning of belief, of the past, the more there is strengthening of the past.

That strengthening of the past is obviously the continuity of itself, which it calls the future. So that is the state of our mind, of our consciousness—a pendulum swinging backwards and forwards between the past and the future.

Beyond Time

The conditioned mind, surely, is incapable of finding out what lies beyond time. That is, sirs, the mind as we know it is conditioned by the past. The past, moving through the present to the future, conditions the mind; and this conditioned mind, being in conflict, in trouble, being fearful, uncertain, seeks something beyond the frontiers of time. That is what we are all doing in various ways, is it not? But how can a mind that is the result of time ever find that which is timeless?

The house of your beliefs, of your properties, of your attachments and comforting ways of thinking is constantly being broken into. But the mind goes on seeking security, so there is a conflict between what you want and what life's process demands of you. This is what is happening to every one of us. . . .

I do not know if this problem interests you at all. Everyday existence, with all its troubles, seems to be sufficient for most of us. Our only concern is to find an immediate answer to our various problems. But sooner or later the immediate answers are found to be unsatisfactory because no problem has an answer apart from the problem itself. But if I can understand the problem, all the intricacies of it, then the problem no longer exists.

A Mind with Problems
Is Not a Serious Mind

One of the principal questions that one has to put to oneself is this: How far or to what depth can the mind penetrate into itself? That is the quality of seriousness because it implies awareness of the whole structure of one's own psychological being, with its urges, its compulsions, its desire to fulfill, and its frustrations, its miseries, strains, and anxieties, its struggles, sorrows, and the innumerable problems that it has. The mind that perpetually has problems is not a serious mind at all, but the mind that understands each problem as it arises and dissolves it immediately so that it is not carried over to the next day—such a mind is serious. . . .

What are most of us interested in? If we have money, we turn to so-called spiritual things, or to intellectual amusements, or we discuss art, or take up a painting to express ourselves. If we have no money, our time is taken up day after day with earning it, and we are caught in that misery, in the endless routine and boredom of it. Most of us are trained to function mechanically in some job, year in and year out. We have responsibilities, a wife and children to provide for, and caught up in this mad world we try to be serious, we try to become religious; we go to church, we join this religious organization or that—or perhaps we hear about these meetings and because we have holidays we turn up here. But none of that will bring about this extraordinary transformation of the mind.

The Religious Mind
Includes the Scientific Mind

A religious mind is free of all authority. And it is extremely difficult to be free from authority—not only the authority imposed by another but also the authority of the experience that one has gathered, which is of the past, which is tradition. And the religious mind has no beliefs; it has no dogmas; it moves from fact to fact, and therefore the religious mind is the scientific mind. But the scientific mind is not the religious mind. The religious mind includes the scientific mind, but the mind that is trained in the knowledge of science is not a religious mind.

A religious mind is concerned with the totality—not with a particular function, but with the total functioning of human existence. The brain is concerned with a particular function; it specializes. It functions in specialization as a scientist, a doctor, an engineer, a musician, an artist, a writer. It is these specialized, narrowed-down techniques that create division, not only inwardly but outwardly. The scientist is probably regarded as the most important man required by society just now, as is the doctor. So function becomes all-important; and with it goes status, status being prestige. So where there is specialization there must be contradiction and a narrowing-down, and that is the function of the brain.

OCTOBER

Time

Perception

Brain

Transformation

Time Provides No Solution

All religions have maintained that time is necessary, the psychological time we are talking about. Heaven is very far away, and one can only come to it through the gradual process of evolution, through suppression, through growth, or through identification with an object, with something superior. Our question is whether it is possible to be free of fear immediately. Otherwise fear breeds disorder; psychological time invariably does breed extraordinary disorder within one.

I am questioning the whole idea of evolution, not of the physical being, but of thought, which has identified itself with a particular form of existence in time. The brain has obviously evolved to come to this present stage, and it may evolve still further, expand still more. But as a human being, I have lived for forty or fifty years in a world made up of all kinds of theories, conflicts, and concepts; in a society in which greed, envy, and competition have bred wars. I am a part of all that. To a man who is in sorrow, there is no significance in looking to time for a solution, in evolving slowly for the next two million years as a human being. Constituted as we are, is it possible to be free from fear and from psychological time? Physical time must exist; you can't get away from that. The question is whether psychological time can bring not only order within the individual but also social order. We are part of society; we are not separate. Where there is order in a human being, there will inevitably be social order outwardly.

A Timeless State

When we are talking about time, we do not mean chronological time, time by the watch. That time exists, must exist. If you want to catch a bus, if you want to get to a train or meet an appointment tomorrow, you must have chronological time. But is there a tomorrow, psychologically, which is the time of the mind? Is there psychologically tomorrow, actually? Or is the tomorrow created by thought because thought sees the impossibility of change, directly, immediately, and invents this process of gradualness? I see for myself, as a human being, that it is terribly important to bring about a radical revolution in my way of life, thinking, feeling, and in my actions, and I say to myself, "I'll take time over it; I'll be different tomorrow, or in a month's time." That is the time we are talking about: the psychological structure of time, of tomorrow, or the future, and in that time we live. Time is the past, the present, and the future, not by the watch. I was, yesterday; yesterday operates through today and creates the future. That's a fairly simple thing. I had an experience a year ago that left an imprint on my mind, and the present I translate according to that experience, knowledge, tradition, conditioning, and I create the tomorrow. I'm caught in this circle. This is what we call living; this is what we call time.

Thought, which is you, with all its memories, conditioning, ideas, hopes, despair, the utter loneliness of existence— all that is this time. . . . And to understand a timeless state, when time has come to a stop, one must inquire whether the mind can be free totally of all experience, which is of time.

The Very Nature of Thought

Time is thought, and thought is the process of memory that creates time as yesterday, today, and tomorrow, as a thing that we use as a means of achievement, as a way of life. Time to us is extraordinarily important, life after life, one life leading to another life that is modified, that continues. Surely, time is the very nature of thought, thought is time. And as long as time exists as a means to something, the mind cannot go beyond itself—the quality of going beyond itself belongs to the new mind, which is free of time. Time is a factor in fear. By time, I don't mean the chronological time, by the watch—second, minute, hour, day, year, but time as a psychological, inward process. It is that fact that brings about fear. Time is fear; as time is thought, it does breed fear; it is time that creates frustration, conflicts, because the immediate perception of the fact, the seeing of the fact is timeless. . . .

So, to understand fear, one must be aware of time—time as distance, space, "me," which thought creates as yesterday, today, and tomorrow, using the memory of yesterday to adjust itself to the present and so to condition the future. So, for most of us fear is an extraordinary reality; and a mind that is entangled with fear, with the complexity of fear, can never be free; it can never understand the totality of fear without understanding the intricacies of time. They go together.

The Disorder That Time Creates

Time means moving from *what is* to "what should be." I am afraid, but one day I shall be free of fear; therefore, time is necessary to be free of fear—at least, that is what we think. To change from *what is* to "what should be" involves time. Now, time implies effort in that interval between *what is* and "what should be." I don't like fear, and I am going to make an effort to understand, to analyze, to dissect it, or I am going to discover the cause of it, or I am going to escape totally from it. All this implies effort—and effort is what we are used to. We are always in conflict between *what is* and "what should be." The "what I should be" is an idea, and the idea is fictitious, it is not "what I am," which is the fact; and the "what I am" can be changed only when I understand the disorder that time creates.

So, is it possible for me to be rid of fear totally, completely, on the instant? If I allow fear to continue, I will create disorder all the time; therefore, one sees that time is an element of disorder, not a means to be ultimately free of fear. So there is no gradual process of getting rid of fear, just as there is no gradual process of getting rid of the poison of nationalism. If you have nationalism and you say that eventually there will be the brotherhood of man, in the interval there are wars, there are hatreds, there is misery, there is all this appalling division between man and man; therefore, time is creating disorder.

Time Is a Poison

In your bathroom you have a bottle marked "poison," and you know it is poison; you are very careful of that bottle, even in the dark. You are always watching out for it. You don't say, "How am I to keep away, how am I to be watchful of that bottle?" You know it is poison, so you are tremendously attentive to it. Time is a poison; it creates disorder. If this is a fact to you, then you can proceed into the understanding of how to be free of fear immediately. But if you are still holding time as a means of freeing yourself, there is no communication between you and me.

You see, there is something much more; there may be a totally different kind of time altogether. We only know two times, physical and psychological, and we are caught in time. Physical time plays an important part in the psyche, and the psyche has an important influence on the physical. We are caught in this battle, in this influence. One must accept physical time in order to catch the bus or the train, but if one rejects psychological time completely, then one may come to a time that is something quite different, a time that is not related to either. I wish you would come on with me into that time! Then time is not disorder; it is tremendous order.

Truth Comes in a Flash

Truth or understanding comes in a flash, and that flash has no continuity; it is not within the field of time. Do see this for yourself. Understanding is fresh, instantaneous; it is not the continuity of something that has been. What has been cannot bring you understanding. As long as one is seeking a continuity—wanting permanency in relationship, in love, longing to find peace everlasting, and all the rest of it—one is pursuing something that is within the field of time and therefore does not belong to the timeless.

A Vain Pursuit

As long as we think in terms of time, there must be fear of death. I have learned, but I have not found the ultimate, and before I die I must find it; or if I do not find it before I die, at least I hope I shall find it in the next life, and so on. All our thinking is based on time. Our thinking is the known, it is the outcome of the known, and the known is the process of time; and with that mind we are trying to find out what it is to be immortal, beyond time, which is a vain pursuit. It has no meaning except to philosophers, theorists, and speculators. If I want to find the truth, not tomorrow, but actually, directly, must not I— the "me," the self that is always gathering, striving, and giving itself a continuity through memory—cease to continue? Is it not possible to die while living—not artificially to lose one's memory, which is amnesia, but actually to cease to accumulate through memory, and thereby cease to give continuance to the "me"? Living in this world, which is of time, is it not possible for the mind to bring about, without any form of compulsion, a state in which the experiencer and the experience have no basis? As long as there is the experiencer, the observer, the thinker, there must be the fear of ending, and therefore of death. . . .

And so, if it is possible for the mind to know all this, to be fully aware of it and not merely say, "Yes, it is simple"—if the mind can be aware of the total process of consciousness, see the whole significance of continuity and of time, and the futility of this search through time to find that which is beyond time—if it can be aware of all that, then there may be a death that is really a creativity totally beyond time.

Perception Acts

You see and I do not see—why does this happen? I think it happens because one is involved in time; you do not see things in time, I see it in time. Your seeing is an action of your whole being, and your whole being is not caught in time; you do not think of gradual arrival; you see something immediately, and that very perception acts. I do not see; I want to find out why I do not see. What is the thing that will make me see something totally so that I have understood the whole thing immediately? You see the whole structure of life: the beauty, the ugliness, the sorrow, the joy, the extraordinary sensitivity, the beauty—you see the whole thing, and I cannot. I see a part of it, but I do not see the whole of it. . . . The man who sees something totally, who sees life totally, must obviously be out of time. Sirs, do listen to this, because this has something actually to do with our daily existence; it is not something spiritual, philosophical, out of daily existence. If we understand this, then we will understand our daily routine, boredom, and sorrows, the nauseating anxieties and fears. So do not brush it away by saying, "What has it to do with our daily existence?" It has. One can see—at least for me, it is very clear—that you can cut, like a surgeon, the whole cord of misery immediately. That is why I want to go into it with you.

At the Edge of All Thought

Has it ever happened to you—I am sure it has—that you suddenly perceive something, and in that moment of perception you have no problems at all? The very moment you have perceived the problem, the problem has completely ceased. Do you understand, sirs? You have a problem, and you think about it, argue with it, worry over it; you exercise every means within the limits of your thought to understand it. Finally you say, "I can do no more." There is nobody to help you to understand, no guru, no book. You are left with the problem, and there is no way out. Having inquired into the problem to the full extent of your capacity, you leave it alone. Your mind is no longer worried, no longer tearing at the problem, no longer saying, "I must find an answer"; so it becomes quiet, does it not? And in that quietness you find the answer. Hasn't that sometimes happened to you? It is not an enormous thing. It happens to great mathematicians and scientists, and people experience it occasionally in everyday life. Which means what? The mind has exercised fully its capacity to think, and has come to the edge of all thought without having found an answer; therefore it becomes quiet—not through weariness, not through fatigue, not by saying, "I will be quiet and thereby find the answer." Having already done everything possible to find the answer, the mind becomes spontaneously quiet. There is an awareness without choice, without any demand, an awareness in which there is no anxiety; and in that state of mind there is perception. It is this perception alone that will resolve all our problems.

This Choiceless Awarenesss

Great seers have always told us to acquire experience. They have said that experience gives us understanding. But it is only the innocent mind, the mind unclouded by experience, totally free from the past—it is only such a mind that can perceive what is reality. If you see the truth of that, if you perceive it for a split second, you will know the extraordinary clarity of a mind that is innocent. This means the falling away of all the encrustations of memory, which is the discarding of the past. But to perceive it, there can be no question of "how." Your mind must not be distracted by the "how," by the desire for an answer. Such a mind is not an attentive mind. As I said earlier in this talk, in the beginning is the end. In the beginning is the seed of the ending of that which we call sorrow. The ending of sorrow is realized in sorrow itself, not away from sorrow. To move away from sorrow is merely to find an answer, a conclusion, an escape; but sorrow continues. Whereas, if you give it your complete attention, which is to be attentive with your whole being, then you will see that there is an immediate perception in which no time is involved, in which there is no effort, no conflict; and it is this immediate perception, this choiceless awareness that puts an end to sorrow.

The Active Still Mind

The mind that is really still is astonishingly active, alive, potent—not towards anything in particular. It is only such a mind which is verbally free—free from experience, from knowledge. Such a mind can perceive what is true, such a mind has direct perception, which is beyond time.

The mind can only be silent when it has understood the process of time and that requires watchfulness, does it not? Must not such a mind be free, not *from* anything, but be free? We only know freedom from something. A mind that is free from something is not a free mind; such freedom, the freedom from something, is only a reaction, and it is not freedom. A mind that is seeking freedom is never free. But the mind is free when it understands the fact, as it is, without translating, without condemning, without judging; and being free, such a mind is an innocent mind, though it lived 100 days, 100 years, having all the experiences. It is innocent because it is free, not from anything, but in itself. It is only such a mind that can perceive that which is true, which is beyond time.

Out of Perception Comes Energy

The problem is, surely, to free the mind totally so that it is in a state of awareness that has no border, no frontier. And how is the mind to discover that state? How is it to come to that freedom?

I hope you are seriously putting this question to yourselves, because I am not putting it to you. I am not trying to influence you; I am merely pointing out the importance of asking oneself this question. The verbal asking of the question by another has no meaning if you don't put it to yourself with insistence, with urgency. The margin of freedom is growing narrower every day, as you must know if you are at all observant. The politicians, the leaders, the priests, the newspapers and books you read, the knowledge you acquire, the beliefs you cling to—all this is making the margin of freedom more and more narrow. If you are aware of this process going on, if you actually perceive the narrowness of the spirit, the increasing slavery of the mind, then you will find that out of perception comes energy; and it is this energy born of perception that is going to shatter the petty mind, the respectable mind, the mind that goes to the temple, the mind that is afraid. So perception is the way of truth.

The Chattering Mind

You know, to perceive something is an astonishing experience. I don't know if you have ever really perceived anything—if you have ever perceived a flower or a face or the sky, or the sea. Of course, you see these things as you pass by in a bus or a car; but I wonder whether you have ever taken the trouble actually to look at a flower? And when you do look at a flower, what happens? You immediately name the flower, you are concerned with what species it belongs to, or you say, "What lovely colours it has. I would like to grow it in my garden; I would like to give it to my wife, or put it in my button-hole," and so on. In other words, the moment you look at a flower, your mind begins chattering about it; therefore you never perceive the flower. You perceive something only when your mind is silent, when there is no chattering of any kind. If you can look at the evening star over the sea without a movement of the mind, then you really perceive the extraordinary beauty of it; and when you perceive beauty, do you not also experience the state of love? Surely, beauty and love are the same. Without love there is no beauty, and without beauty there is no love. Beauty is in form, beauty is in speech, beauty is in conduct. If there is no love, conduct is empty; it is merely the product of society, of a particular culture, and what is produced is mechanical, lifeless. But when the mind perceives without the slightest flutter, then it is capable of looking into the total depth of itself; and such perception is really timeless. You don't have to do something to bring it about; there is no discipline, no practice, no method by which you can learn to perceive.

Knowledge Diverts the Mind

You have only one instrument, which is the mind; and the mind is the brain also. Therefore, to find out the truth of this matter, you must understand the ways of the mind, must you not? If the mind is crooked you will never see straight; if the mind is very limited you cannot perceive the illimitable. The mind is the instrument of perception and, to perceive truly, the mind must be made straight, it must be cleansed of all conditioning, of all fear. The mind must also be free of knowledge, because knowledge diverts the mind and makes things twisted. The enormous capacity of the mind to invent, to imagine, to speculate, to think—must not this capacity be put aside so that the mind is very clear and very simple? Because it is only the innocent mind, the mind that has experienced vastly and yet is free of knowledge and experience—it is only such a mind that can discover that which is more than brain and mind. Otherwise, what you discover will be colored by what you have already experienced, and your experience is the result of your conditioning.

Drowned by Influence

Why does the mind grow old? It is old, is it not, in the sense of getting decrepit, deteriorating, repeating itself, caught in habits—sexual habits, religious habits, job habits, or various habits of ambition. The mind is so burdened with innumerable experiences and memories, so marred and scarred with sorrow that it cannot see anything freshly, but is always translating what it sees in terms of its own memories, conclusions, formulas, always quoting; it is authority-bound; it is an old mind. You can see why it happens. All our education is merely the cultivation of memory; and there is this mass communication through journals, the radio, the television; there are the professors who read lectures and repeat the same thing over and over again until your brain soaks in what they have repeated, and you vomit it up in an examination and get your degree and go on with the process—the job, the routine, the incessant repetition. Not only that, but there is also our own inward struggle of ambition with its frustrations, the competition not only for jobs but for God, wanting to be near him, asking the quick road to him. . . .

So, what is happening is that through pressure, through stress, through strain, our minds are being crowded, drowned by influence, by sorrow, consciously or unconsciously. . . . We are wearing down the mind, not using it.

The Old Brain, Our Animalistic Brain

I think it is important to understand the operation, the functioning, the activity of the old brain. When the new brain operates, the old brain cannot possibly understand the new brain. It is only when the old brain, which is our conditioned brain, our animalistic brain, the brain that has been cultivated through centuries of time, which is everlastingly seeking its own security, its own comfort—it is only when that old brain is quiet that you will see that there is a different kind of movement altogether, and it is this movement that is going to bring clarity. It is this movement that is clarity itself. To understand, you must understand the old brain, be aware of it, know all its movements, its activities, its demands, its pursuits, and that is why meditation is very important. I do not mean the absurd, systematized cultivation of a certain habit of thought, and the rest of it; that's all too immature and childish. By meditation I mean to understand the operations of the old brain, to watch it, to know how it reacts, what its responses are, its tendencies, its demands, its aggressive pursuits—to know the whole of that, the unconscious as well as the conscious part of it. When you know it, when there is an awareness of it, without controlling it, without directing it, without saying, "This is good; this is bad; I'll keep this; I won't keep that"—when you see the total movement of the old mind, when you see it totally, then it becomes quiet.

A Fresh Mind

I think constant endeavor to be something, to become something, is the real cause of the destructiveness and the aging of the mind. Look how quickly we are aging, not only the people who are over sixty, but also the young people. How old they are already mentally! Very few sustain or maintain the quality of a mind that is young. I mean by young not the mind that merely wants to enjoy itself, to have a good time, but the mind that is uncontaminated, that is not scratched, warped, twisted by the accidents and incidents of life, a mind that is not worn out by struggle, by grief, by constant strivings. Surely it is necessary to have a young mind because the old mind is so full of the scars of memories that it cannot live, it cannot be earnest; it is a dead mind, a decided mind. A mind that has decided and lives according to its decisions is dead. But a young mind is always deciding anew, and a fresh mind does not burden itself with innumerable memories. A mind that carries no shadow of suffering, though it may pass through the valley of sorrow, remains unscratched. . . .

I do not think such a young mind is to be acquired. It is not a thing that you can purchase through endeavor, through sacrifice. There is no coin to it and it is not a marketable thing, but if you see the importance of it, the necessity of it, if you see the truth of it, then something else takes place.

Discard All Methods

How is the religious mind or the new mind to come into being? Will you have a system, a method? Through a method—a method being a system, a practice, a repetitive thing day after day? Will a method produce a new mind? . . . Surely, a method implies a continuity of a practice, directed along a certain line towards a certain result—which is to acquire a mechanical habit, and through that mechanical habit to realize a mind that is not mechanical. . . .

When you say, "discipline," all discipline is based on a method according to a certain pattern; and the pattern promises you a result that is predetermined by a mind that has already a belief, which has already taken a position. So, will a method, in the widest or the narrowest sense of that word, bring about this new mind? If it does not, then method as habit must go completely because it is false. . . . Method only conditions the mind according to the result that is desired. You have to discard all the mechanical processes of the mind. . . . The mind must discard all the mechanical processes of thought. So, the idea that a method, a system, a discipline, a continuity of habit will bring about this mind is not true. So, all that is to be discarded totally as being mechanical. A mind that is mechanical is a traditional mind; it cannot meet life, which is nonmechanical; so, the method is to be put aside.

A Mind Without Anchorage or Haven

You need a new mind, a mind that is free of time, a mind that no longer thinks in terms of distance or space, a mind that has no horizon, a mind that has no anchorage or haven. You need such a mind to deal not only with the everlasting, but also with the immediate problems of existence.

Therefore the issue is: Is it possible for each one of us to have such a mind? Not gradually, not to cultivate it, because cultivation, development, a process, implies time. It must take place immediately; there must be a transformation now, in the sense of a timeless quality. Life is death, and death is awaiting you; you cannot argue with death as you can argue with life. So is it possible to have such a mind?—not as an achievement, not as a goal, not as a thing to be aimed at, not as something to be arrived at, because all that implies time and space. We have a very convenient, luxurious theory that there is time to progress, to arrive, to achieve, to come near truth. That is a fallacious idea, it is an illusion completely—time is an illusion in that sense.

Active but Quiet

To discover the new mind, not only is it necessary for us to understand the responses of the old brain, it is also necessary for the old brain to be quiet. The old brain must be active but quiet. You are following what I am saying? Look, sir! If you would discover for yourself firsthand—not what somebody else says—if there is a reality, if there is such a thing as God—the word *God* is not the fact—your old brain, which has been nurtured in a tradition, either anti-God or pro-God, in a culture, in an environmental influence and propaganda, through centuries of social assertion, must be quiet. Because otherwise it will only project its own images, its own concepts, its own values. But those values, those concepts, those beliefs are the result of what you have been told, or are the result of your reactions to what you have been told; so, unconsciously, you say, This is my experience!

So you have to question the very validity of experience—your own experience or the experience of anybody else; it does not matter who it is. Then by questioning, enquiring, asking, demanding, looking, listening attentively, the reactions of the old brain become quiet. But the brain is not asleep; it is very active, but it is quiet. It has come to that quietness through observation, through investigation. And to investigate, to observe, you must have light; and the light is your constant alertness.

There Is a Quietness

I hope that you will listen, but not with the memory of what you already know; and this is very difficult to do. You listen to something, and your mind immediately reacts with its knowledge, its conclusions, its opinions, its past memories. It listens, inquiring for a future understanding. Just observe yourself, how you are listening, and you will see that this is what is taking place. Either you are listening with a conclusion, with knowledge, with certain memories, experiences, or you want an answer, and you are impatient. You want to know what it is all about, what life is all about, the extraordinary complexity of life. You are not actually listening at all. You can only listen when the mind is quiet, when the mind doesn't react immediately, when there is an interval between your reaction and what is being said. Then in that interval there is a quietness, there is a silence in which alone there is a comprehension, which is not intellectual understanding. If there is a gap between what is said and your own reaction to what is said, in that interval, whether you prolong it indefinitely, for a long period, or for a few seconds—in that interval, if you observe, there comes clarity. It is the interval that is the new brain. The immediate reaction is the old brain, and the old brain functions in its own traditional, accepted, reactionary, animalistic sense. When there is an abeyance of that, when the reaction is suspended, when there is an interval, then you will find that the new brain acts, and it is only the new brain that can understand, not the old brain.

Our Responsibility

To transform the world, we must begin with ourselves; and what is important in beginning with ourselves is the intention. The intention must be to understand ourselves and not to leave it to others to transform themselves or to bring about a modified change through revolution, either of the left or of the right. It is important to understand that this is our responsibility, yours and mine; because, however small may be the world we live in, if we can transform ourselves, bring about a radically different point of view in our daily existence, then perhaps we shall affect the world at large, the extended relationship with others.

If the Mind Is Occupied

Whether change is brought about consciously or unconsciously it is still the same. Conscious change implies effort; and unconscious endeavor to bring about a change also implies an effort, a struggle. So long as there is a struggle, conflict, the change is merely enforced, and there is no understanding; and therefore it is no longer a change at all. So, is the mind capable of meeting the problem of change—of acquisitiveness, for example—without making an effort, just seeing the whole implication of acquisitiveness? Because you cannot see the whole content of acquisitiveness totally so long as there is any endeavor to change it. Real change can only take place when the mind comes to the problem afresh, not with all the jaded memories of a thousand yesterdays. Obviously you cannot have a fresh, eager mind if the mind is occupied. And the mind ceases to be occupied only when it sees the truth about its own occupation. You cannot see the truth if you are not giving your whole attention, if you are translating what is being said into something that will suit you, or translating it into your own terms. You must come to something new with a fresh mind, and a mind is not fresh when it is occupied, consciously or unconsciously.

Knowledge Is a Detriment to Change

This requires a great deal of insight, inquiry. Don't agree with me, but go into it, meditate, tear your mind apart to find out the truth or the falseness of all this. Does knowledge, which is the known, bring about change? I must have knowledge to build a bridge; but must my mind know towards what it is changing? Surely, if I know what the state of the mind will be when it is changed, it is no longer change. Such knowledge is a detriment to change because it becomes a means of satisfaction, and as long as there is a center seeking satisfaction, reward, or security, there is no change at all. And all our efforts are based on that center of reward, punishment, success, gain, are they not? That is all most of us are concerned with, and if it will help us get what we want, we will change; but such change is no change at all. So the mind that wishes to be fundamentally, deeply, in a state of change, in a state of revolution, must be free from the known. Then the mind becomes astonishingly still, and only such a mind will experience the radical transformation that is so necessary.

Complete Emptiness

For the complete mutation in consciousness to take place you must deny analysis and search, and no longer be under any influence—which is immensely difficult. The mind, seeing what is false, has put the false aside completely, not knowing what is true. If you already know what is true, then you are merely exchanging what you consider is false for what you imagine is true. There is no renunciation if you know what you are going to get in return. There is only renunciation when you drop something not knowing what is going to happen. That state of negation is completely necessary. Please follow this carefully, because if you have gone so far you will see that in that state of negation you discover what is true; because negation is the emptying of consciousness of the known. After all, consciousness is based on knowledge, on experience, on racial inheritance, on memory, on the things one has experienced. Experiences are always of the past, operating on the present, being modified by the present and continuing into the future. All that is consciousness, the vast storehouse of centuries. It has its usefulness in mechanical living only. It would be absurd to deny all the scientific knowledge acquired through the long past. But to bring about a mutation in consciousness, a revolution in this whole structure, there must be complete emptiness. And that emptiness is possible only when there is the discovery, the actual seeing of what is false. Then you will see, if you have gone so far, that emptiness itself brings about a complete revolution in consciousness: it has taken place.

Deliberate Change
Is No Change at All

In the very action of the individual changing, surely, the collective will also change. They are not two separate things opposed to each other, the individual and the collective, though certain political groups try to separate the two and to force the individual to conform to the so-called collective.

If we could unravel together the whole problem of change, how to bring about a change in the individual and what that change implies, then perhaps, in the very act of listening, participating in the inquiry, there might come about a change that is without your volition. For me, a deliberate change, a change that is compulsory, disciplinary, conformative, is no change at all. Force, influence, some new invention, propaganda, a fear, a motive compels you to change—that is no change at all. And though intellectually you may agree very easily with this, I assure you that to fathom the actual nature of change without a motive is quite extraordinary.

Outside the Field of Thought

You have changed your ideas, you have changed your thought, but thought is always conditioned. Whether it is the thought of Jesus, Buddha, X, Y, or Z, it is still thought, and therefore one thought can be in opposition to another thought; and when there is opposition, a conflict between two thoughts, the result is a modified continuity of thought. In other words, the change is still within the field of thought, and change within the field of thought is no change at all. One idea or set of ideas has merely been substituted for another.

Seeing this whole process, is it possible to leave thought and bring about a change outside the field of thought? All consciousness, surely, whether it is of the past, the present, or the future, is within the field of thought; and any change within that field, which sets the boundaries of the mind, is no real change. A radical change can take place only outside the field of thought, not within it, and the mind can leave the field only when it sees the confines, the boundaries of the field, and realizes that any change within the field is no change at all. This is real meditation.

Real Change

A change is possible only from the known to the unknown, not from the known to the known. Do please think this over with me. In the change from the known to the known, there is authority, there is a hierarchical outlook of life—You know, I do not know. Therefore, I worship you, I create a system, I go after a guru, I follow you because you are giving me what I want to know, you are giving me a certainty of conduct that will produce the result, the success and the result. Success is the known. I know what it is to be successful. That is what I want. So we proceed from the known to the known, in which authority must exist—the authority of sanction, the authority of the leader, the guru, the hierarchy, the one who knows and the other who does not know—and the one who knows must guarantee me the success, the success in my endeavor, in change, so that I will be happy, I will have what I want. Is that not the motive for most of us to change? Do please observe your own thinking, and you will see the ways of your own life and conduct. . . . When you look at it, is that change? Change, revolution, is something from the known to the unknown, in which there is no authority, in which there may be total failure. But if you are assured that you will achieve, you will succeed, you will be happy, you will have everlasting life, then there is no problem. Then you pursue the well-known course of action, which is, yourself being always at the center of things.

Can a Human Being Change?

One must have asked oneself, I'm quite sure, whether one changes at all. I know that outward circumstances change; we marry, divorce, have children; there is death, a better job, the pressure of new inventions, and so on. Outwardly there is a tremendous revolution going on in cybernetics and automation. One must have asked oneself whether it is at all possible for one to change at all, not in relation to outward events, not a change that is a mere repetition or a modified continuity, but a radical revolution, a total mutation of the mind. When one realizes, as one must have noticed within oneself, that actually one doesn't change, one gets terribly depressed, or one escapes from oneself. So the inevitable question arises: can there be change at all? We go back to a period when we were young, and that comes back to us again. Is there change at all in human beings? Have you changed at all? Perhaps there has been a modification on the periphery, but deeply, radically, have you changed? Perhaps we do not want to change because we are fairly comfortable. . . .

I want to change. I see that I am terribly unhappy, depressed, ugly, violent, with an occasional flash of something other than the mere result of a motive; and I exercise my will to do something about it. I say I must be different, I must drop this habit, that habit; I must think differently; I must act in a different way; I must be more this and less that. One makes a tremendous effort and at the end of it one is still shoddy, depressed, ugly, brutal, without any sense of quality. So one then asks oneself if there is change at all. Can a human being change?

Transformation Without Motivation

How am I to transform? I see the truth—at least, I see something in it—that a change, a transformation, must begin at a level that the mind, as the conscious or the unconscious, cannot reach, because my consciousness as a whole is conditioned. So, what am I to do? I hope I am making the problem clear? If I may put it differently, Can my mind, the conscious as well as the unconscious, be free of society?—society being all the education, the culture, the norm, the values, the standards. Because if it is not free, then whatever change it tries to bring about within that conditioned state is still limited, and therefore no change at all.

So, can I look without any motive? Can my mind exist without any incentive, without any motive to change or not to change? Because any motive is the outcome of the reaction of a particular culture, is born out of a particular background. So, can my mind be free from the given culture in which I have been brought up? This is really quite an important question. Because if the mind is not free from the culture in which it has been reared, nurtured, surely the individual can never be at peace, can never have freedom. His gods and his myths, his symbols, and all his endeavors are limited, for they are still within the field of the conditioned mind. Whatever efforts he makes, or does not make, within that limited field, are really futile in the deepest sense of that word. There may be a better decoration of the prison—more light, more windows, better food—but it is still the prison of a particular culture.

A Psychological Revolution

Is it possible for the thinker and the thought, for the observer and the observed, to be one? You will never find out if you merely glance at this problem and superficially ask me to explain what I mean by this or that. Surely, this is your problem, it is not my problem only; you are not here to find out how I look at this problem or the problems of the world. This constant battle within, which is so destructive, so deteriorating—it is your problem, is it not? And it is also your problem how to bring about a radical change in yourself and not be satisfied with superficial revolutions in politics, in economics, in different bureaucracies. You are not trying to understand me or the way I look at life. You are trying to understand yourself, and these are your problems which you have to face; and by considering them together, which is what we are doing in these talks, we can perhaps help each other to look at them more clearly, see them more distinctly. But to see clearly merely at the verbal level is not enough. That does not bring about a creative psychological change. We must go beyond the words, beyond all symbols and their sensations . . .

We must put aside all these things and come to the central issue—how to dissolve the "me," which is time-binding, in which there is no love, no compassion. It is possible to go beyond only when the mind does not separate itself as the thinker and the thought. When the thinker and the thought are one, only then is there silence, the silence in which there is no image-making or waiting for further experience. In that silence there is no experiencer who is experiencing, and only then is there a psychological revolution that is creative.

◈

NOVEMBER

Living

Dying

Rebirth

Love

◈

Breaking Habits

Let us find out how to understand this whole process of habit forming and habit breaking. We can take the example of smoking, and you can substitute your own habit, your own particular problem, and experiment with your own problem directly as I am experimenting with the problem of smoking. It is a problem, it becomes a problem, when I want to give it up; as long as I am satisfied with it, it is not a problem. The problem arises when I have to do something about a particular habit, when the habit becomes a disturbance. Smoking has created a disturbance, so I want to be free of it. I want to stop smoking; I want to be rid of it, to put it aside, so my approach to smoking is one of resistance or condemnation. That is, I don't want to smoke, so my approach is either to suppress it, condemn it, or to find a substitute for it—instead of smoking, to chew. Now, can I look at the problem free of condemnation, justification, or suppression? Can I look at my smoking without any sense of rejection? Try to experiment with it now as I am talking, and you will see how extraordinarily difficult it is not to reject or accept. Because, our whole tradition, our whole background, is urging us to reject or to justify rather than to be curious about it. Instead of being passively watchful, the mind always operates on the problem.

Live the Four Seasons in a Day

Is it not essential that there should be a constant renewal, a rebirth? If the present is burdened with the experience of yesterday there can be no renewal. Renewal is not the action of birth and death; it is beyond the opposites; only freedom from the accumulation of memory brings renewal, and there is no understanding save in the present.

The mind can understand the present only if it does not compare, judge; the desire to alter or condemn the present without understanding it gives continuance to the past. Only in comprehending the reflection of the past in the mirror of the present, without distortion, is there renewal. . . .

If you have lived an experience fully, completely, have you not found that it leaves no traces behind? It is only the incomplete experiences that leave their mark, giving continuity to self-identified memory. We consider the present as a means to an end, so the present loses its immense significance. The present is the eternal. But how can a mind that is made up, put together, understand that which is not put together, which is beyond all value, the eternal?

As each experience arises, live it out as fully and deeply as possible; think it out, feel it out extensively and profoundly; be aware of its pain and pleasure, of your judgments and identifications. Only when experience is completed is there a renewal. We must be capable of living the four seasons in a day; to be keenly aware, to experience, to understand and be free of the gatherings of each day.

Anonymous Creativity

Have you ever thought about it? We want to be famous as a writer, as a poet, as a painter, as a politician, as a singer, or what you will. Why? Because we really don't love what we are doing. If you loved to sing, or to paint, or to write poems—if you really loved it—you would not be concerned with whether you are famous or not. To want to be famous is tawdry, trivial, stupid, it has no meaning; but, because we don't love what we are doing, we want to enrich ourselves with fame. Our present education is rotten because it teaches us to love success and not what we are doing. The result has become more important than the action.

You know, it is good to hide your brilliance under a bushel, to be anonymous, to love what you are doing and not to show off. It is good to be kind without a name. That does not make you famous, it does not cause your photograph to appear in the newspapers. Politicians do not come to your door. You are just a creative human being living anonymously, and in that there is richness and great beauty.

Empty Techniques

You cannot reconcile creativeness with technical achievement. You may be perfect in playing the piano, and not be creative; you may play the piano most brilliantly, and not be a musician. You may be able to handle color, to put paint on canvas most cleverly, and not be a creative painter. You may create a face, an image out of a stone, because you have learned the technique, and not be a master creator. Creation comes first, not technique, and that is why we are miserable all our lives. We have technique—how to put up a house, how to build a bridge, how to assemble a motor, how to educate our children through a system—we have learned all these techniques, but our hearts and minds are empty. We are first class machines; we know how to operate most beautifully, but we do not love a living thing. You may be a good engineer, you may be a pianist, you may write in a good style in English or Marathi or whatever your language is, but creativeness is not found through technique. If you have something to say, you create your own style; but when you have nothing to say, even if you have a beautiful style, what you write is only the traditional routine, a repetition in new words of the same old thing. . . .

So, having lost the song, we pursue the singer. We learn from the singer the technique of song, but there is no song; and I say the song is essential, the joy of singing is essential. When the joy is there, the technique can be built up from nothing; you will invent your own technique, you won't have to study elocution or style. When you have, you see, and the very seeing of beauty is an art.

Know When Not to Cooperate

Reformers—political, social, and religious—will only cause more sorrow for man unless man understands the workings of his own mind. In the understanding of the total process of the mind, there is a radical, inward revolution, and from that inward revolution springs the action of true cooperation, which is not cooperation with a pattern, with authority, with somebody who "knows." When you know how to co-operate because there is this inward revolution, then you will also know when not to cooperate, which is really very important, perhaps more important. We now cooperate with any person who offers a reform, a change, which only perpetuates conflict and misery, but if we can know what it is to have the spirit of cooperation that comes into being with the understanding of the total process of the mind and in which there is freedom from the self, then there is a possibility of creating a new civilization, a totally different world in which there is no acquisitiveness, no envy, no comparison. This is not a theoretical utopia but the actual state of the mind that is constantly inquiring and pursuing that which is true and blessed.

Why Is There Crime?

You see, there is either a revolt within the pattern of society, or a complete revolution outside of society. The complete revolution outside of society is what I call religious revolution. Any revolution that is not religious is within society and is therefore no revolution at all, but only a modified continuation of the old pattern. What is happening throughout the world, I believe, is revolt within society, and this revolt often takes the form of what is called crime. There is bound to be this kind of revolt so long as our education is concerned only with training youth to fit into society—that is, to get a job, to earn money, to be acquisitive, to have more, to conform.

That is what our so-called education everywhere is doing—teaching the young to conform, religiously, morally, economically; so naturally their revolt has no meaning, except that it must be suppressed, reformed, or controlled. Such revolt is still within the framework of society, and therefore it is not creative at all. But through right education we could perhaps bring about a different understanding by helping to free the mind from all conditioning—that is, by encouraging the young to be aware of the many influences which condition the mind and make it conform.

 NOVEMBER 6

Life's Purpose

There are many people who will give you the purpose of life; they will tell you what the sacred books say. Clever people will go on inventing what the purpose of life is. The political group will have one purpose, the religious group will have another purpose, and so on and on. So, what is the purpose of life when you yourself are confused? When I am confused, I ask you this question, "What is the purpose of life?" because I hope that through this confusion, I shall find an answer. How can I find a true answer when I am confused? Do you understand? If I am confused, I can only receive an answer that is also confused. If my mind is confused, if my mind is disturbed, if my mind is not beautiful, quiet, whatever answer I receive will be through this screen of confusion, anxiety, and fear; therefore, the answer will be perverted. So, what is important is not to ask, "What is the purpose of life, of existence?" but to clear the confusion that is within you. It is like a blind man who asks, "What is light?" If I tell him what light is, he will listen according to his blindness, according to his darkness; but suppose he is able to see, then he will never ask the question, "What is light?" It is there.

Similarly, if you can clarify the confusion within yourself, then you will find what the purpose of life is; you will not have to ask, you will not have to look for it; all that you have to do is to be free from those causes that bring about confusion.

Live in This World Anonymously

Is it not possible to live in this world without ambition, just being what you are? If you begin to understand what you are without trying to change it, then what you are undergoes a transformation. I think one can live in this world anonymously, completely unknown, without being famous, ambitious, cruel. One can live very happily when no importance is given to the self; and this also is part of right education.

The whole world is worshipping success. You hear stories of how the poor boy studied at night and eventually became a judge, or how he began by selling newspapers and ended up a multimillionaire. You are fed on the glorification of success. With achievement of great success there is also great sorrow; but most of us are caught up in the desire to achieve, and success is much more important to us than the understanding and dissolution of sorrow.

Only One Hour to Live

If you had only one hour to live, what would you do? Would you not arrange what is necessary outwardly, your affairs, your will, and so on? Would you not call your family and friends together and ask their forgiveness for the harm that you might have done to them, and forgive them for whatever harm they might have done to you? Would you not die completely to the things of the mind, to desires and to the world? And if it can be done for an hour, then it can also be done for the days and years that may remain. . . Try it and you will find out.

Die Every Day

What is age? Is it the number of years you have lived? That is part of age; you were born in such and such a year, and now you are fifteen, forty, or sixty years old. Your body grows old—and so does your mind when it is burdened with all the experiences, miseries, and weariness of life; and such a mind can never discover what is truth. The mind can discover only when it is young, fresh, innocent; but innocence is not a matter of age. It is not only the child that is innocent—he may not be—but the mind that is capable of experiencing without accumulating the residue of experience. The mind must experience, that is inevitable. It must respond to everything—to the river, to the diseased animal, to the dead body being carried away to be burned, to the poor villagers carrying their burdens along the road, to the tortures and miseries of life—otherwise it is already dead; but it must be capable of responding without being held by the experience. It is tradition, the accumulation of experience, the ashes of memory, that make the mind old. The mind that dies every day to the memories of yesterday, to all the joys and sorrows of the past—such a mind is fresh, innocent, it has no age; and without that innocence, whether you are ten or sixty, you will not find God.

Feel the State of Death

We are afraid to die. To end the fear of death we must come into contact with death, not with the image that thought has created about death, but we must actually feel the state. Otherwise there is no end to fear, because the word *death* creates fear, and we don't even want to talk about it. Being healthy, normal, with the capacity to reason clearly, to think objectively, to observe, is it possible for us to come into contact with the fact, totally? The organism, through usage, through disease, will eventually die. If we are healthy, we want to find out what death means. It's not a morbid desire, because perhaps by dying we shall understand living. Living, as it is now, is torture, endless turmoil, a contradiction, and therefore there is conflict, misery, and confusion. The everyday going to the office, the repetition of pleasure, with its pains, the anxiety, the groping, the uncertainty—that's what we call living. We have become accustomed to that kind of living. We accept it; we grow old with it and die.

To find out what living is as well as to find out what dying is, one must come into contact with death; that is, one must end every day everything one has known. One must end the image that one has built up about oneself, about one's family, about one's relationship, the image that one has built through pleasure, through one's relationship to society, everything. That is what is going to take place when death occurs.

Fear of Death?

Why are you afraid of death? Is it perhaps because you do not know how to live? If you knew how to live fully, would you be afraid of death? If you loved the trees, the sunset, the birds, the falling leaf; if you were aware of men and women in tears, of poor people, and really felt love in your heart, would you be afraid of death? Would you? Don't be persuaded by me. Let us think about it together. You do not live with joy, you are not happy, you are not vitally sensitive to things; and is that why you ask what is going to happen when you die? Life for you is sorrow, and so you are much more interested in death. You feel that perhaps there will be happiness after death. But that is a tremendous problem, and I do not know if you want to go into it. After all, fear is at the bottom of all this—fear of dying, fear of living, fear of suffering. If you cannot understand what it is that causes fear and be free of it, then it does not matter very much whether you are living or dead.

I Am Afraid

My inquiry now is how to be free from the fear of the known, which is the fear of losing my family, my reputation, my character, my bank account, my appetites, and so on. You may say that fear arises from conscience; but your conscience is formed by your conditioning, so conscience is still the result of the known. What do I know? Knowledge is having ideas, having opinions about things, having a sense of continuity as in relation to the known, and no more. . . .

There is fear of pain. Physical pain is a nervous response, but psychological pain arises when I hold on to things that give me satisfaction, for then I am afraid of anyone or anything that may take them away from me. The psychological accumulations prevent psychological pain as long as they are undisturbed; that is, I am a bundle of accumulations, experiences, which prevent any serious form of disturbance—and I do not want to be disturbed. Therefore, I am afraid of anyone who disturbs them. Thus my fear is of the known, I am afraid of the accumulations, physical or psychological, that I have gathered as a means of warding off pain or preventing sorrow. . . . Knowledge also helps to prevent pain. As medical knowledge helps to prevent physical pain, so beliefs help to prevent psychological pain, and that is why I am afraid of losing my beliefs, though I have no perfect knowledge or concrete proof of the reality of such beliefs.

Only That Which
Dies Can Renew Itself

When we talk of a spiritual entity, we mean by that something that is not within the field of the mind, obviously. Now, is the "I" such a spiritual entity? If it is a spiritual entity, it must be beyond all time; therefore, it cannot be reborn or continued. Thought cannot think about it because thought comes within the measure of time, thought is from yesterday, thought is a continuous movement, the response of the past; so thought is essentially a product of time. If thought can think about the "I," then it is part of time; therefore, that "I" is not free of time, therefore it is not spiritual—which is obvious. So, the "I," the "you" is only a process of thought; and you want to know whether that process of thought, continuing apart from the physical body, is born again, is reincarnated in a physical form. Now go a little further. That which continues—can it ever discover the real, which is beyond time and measurement. That "I," that entity which is a thought-process—can it ever be new? If it cannot, then there must be an ending to thought. Is not anything that continues inherently destructive? That which has continuity can never renew itself. As long as thought continues through memory, through desire, through experience, it can never renew itself; therefore, that which is continued cannot know the real. You may be reborn a thousand times, but you can never know the real, for only that which dies, that which comes to an end, can renew itself.

To Die Without Argument

Do you know what it means to come into contact with death, to die without argument? Because death, when it comes, does not argue with you. To meet it, you have to die every day to everything: to your agony, to your loneliness, to the relationship you cling to; you have to die to your thought, to die to your habit, to die to your wife so that you can look at your wife anew; you have to die to your society so that you, as a human being, are new, fresh, young, and you can look at it. But you cannot meet death if you don't die every day. It is only when you die that there is love. A mind that is frightened has no love—it has habits, it has sympathy, it can force itself to be kind and super-ficially considerate. But fear breeds sorrow, and sorrow is time as thought.

So to end sorrow is to come into contact with death while living, by dying to your name, to your house, to your property, to your cause, so that you are fresh, young, clear, and you can see things as they are without any distortion. That is what is going to take place when you die. But we have a limited death to the physical. We know very well logically, sanely, that the organism is going to come to an end. So we invent a life that we have lived of daily agony, daily insensitivity, the increase of problems, and its stupidity; that life we want to carry over, which we call the "soul"—which we say is the most sacred thing, a part of the divine, but it is still part of your thought and there-fore it has nothing to do with divinity. It is your life!

So one has to live every day dying—dying because you are then in contact with life.

In Death Is Immortality

Surely, in ending there is renewal, is there not? It's only in death that a new thing comes into being. I am not giving you comfort. This is not something to be believed or thought about or intellectually examined and accepted, for then you will make it into another comfort, as you now believe in reincarnation or continuity in the hereafter, and so on. But the actual fact is that that which continues has no rebirth, no renewal. Therefore, in dying every day there is renewal, there is a rebirth. That is immortality. In death there is immortality—not the death of which you are afraid, but the death of previous conclusions, memories, experiences, with which you are identified as the "me." In the dying of the "me" every minute there is eternity, there is immortality, there is a thing to be experienced—not to be speculated upon or lectured about, as you do about reincarnation and all that kind of stuff. . . .

When you are no longer afraid, because every minute there is an ending and therefore a renewal, then you are open to the unknown. Reality is the unknown. Death is also the unknown. But to call death beautiful, to say how marvelous it is because we shall continue in the hereafter and all that nonsense, has no reality. What has reality is seeing death as it is—an ending; an ending in which there is renewal, a rebirth, not a continuity. For that which continues decays; and that which has the power to renew itself is eternal.

Reincarnation Is Essentially Egotistic

You want me to give you an assurance that you will live another life, but in that there is no happiness or wisdom. The search for immortality through reincarnation is essentially egotistic, and therefore not true. Your search for immortality is only another form of the desire for the continuance of self-defensive reactions against life and intelligence. Such a craving can only lead to illusion. So what matters is not whether there is reincarnation, but to realize complete fulfillment in the present. And you can do that only when your mind and heart are no longer protecting themselves against life. The mind is cunning and subtle in its self-defense, and it must discern for itself the illusory nature of self-protection. This means that you must think and act completely anew. You must liberate yourself from the net of false values that environment has imposed upon you. There must be utter nakedness. Then there is immortality, reality.

What Is Reincarnation?

Let us find out what you mean by reincarnation—the truth of it, not what you like to believe, not what someone has told you, or what your teacher has said. Surely, it is the truth that liberates, not your own conclusion, your own opinion. . . . When you say, "I shall be reborn," you must know what the "I" is. . . . Is the "I" a spiritual entity, is the "I" something continuous, is the "I" something independent of memory, experience, knowledge? Either the "I" is a spiritual entity or it is merely a thought process. Either it is something out of time, which we call spiritual, not measurable in terms of time, or it is within the field of time, the field of memory, thought. It cannot be something else. Let us find out if it is beyond the measurement of time. I hope you are following all this. Let us find out if the "I" is in essence something spiritual. Now by "spiritual" we mean, do we not, something not capable of being conditioned, something that is not the projection of the human mind, something that is not within the field of thought, something that does not die. When we talk of a spiritual entity, we mean by that something that is not within the field of the mind, obviously. Now, is the "I" such a spiritual entity? If it is a spiritual entity, it must be beyond all time; therefore, it cannot be reborn or continued. . . . That which has continuity can never renew itself. As long as thought continues through memory, through desire, through experience, it can never renew itself; therefore, that which is continued cannot know the real.

Is There Such a Thing as a Soul?

So to understand this question of death, we must be rid of fear, which invents the various theories of afterlife or immortality or reincarnation. So we say, those in the East say, that there is reincarnation, there is a rebirth, a constant renewal going on and on and on—the soul, the so-called soul. Now please listen carefully.

Is there such a thing? We like to think there is such a thing, because it gives us pleasure, because that is something that we have set beyond thought, beyond words, beyond; it is something eternal, spiritual, that can never die, and so thought clings to it. But is there such a thing as a soul, which is something beyond time, something beyond thought, something that is not invented by man, something that is beyond the nature of man, something that is not put together by the cunning mind? Because the mind sees such enormous uncertainty, confusion, nothing permanent in life—nothing. Your relationship to your wife, your husband, your job—nothing is permanent. And so the mind invents a something which is permanent, which it calls the soul. But since the mind can think about it, thought can think about it; as thought can think about it, it is still within the field of time—naturally. If I can think about something, it is part of my thought. And my thought is the result of time, of experience, of knowledge. So, the soul is still within the field of time. . . .

So the idea of a continuity of a soul that will be reborn over and over and over again has no meaning because it is the invention of a mind that is frightened, of a mind that wants, that seeks a duration through permanency, that wants certainty, because in that there is hope.

What Do You Mean by Karma?

Karma implies, does it not, cause and effect?—action based on cause, producing a certain effect; action born out of conditioning, producing further results. So karma implies cause and effect. And are cause and effect static, are cause and effect ever fixed? Does not effect become cause also? So there is no fixed cause or fixed effect. Today is a result of yesterday, is it not? Today is the outcome of yesterday, chronologically as well as psychologically; and today is the cause of tomorrow. So cause is effect, and effect becomes cause—it is one continuous movement . . . there is no fixed cause or fixed effect. If there were a fixed cause and a fixed effect, there would be specialization; and is not specialization death? Any species that specializes obviously comes to an end. The greatness of man is that he cannot specialize. He may specialize technically, but in structure he cannot specialize. An acorn seed is specialized—it cannot be anything but what it is. But the human being does not end completely. There is the possibility of constant renewal; he is not limited by specialization. As long as we regard the cause, the background, the conditioning, as unrelated to the effect, there must be conflict between thought and the background. So the problem is much more complex than whether to believe in reincarnation or not, because the question is how to act, not whether you believe in reincarnation or in karma. That is absolutely irrelevant.

Action Based on Idea

Can action ever bring about freedom from this chain of cause-effect? I have done something in the past; I have had experience, which obviously conditions my response today; and today's response conditions tomorrow. That is the whole process of karma, cause and effect; and obviously, though it may temporarily give pleasure, such a process of cause and effect ultimately leads to pain. That is the real crux of the matter: Can thought be free? Thought or action that is free does not produce pain, does not bring about conditioning. That is the vital point of this whole question. So, can there be action unrelated to the past? Can there be action not based on idea? Idea is the continuation of yesterday in a modified form, and that continuation will condition tomorrow, which means action based on idea can never be free. As long as action is based on idea, it will inevitably produce further conflict. Can there be action unrelated to the past? Can there be action without the burden of experience, the knowledge of yesterday? As long as action is the outcome of the past, action can never be free, and only in freedom can you discover what is true. What happens is that, as the mind is not free, it cannot act; it can only react, and reaction is the basis of our action. Our action is not action but merely the continuation of reaction because it is the outcome of memory, of experience, of yesterday's response. So, the question is, can the mind be free from its conditioning?

Love Is Not Pleasure

Without the understanding of pleasure you will never be able to understand love. Love is not pleasure. Love is something entirely different. And to understand pleasure, as I said, you have to learn about it. Now, for most of us, for every human being, sex is a problem. Why? Listen to this very carefully. Because you are not able to solve it, you run away from it. The sannyasi runs away from it by taking a vow of celibacy, by denying. Please see what happens to such a mind. By denying something that is a part of your whole structure—the glands and so on—by suppressing it, you have made yourself arid, and there is a constant battle going on within yourself.

As we were saying, we have only two ways of meeting any problem, apparently: either suppressing it or running away from it. Suppressing it is really the same thing as running away from it. And we have a whole network of escapes—very intricate, intellectual, emotional—and ordinary everyday activity. There are various forms of escapes into which we will not go for the moment. But we have this problem. The sannyasi escapes from it in one way, but he has not resolved it; he has suppressed it by taking a vow, and the whole problem is boiling in him. He may put on the outward robe of simplicity, but this becomes an extraordinary issue for him too, as it is for the man who lives an ordinary life. How do you solve that problem?

Love Is Not Cultivated

Love is not to be cultivated. Love cannot be divided into divine and physical; it is only love—not that you love many or the one. That again is an absurd question to ask: "Do you love all?" You know, a flower that has perfume is not concerned who comes to smell it, or who turns his back upon it. So is love. Love is not a memory. Love is not a thing of the mind or the intellect. But it comes into being naturally as compassion, when this whole problem of existence—as fear, greed, envy, despair, hope—has been understood and resolved. An ambitious man cannot love. A man who is attached to his family has no love. Nor has jealousy anything to do with love. When you say, "I love my wife," you really do not mean it, because the next moment you are jealous of her.

Love implies great freedom—not to do what you like. But love comes only when the mind is very quiet, disinterested, not self-centered. These are not ideals. If you have no love, do what you will—go after all the gods on earth, do all the social activities, try to reform the poor, the politics, write books, write poems—you are a dead human being. And without love your problems will increase, multiply endlessly. And with love, do what you will, there is no risk; there is no conflict. Then love is the essence of virtue. And a mind that is not in a state of love is not a religious mind at all. And it is only the religious mind that is freed from problems, and that knows the beauty of love and truth.

Love Without Incentive

What is love without motive? Can there be love without any incentive, without wanting something for oneself out of love? Can there be love in which there is no sense of being wounded when love is not returned? If I offer you my friendship and you turn away, am I not hurt? Is that feeling of being hurt the outcome of friendship, of generosity, of sympathy? Surely, as long as I feel hurt, as long as there is fear, as long as I help you hoping that you may help me—which is called service—there is no love.

If you understand this, the answer is there.

Love Is Dangerous

How can man live without love? We can only exist, and existence without love is control, confusion, and pain—and that is what most of us are creating. We organize for existence and we accept conflict as inevitable because our existence is a ceaseless demand for power. Surely, when we love, organization has its own place, its right place; but without love, organization becomes a nightmare, merely mechanical and efficient, like the army; but as modern society is based on mere efficiency, we have to have armies—and the purpose of an army is to create war. Even in so-called peace, the more intellectually efficient we are, the more ruthless, the more brutal, the more callous we become. That is why there is confusion in the world, why bureaucracy is more and more powerful, why more and more governments are becoming totalitarian. We submit to all this as being inevitable because we live in our brains and not in our hearts, and therefore love does not exist. Love is the most dangerous and uncertain element in life; and because we do not want to be uncertain, because we do not want to be in danger, we live in the mind. A man who loves is dangerous, and we do not want to live dangerously; we want to live efficiently, we want to live merely in the framework of organization because we think organizations are going to bring order and peace in the world. Organizations have never brought order and peace. Only love, only goodwill, only mercy can bring order and peace, ultimately and therefore now.

What Is Your Reaction?

When you observe those poor women carrying a heavy load to the market, or watch the peasant children playing in the mud with very little else to play with, [children] who will not have the education that you are getting, who have no proper home, no cleanliness, insufficient clothing, inadequate food—when you observe all that, what is your reaction? It is very important to find out for yourself what your reaction is. I will tell you what mine was.

Those children have no proper place to sleep; the father and the mother are occupied all day long, with never a holiday; the children never know what it is to be loved, to be cared for; the parents never sit down with them and tell them stories about the beauty of the earth and the heavens. And what kind of society is it that has produced these circumstances—where there are immensely rich people who have everything on earth they want, and at the same time there are boys and girls who have nothing? What kind of society is it, and how has it come into being? You may revolutionize, break the pattern of this society, but in the very breaking of it a new one is born, which is again the same thing in another form—the commissars with their special houses in the country, the privileges, the uniforms, and so on down the line. This has happened after every revolution, the French, the Russian, and the Chinese. And is it possible to create a society in which all this corruption and misery does not exist? It can be created only when you and I as individuals break away from the collective, when we are free of ambition and know what it means to love. That was my whole reaction, in a flash.

Compassion Is Not the Word

Thought cannot, by any means whatsoever, cultivate compassion. I am not using that word *compassion* to mean the opposite, the antithesis of hate or violence. But unless each one of us has a deep sense of compassion, we shall become more and more brutal, inhuman to each other. We shall have mechanical, computer-like minds that have merely been trained to perform certain functions; we shall go on seeking security, both physical and psychological, and we shall miss the extraordinary depth and beauty, the whole significance of life.

By compassion I do not mean a thing to be acquired. Compassion is not the word, which is merely of the past, but something that is of the active present; it is the verb and not the word, the name, or the noun. There is a difference between the verb and the word. The verb is of the active present, whereas the word is always of the past and therefore static. You may give vitality or movement to the name, to the word, but it is not the same as the verb, which is actively present. . . .

Compassion is not sentiment; it is not this woolly sympathy or empathy. Compassion is not something that you can cultivate through thought, through discipline, control, suppression, nor by being kind, polite, gentle, and all the rest of it. Compassion comes into being only when thought has come to an end at its very root.

Compassion and Goodness

Can compassion, that sense of goodness, that feeling of the sacredness of life about which we were talking last time we met—can that feeling be brought into being through compulsion? Surely, when there is compulsion in any form, when there is propaganda or moralizing, there is no compassion, nor is there compassion when change is brought about merely through seeing the necessity of meeting the technological challenge in such a way that human beings will remain human beings and not become machines. So there must be a change without any causation. A change that is brought about through causation is not compassion; it is merely a thing of the marketplace. So that is one problem.

Another problem is: if I change, how will it affect society? Or am I not concerned with that at all? Because the vast majority of people are not interested in what we are talking about—nor are you if you listen out of curiosity or some kind of impulse, and pass by. The machines are progressing so rapidly that most human beings are merely pushed along and are not capable of meeting life with the enrichment of love, with compassion, with deep thought. And if I change, how will it affect society, which is my relationship with you? Society is not some extraordinary mythical entity; it is our relationship with each other, and if two or three of us change, how will it affect the rest of the world? Or is there a way of affecting the total mind of man?

That is, is there a process by which the individual who is changed can touch the unconscious of man?

Transmitting Compassion

If I am concerned with compassion, . . . with love, with the real feeling of something sacred, then how is that feeling to be transmitted? Please follow this. If I transmit it through the microphone, through the machinery of propaganda, and thereby convince another, his heart will still be empty. The flame of ideology will operate, and he will merely repeat, as you are all repeating, that we must be kind, good, free—all the nonsense that the politicians, the socialists, and the rest of them talk. So, seeing that any form of compulsion, however subtle, does not bring this beauty, this flowering of goodness, of compassion, what is the individual to do? . . .

What is the relationship between the man who has this sense of compassion, and the man whose mind is entrenched in the collective, in the traditional? How are we to find the relationship between these two, not theoretically, but actually? . . .

That which conforms can never flower in goodness. There must be freedom, and freedom comes only when you understand the whole problem of envy, greed, ambition, and the desire for power. It is freedom from those things that allows the extraordinary thing called character to flower. Such a man has compassion, he knows what it is to love—not the man who merely repeats a lot of words about morality.

So the flowering of goodness does not lie within society, because society in itself is always corrupt. Only the man who understands the whole structure and process of society, and is freeing himself from it, has character, and he alone can flower in goodness.

Come to It Empty-Handed

Compassion is not hard to come by when the heart is not filled with the cunning things of the mind. It is the mind with its demands and fears, its attachments and denials, its determinations and urges, that destroys love. And how difficult it is to be simple about all this! You don't need philosophies and doctrines to be gentle and kind. The efficient and the powerful of the land will organize to feed and clothe the people, to provide them with shelter and medical care. This is inevitable with the rapid increase of production; it is the function of well-organized government and a balanced society. But organization does not give the generosity of the heart and hand. Generosity comes from quite a different source, a source beyond all measure. Ambition and envy destroy it as surely as fire burns. This source must be touched, but one must come to it empty-handed, without prayer, without sacrifice. Books cannot teach, nor can any guru lead to, this source. It cannot be reached through the cultivation of virtue, though virtue is necessary, nor through capacity and obedience. When the mind is serene, without any movement, it is there. Serenity is without motive, without the urge for the more.

DECEMBER

◇

Aloneness

Religion

God

Meditation

◇

Alone Has Beauty

I do not know if you have ever been lonely; when you suddenly realize that you have no relationship with anybody—not an intellectual realization but a factual realization . . . and you are completely isolated. Every form of thought and emotion is blocked; you cannot turn anywhere; there is nobody to turn to; the gods, the angels, have all gone beyond the clouds, and as the clouds vanish they have also vanished; you are completely lonely—I will not use the word alone.

Alone has quite a different meaning; alone has beauty. To be alone means something entirely different. And you must be alone. When man frees himself from the social structure of greed, envy, ambition, arrogance, achievement, status—when he frees himself from those, then he is completely alone. That is quite a different thing. Then there is great beauty, the feeling of great energy.

Aloneness Is Not Loneliness

Though we are all human beings, we have built walls between ourselves and our neighbors through nationalism, through race, caste, and class—which again breeds isolation, loneliness.

Now a mind that is caught in loneliness, in this state of isolation, can never possibly understand what religion is. It can believe, it can have certain theories, concepts, formulas, it can try to identify itself with that which it calls God; but religion, it seems to me, has nothing whatsoever to do with any belief, with any priest, with any church or so-called sacred book. The state of the religious mind can be understood only when we begin to understand what beauty is; and the understanding of beauty must be approached through total aloneness. Only when the mind is completely alone can it know what is beauty, and not in any other state.

Aloneness is obviously not isolation, and it is not uniqueness. To be unique is merely to be exceptional in some way, whereas to be completely alone demands extraordinary sensitivity, intelligence, understanding. To be completely alone implies that the mind is free of every kind of influence and is therefore uncontaminated by society; and it must be alone to understand what is religion—which is to find out for oneself whether there is something immortal, beyond time.

Knowing Loneliness

Loneliness is entirely different from aloneness. That loneliness must be passed to be alone. Loneliness is not comparable with aloneness. The man who knows loneliness can never know that which is alone. Are you in that state of aloneness? Our minds are not integrated to be alone. The very process of the mind is separative. And that which separates knows loneliness.

But aloneness is not separative. It is something that is not the many, which is not influenced by the many, which is not the result of the many, which is not put together as the mind is; the mind is of the many. Mind is not an entity that is alone, being put together, brought together, manufactured through centuries. Mind can never be alone. Mind can never know aloneness. But being aware of the loneliness when going through it, there comes into being that aloneness. Then only can there be that which is immeasurable. Unfortunately most of us seek dependence. We want companions, we want friends, we want to live in a state of separation, in a state that brings about conflict. That which is alone can never be in a state of conflict. But mind can never perceive that, can never understand that, it can only know loneliness.

Only in Aloneness Is There Innocence

Most of us are never alone. You may withdraw into the mountains and live as a recluse, but when you are physically by yourself, you will have with you all your ideas, your experiences, your traditions, your knowledge of what has been. The Christian monk in a monastery cell is not alone; he is with his conceptual Jesus, with his theology, with the beliefs and dogmas of his particular conditioning. Similarly, the sannyasi in India who withdraws from the world and lives in isolation is not alone, for he too lives with his memories.

I am talking of an aloneness in which the mind is totally free from the past, and only such a mind is virtuous, for only in this aloneness is there innocence. Perhaps you will say, "That is too much to ask. One cannot live like that in this chaotic world, where one has to go to the office every day, earn a livelihood, bear children, endure the nagging of one's wife or husband, and all the rest of it." But I think what is being said is directly related to everyday life and action; otherwise, it has no value at all. You see, out of this aloneness comes a virtue that is virile and which brings an extraordinary sense of purity and gentleness. It doesn't matter if one makes mistakes; that is of very little importance. What matters is to have this feeling of being completely alone, uncontaminated, for it is only such a mind that can know or be aware of that which is beyond the word, beyond the name, beyond all the projections of imagination.

The One Who Is Alone Is Innocent

One of the factors of sorrow is the extraordinary loneliness of man. You may have companions, you may have gods, you may have a great deal of knowledge, you may be extraordinarily active socially, talking endless gossip about politics—and most politicians gossip anyhow—and still this loneliness remains. Therefore, man seeks to find significance in life and invents a significance, a meaning. But the loneliness still remains. So can you look at it without any comparison, just see it as it is, without trying to run away from it, without trying to cover it up, or to escape from it? Then you will see that loneliness becomes something entirely different.

We are not alone. We are the result of a thousand influences, a thousand conditionings, psychological inheritances, propaganda, culture. We are not alone, and therefore we are secondhand human beings. When one is alone, totally alone, neither belonging to any family, though one may have a family, nor belonging to any nation, to any culture, to any particular commitment, there is the sense of being an outsider—outsider to every form of thought, action, family, nation. And it is only the one who is completely alone who is innocent. It is this innocency that frees the mind from sorrow.

Create a New World

If you have to create a new world, a new civilization, a new art, everything new, not contaminated by tradition, by fear, by ambitions, if you have to create something anonymous which is yours and mine, a new society, together, in which there is not you and me but an "ourness," must there not be a mind that is completely anonymous, therefore alone? This implies, does it not, that there must be a revolt against conformity, a revolt against respectability, because the respectable man is the mediocre man because he wants something—he is dependent on influence for his happiness, on what his neighbor thinks, on what his guru thinks, on what the Bhagavad-Gita or the Upanishads or the Bible or the Christ says. His mind is never alone. He never walks alone, but he always walks with a companion, the companion of his ideas.

Is it not important to find out, to see, the whole significance of interference, of influence, the establishment of the "me," which is the contradiction of the anonymous? Seeing the whole of that, does not the question inevitably arise: Is it possible immediately to bring about that state of mind that is not influenced, which cannot be influenced by its own experience or by the experience of others, a mind that is incorruptible, that is alone? Then only is there a possibility of bringing about a different world, a different culture, a different society in which happiness is possible.

Aloneness in Which There Is No Fear

It is only when the mind is capable of shedding all influences, all interferences, of being completely alone . . . there is creativeness.

In the world, more and more technique is being developed—the technique of how to influence people through propaganda, through compulsion, through imitation. . . . There are innumerable books written on how to do a thing, how to think efficiently, how to build a house, how to put machinery together; so gradually we are losing initiative, the initiative to think out something original for ourselves. In our education, in our relationship with government, through various means, we are being influenced to conform, to imitate. And when we allow one influence to persuade us to a particular attitude or action, naturally we create resistance to other influences. In that very process of creating a resistance to another influence, are we not succumbing to it negatively?

Should not the mind always be in revolt so as to understand the influences that are always impinging, interfering, controlling, shaping? Is it not one of the factors of the mediocre mind that it is always fearful and, being in a state of confusion, it wants order, it wants consistency, it wants a form, a shape by which it can be guided and controlled. And yet these forms, these various influences create contradictions in the individual, create confusion in the individual. . . . Any choice between influences is surely still a state of mediocrity.

. . . Must not the mind have the capacity to fathom—not to imitate, not to be shaped—and to be without fear? Should not such a mind be alone and therefore creative? That creativeness is not yours or mine, it is anonymous.

Begin Here

A religious man does not seek God. The religious man is concerned with the transformation of society, which is himself. The religious man is not the man that does innumerable rituals, follows traditions, lives in a dead, past culture, explaining endlessly the Gita or the Bible, endlessly chanting, or taking sannyasa—that is not a religious man; such a man is escaping from facts. The religious man is concerned totally and completely with the understanding of society, which is himself. He is not separate from society. Bringing about in himself a complete, total mutation means complete cessation of greed, envy, ambition; and therefore he is not dependent on circumstances, though he is the result of circumstance—the food he eats, the books he reads, the cinemas he goes to, the religious dogmas, beliefs, rituals, and all that business. He is responsible, and therefore the religious man must understand himself, who is the product of society that he himself has created. Therefore, to find reality he must begin here, not in a temple, not in an image—whether the image is graven by the hand or by the mind. Otherwise, how can he find something totally new, a new state?

The Religious Mind Is Explosive

Can we discover for ourselves what is the religious mind? The scientist in his laboratory is really a scientist; he is not persuaded by his nationalism, by his fears, by his vanities, ambitions, and local demands; there, he is merely investigating. But outside the laboratory, he is like anybody else with his prejudices, with his ambitions, with his nationality, with his vanities, with his jealousies, and all the rest of it. Such a mind cannot approach the religious mind. The religious mind does not function from a center of authority, whether it is accumulated knowledge as tradition, or it is experience—which is really the continuation of tradition, the continuation of conditioning. The religious spirit does not think in terms of time, the immediate results, the immediate reformation within the pattern of society. . . . We said the religious mind is not a ritualistic mind; it does not belong to any church, to any group, to any pattern of thinking. The religious mind is the mind that has entered into the unknown, and you cannot come to the unknown except by jumping; you cannot carefully calculate and enter the unknown. The religious mind is the real revolutionary mind, and the revolutionary mind is not a reaction to what has been. The religious mind is really explosive, creative—not in the accepted sense of the word *creative,* as in a poem, decoration, or building, as in architecture, music, poetry, and all the rest of it—it is in a state of creation.

Prayer Is a Complex Affair

Like all deep human problems, prayer is a complex affair and not to be rushed at; it needs patience, careful and tolerant probing, and one cannot demand definite conclusions and decisions. Without understanding himself, he who prays may through his very prayer be led to self-delusion. We sometimes hear people say, and several have told me, that when they pray to what they call God for worldly things, their prayers are often granted. If they have faith, and depending upon the intensity of their prayer, what they seek—health, comfort, worldly possessions—they eventually get. If one indulges in petitionary prayer it brings its own reward, the thing asked for is often granted, and this further strengthens supplications. Then there is the prayer, not for things or for people, but to experience reality, God, which is also frequently answered; and there are still other forms of petitionary prayer, more subtle and devious, but nevertheless supplicating, begging, and offering. All such prayers have their own reward, they bring their own experiences; but do they lead to the realization of the ultimate reality?

Are we not the result of the past, and are we not therefore related to the enormous reservoir of greed and hate, with their opposites? Surely, when we make an appeal, or offer a petitionary prayer, we are calling upon this reservoir of accumulated greed, and so on, which does bring its own reward, and has its own price. . . . Does supplication to another, to something outside, bring about the understanding of truth?

The Answer to Prayer

Prayer, which is a supplication, a petition, can never find that reality which is not the outcome of a demand. We demand, supplicate, pray, only when we are in confusion, in sorrow; and not understanding that confusion and sorrow, we turn to somebody else. The answer to prayer is our own projection; in one way or another it is always satisfactory, gratifying, otherwise we would reject it. So, when one has learned the trick of quieting the mind through repetition, one keeps on with that habit, but the answer to supplication must obviously be shaped according to the desire of the person who supplicates.

Now, prayer, supplication, petition, can never uncover that which is not the projection of the mind. To find that which is not the fabrication of the mind, the mind must be quiet—not made quiet by the repetition of words, which is self-hypnosis, nor by any other means of inducing the mind to be still.

Stillness that is induced, enforced, is not stillness at all. It is like putting a child in the corner—superficially he may be quiet, but inwardly he is boiling. So, a mind that is made quiet by discipline is never really quiet, and stillness that is induced can never uncover that creative state in which reality comes into being.

Is Religion a Matter of Belief?

Religion as we generally know it or acknowledge it, is a series of beliefs, of dogmas, of rituals, of superstitions, of worship of idols, of charms and gurus that will lead you to what you want as an ultimate goal. The ultimate truth is your projection, that is what you want, which will make you happy, which will give a certainty of the deathless state. So the mind caught in all this creates a religion, a religion of dogmas, of priest-craft, of superstitions and idol-worship—and in that, you are caught, and the mind stagnates. Is that religion? Is religion a matter of belief, a matter of knowledge of other people's experiences and assertions? Or is religion merely the following of morality? You know it is comparatively easy to be moral—to do this and not to do that. Because it is easy, you can imitate a moral system. Behind that morality lurks the self, growing, expanding, aggressive, dominating. But is that religion?

You have to find out what truth is because that is the only thing that matters, not whether you are rich or poor, not whether you are happily married and have children, because they all come to an end, there is always death. So, without any form of belief, you must find out; you must have the vigor, the self-reliance, the initiative, so that for yourself you know what truth is, what God is. Belief will not give you anything; belief only corrupts, binds, darkens. The mind can only be free through vigor, through self-reliance.

Is There Truth in Religions?

The question is: Is there not truth in religions, in theories, in ideals, in beliefs? Let us examine. What do we mean by religion? Surely, not organized religion, not Hinduism, Buddhism, or Christianity—which are all organized beliefs with their propaganda, conversion, proselytism, compulsion, and so on. Is there any truth in organized religion? It may engulf, enmesh truth, but the organized religion itself is not true. Therefore, organized religion is false, it separates man from man. You are a Muslim, I am a Hindu, another is a Christian or a Buddhist—and we are wrangling, butchering each other. Is there any truth in that? We are not discussing religion as the pursuit of truth, but we are considering if there is any truth in organized religion. We are so conditioned by organized religion to think there is truth in it that we have come to believe that by calling oneself a Hindu, one is somebody, or one will find God. How absurd, sir; to find God, to find reality, there must be virtue. Virtue is freedom, and only through freedom can truth be discovered—not when you are caught in the hands of organized religion, with its beliefs. And is there any truth in theories, in ideals, in beliefs? Why do you have beliefs? Obviously, because beliefs give you security, comfort, safety, a guide. In yourself you are frightened, you want to be protected, you want to lean on somebody, and therefore, you create the ideal, which prevents you from understanding that *which is*. Therefore, an ideal becomes a hindrance to action.

To Climb High One Must Begin Low

Religious organizations become as fixed and as rigid as the thoughts of those who belong to them. Life is a constant change, a continual becoming, a ceaseless revolution, and because an organization can never be pliable, it stands in the way of change; it becomes reactionary to protect itself. The search for truth is individual, not congregational. To commune with the real there must be aloneness; not isolation, but freedom from all influence and opinion. Organizations of thought inevitably become hindrances to thought.

As you yourself are aware, the greed for power is almost inexhaustible in a so-called spiritual organization; this greed is covered over by all kinds of sweet and official-sounding words, but the canker of avariciousness, pride, and antagonism is nourished and shared. From this grow conflict, intolerance, sectarianism, and other ugly manifestations.

Would it not be wiser to have small informed groups of twenty or twenty-five persons, without dues or membership, meeting where it is convenient to discuss gently the approach to reality? To prevent any group from becoming exclusive, each member could from time to time encourage and perhaps join another small group; thus, it would be extensive, not narrow and parochial.

To climb high one must begin low. Out of this small beginning one may help to create a more sane and happy world.

Your Gods Are Dividing You

What is happening in the world? You have a Christian God, Hindu gods, Mohammedans with their particular conception of God—each little sect with its particular truth; and all these truths are becoming like so many diseases in the world, separating people. These truths, in the hands of the few, are becoming the means of exploitation. You go to each, one after the other, tasting them all, because you begin to lose all sense of discrimination, because you are suffering and you want a remedy, and you accept any remedy that is offered by any sect, whether Christian, Hindu, or any other sect. So, what is happening? Your gods are dividing you, your beliefs in God are dividing you and yet you talk about the brotherhood of man, unity in God, and at the same time deny the very thing that you want to find out, because you cling to these beliefs as the most potent means of destroying limitation, whereas they but intensify it. These things are so obvious.

True Religion

Do you know what religion is? It is not in the chant, it is not in the performance of *puja,* or any other ritual, it is not in the worship of tin gods or stone images, it is not in the temples and churches, it is not in the reading of the Bible or the *Gita,* it is not in the repeating of a sacred name or in the following of some other superstition invented by men. None of this is religion.

Religion is the feeling of goodness, that love which is like the river, living, moving everlastingly. In that state you will find there comes a moment when there is no longer any search at all; and this ending of search is the beginning of something totally different. The search for God, for truth, the feeling of being completely good—not the cultivation of goodness, of humility, but the seeking out of something beyond the inventions and tricks of the mind, which means having a feeling for that something, living in it, being it—*that* is true religion. But you can do that only when you leave the pool you have dug for yourself and go out into the river of life. Then life has an astonishing way of taking care of you, because then there is no taking care on your part. Life carries you where it will because you are part of itself; then there is no problem of security, of what people say or don't say, and that is the beauty of life.

A Marvelous Escape

What is the impetus behind the search for God, and is that search real? For most of us, it is an escape from actuality. So, we must be very clear in ourselves whether this search after God is an escape, or whether it is a search for truth in everything—truth in our relationships, truth in the value of things, truth in ideas. If we are seeking God merely because we are tired of this world and its miseries, then it is an escape. Then we create God, and therefore it is not God. The God of the temples, of the books, is not God, obviously—it is a marvelous escape. But if we try to find the truth, not in one exclusive set of actions, but in all our actions, ideas, and relationships, if we seek the right evaluation of food, clothing, and shelter, then because our minds are capable of clarity and understanding, when we seek reality we shall find it. It will not then be an escape. But if we are confused with regard to the things of the world—food, clothing, shelter, relationship, and ideas—how can we find reality? We can only invent reality. So, God, truth, or reality, is not to be known by a mind that is confused, conditioned, limited. How can such a mind think of reality or God? It has first to decondition itself. It has to free itself from its own limitations, and only then can it know what God is, obviously not before. Reality is the unknown, and that which is known is not the real.

Your God Is Not God

A man who believes in God can never find God. If you are open to reality, there can be no belief in reality. If you are open to the unknown, there can be no belief in it. After all, belief is a form of self-protection, and only a petty mind can believe in God. Look at the belief of the aviators during the war who said God was their companion as they were dropping bombs! So you believe in God when you kill, when you are exploiting people. You worship God and go on ruthlessly extorting money, supporting the army—yet you say you believe in mercy, compassion, kindliness. . . . As long as belief exists, there can never be the unknown; you cannot think about the unknown, thought cannot measure it. The mind is the product of the past, it is the result of yesterday, and can such a mind be open to the unknown? It can only project an image, but that projection is not real; so your God is not God—it is an image of your own making, an image of your own gratification. There can be reality only when the mind understands the total process of itself and comes to an end. When the mind is completely empty—only then is it capable of receiving the unknown. The mind is not purged until it understands the content of relationship—its relationship with property, with people—until it has established the right relationship with everything. Until it understands the whole process of conflict in relationship, the mind cannot be free. Only when the mind is wholly silent, completely inactive, not projecting, when it is not seeking and is utterly still—only then that which is eternal and timeless comes into being.

The Religious Man

What is the state of the mind that says, "I do not know whether there is God, whether there is love," that is, when there is no response of memory? Please don't immediately answer the question to yourselves because if you do, your answer will be merely the recognition of what you think it should or should not be. If you say, "It is a state of negation," you are comparing it with something that you already know; therefore, that state in which you say, "I do not know" is nonexistent. . . .

So the mind that is capable of saying, "I do not know," is in the only state in which anything can be discovered. But the man who says, "I know," the man who has studied infinitely the varieties of human experience and whose mind is burdened with information, with encyclopedic knowledge, can he ever experience something that is not to be accumulated? He will find it extremely hard. When the mind totally puts aside all the knowledge that it has acquired, when for it there are no Buddhas, no Christs, no Masters, no teachers, no religions, no quotations; when the mind is completely alone, uncontaminated, which means that the movement of the known has come to an end—it is only then that there is a possibility of a tremendous revolution, a fundamental change. . . . The religious man is he who does not belong to any religion, to any nation, to any race, who is inwardly completely alone, in a state of not-knowing, and for him the blessing of the sacred comes into being.

I Do Not Know

If one can really come to that state of saying, "I do not know," it indicates an extraordinary sense of humility; there is no arrogance of knowledge; there is no self-assertive answer to make an impression. When you can actually say, "I do not know," which very few are capable of saying, then in that state all fear ceases because all sense of recognition, the search into memory, has come to an end; there is no longer inquiry into the field of the known. Then comes the extraordinary thing. If you have so far followed what I am talking about, not just verbally, but if you are actually experiencing it, you will find that when you can say, "I do not know," all conditioning has stopped. And what then is the state of the mind? . . .

We are seeking something permanent—permanent in the sense of time, something enduring, everlasting. We see that everything about us is transient, in flux, being born, withering, and dying, and our search is always to establish something that will endure within the field of the known. But that which is truly sacred is beyond the measure of time; it is not to be found within the field of the known. The known operates only through thought, which is the response of memory to challenge. If I see that, and I want to find out how to end thinking, what am I to do? Surely I must, through self-knowledge, be aware of the whole process of my thinking. I must see that every thought, however subtle, however lofty, or however ignoble, stupid, has its roots in the known, in memory. If I see that very clearly, then the mind, when confronted with an immense problem, is capable of saying, "I do not know," because it has no answer.

Beyond the Limitations of Beliefs

To be a theist or an atheist, to me, are both absurd. If you knew what truth is, what God is, you would neither be a theist nor an atheist, because in that awareness belief is unnecessary. It is the man who is not aware, who only hopes and supposes, who looks to belief or to disbelief to support him, and to lead him to act in a particular way.

Now, if you approach it quite differently, you will find out for yourselves, as individuals, something real that is beyond all the limitations of beliefs, beyond the illusion of words. But that—the discovery of truth, or God—demands great intelligence, which is not assertion of belief or disbelief, but the recognition of the hindrances created by lack of intelligence. So to discover God or truth—and I say such a thing does exist, I have realized it—to recognize that, to realize that, the mind must be free of all the hindrances that have been created throughout the ages, based on self-protection and security. You cannot be free of security by merely saying that you are free. To penetrate the walls of these hindrances, you need to have a great deal of intelligence, not mere intellect. Intelligence, to me, is mind and heart in full harmony; and then you will find out for yourself, without asking anyone, what that reality is.

Free from the Net of Time

Without meditation, there is no self-knowledge; without self-knowledge, there is no meditation. So you must begin to know what you are. You cannot go far without beginning near, without understanding your daily process of thought, feeling, and action. In other words, thought must understand its own working, and when you see yourself in operation, you will observe that thought moves from the known to the known. You cannot think about the unknown. That which you know is not real because what you know is only in time. To be free from the net of time is the important concern, not to think about the unknown, because you cannot think about the unknown. The answers to your prayers are of the known. To receive the unknown, the mind itself must become the unknown. The mind is the result of the thought process, the result of time, and this thought process must come to an end. The mind cannot think of that which is eternal, timeless; therefore, the mind must be free of time, the time process of the mind must be dissolved. Only when the mind is completely free from yesterday, and is therefore not using the present as a means to the future, is it capable of receiving the eternal. . . . Therefore, our concern in meditation is to know oneself, not only superficially, but the whole content of the inner, hidden consciousness. Without knowing all that and being free of its conditioning, you cannot possibly go beyond the mind's limits. That is why the thought process must cease, and for this cessation there must be knowledge of oneself. Therefore meditation is the beginning of wisdom, which is the understanding of one's own mind and heart.

Meditation

I am going step-by-step into what meditation is. Please don't wait till the end, hoping to have a complete description of how to meditate. What we are doing now is part of meditation.

Now, what one has to do is to be aware of the thinker, and not try to resolve the contradiction and bring about an integration between thought and the thinker. The thinker is the psychological entity who has accumulated experience as knowledge; he is the time-bound center that is the result of ever-changing environmental influence, and from this center he looks, he listens, he experiences. As long as one does not understand the structure and the anatomy of this center, there must always be conflict, and a mind in conflict cannot possibly understand the depth and the beauty of meditation.

In meditation there can be no thinker, which means that thought must come to an end—the thought that is urged forward by the desire to achieve a result. Meditation has nothing to do with achieving a result. It is not a matter of breathing in a particular way, or looking at your nose, or awakening the power to perform certain tricks, or any of the rest of that immature nonsense. . . . Meditation is not something apart from life. When you are driving a car or sitting in a bus, when you are chatting aimlessly, when you are walking by yourself in a wood or watching a butterfly being carried along by the wind—to be choicelessly aware of all that is part of meditation.

Know the Whole Content
of One Thought

Not being anything is the beginning of freedom. So if you are capable of feeling, of going into this you will find, as you become aware, that you are not free, that you are bound to very many different things, and that at the same time the mind hopes to be free. And you can see that the two are contradictory. So the mind has to investigate why it clings to anything. All this implies hard work. It is much more arduous than going to an office, than any physical labour, than all the sciences put together. Because the humble, intelligent mind is concerned with itself without being self-centered; therefore it has to be extraordinarily alert, aware, and that means real hard work every day, every hour, every minute. . . . This demands insistent work because freedom does not come easily. Everything impedes—your wife, your husband, your son, your neighbor, your Gods, your religions, your tradition. All these impede you, but you have created them because you want security. And the mind that is seeking security can never find it. If you have watched a little in the world, you know there is no such thing as security. The wife dies, the husband dies, the son runs away—something happens. Life is not static, though we would like to make it so. No relationship is static because all life is movement. That is a thing to be grasped, the truth to be seen, felt, not something to be argued about. Then you will see, as you begin to investigate, that it is really a process of meditation.

But do not be mesmerized by that word. To be aware of every thought, to know from what source it springs and what is its intention—that is meditation. And to know the whole content of one thought reveals the whole process of the mind.

Igniting the Flame of Self-Awareness

If you find it difficult to be aware, then experiment with writing down every thought and feeling that arises throughout the day; write down your reactions of jealousy, envy, vanity, sensuality, the intentions behind your words, and so on.

Spend some time before breakfast in writing them down—which may necessitate going to bed earlier and putting aside some social affair. If you write these things down whenever you can, and in the evening before sleeping look over all that you have written during the day, study and examine it without judgment, without condemnation, you will begin to discover the hidden causes of your thoughts and feelings, desires and words. . . .

Now, the important thing in this is to study with free intelligence what you have written down, and in studying it you will become aware of your own state. In the flame of self-awareness, of self-knowledge, the causes of conflict are discovered and consumed. You should continue to write down your thoughts and feelings, intentions and reactions, not once or twice, but for a considerable number of days until you are able to be aware of them instantly. . . .

Meditation is not only constant self-awareness, but constant abandonment of the self. Out of right thinking there is meditation, from which there comes the tranquillity of wisdom; and in that serenity the highest is realized.

Writing down what one thinks and feels, one's desires and reactions, brings about an inward awareness, the cooperation of the unconscious with the conscious, and this in turn leads to integration and understanding.

The Way of Meditation

Is truth something final, absolute, fixed? We would like it to be absolute because then we could take shelter in it. We would like it to be permanent because then we could hold on to it, find happiness in it. But is truth absolute, continuous, to be experienced over and over again? The repetition of experience is the mere cultivation of memory, is it not? In moments of quietness, I may experience a certain truth, but if I cling to that experience through memory and make it absolute, fixed—is that truth? Is truth the continuation, the cultivation of memory? Or, is truth to be found only when the mind is utterly still? When the mind is not caught in memories, not cultivating memory as the center of recognition, but is aware of everything I am saying, everything I am doing in my relationships, in my activities, seeing the truth of everything as it is from moment to moment—surely, that is the way of meditation, is it not? There is comprehension only when the mind is still, and the mind cannot be still as long as it is ignorant of itself. That ignorance is not dispelled through any form of discipline, through pursuing any authority, ancient or modern. Belief only creates resistance, isolation, and where there is isolation, there is no possibility of tranquillity. Tranquillity comes only when I understand the whole process of myself—the various entities in conflict with each other which compose the "me." As that is an arduous task, we turn to others to learn various tricks, which we call meditation. The tricks of the mind are not meditation. Meditation is the beginning of self-knowledge, and without meditation, there is no self-knowledge.

A Mind in the State of Creation

Meditation is the emptying of the mind of all the things that the mind has put together. If you do that—perhaps you won't, but it doesn't matter, just listen to this—you will find that there is an extraordinary space in the mind, and that space is freedom. So you must demand freedom at the very beginning, and not just wait, hoping to have it at the end. You must seek out the significance of freedom in your work, in your relationships, in everything that you do. Then you will find that meditation is creation.

Creation is a word that we all use so glibly, so easily. A painter puts on canvas a few colours and gets tremendously excited about it. It is his fulfillment, the means through which he expresses himself; it is his market in which to gain money or reputation—and he calls that "creation"! Every writer "creates," and there are schools of "creative" writing, but none of that has anything to do with creation. It is all the conditioned response of a mind that lives in a particular society.

The creation of which I am speaking is something entirely different. It is a mind that is in the state of creation. It may or it may not express that state. Expression has very little value. That state of creation has no cause, and therefore a mind in that state is every moment dying and living and loving and being. The whole of this is meditation.

Lay the Foundation Instantly

A still mind is not seeking experience of any kind. And if it is not seeking and therefore is completely still, without any movement from the past and therefore free from the known, then you will find, if you have gone that far, that there is a movement of the unknown that is not recognized, that is not translatable, that cannot be put into words—then you will find that there is a movement which is of the immense. That movement is of the timeless because in that there is no time, nor is there space, nor something in which to experience, nor something to gain, to achieve. Such a mind knows what is creation—not the creation of the painter, the poet, the verbalizer; but that creation which has no motive, which has no expression. That creation is love and death.

This whole thing from the beginning to the end is the way of meditation. A man who would meditate must understand himself. Without knowing yourself, you cannot go far. However much you may attempt to go far, you can go only so far as your own projection; and your own projection is very near, is very close, and does not lead you anywhere. Meditation is that process of laying the foundation instantly, immediately, and bringing about—naturally, without any effort—that state of stillness. And only then is there a mind which is beyond time, beyond experience, and beyond knowing.

Finding Silence

If you have followed this inquiry into what is meditation, and have understood the whole process of thinking, you will find that the mind is completely still. In that total stillness of the mind, there is no watcher, no observer, and therefore no experiencer at all; there is no entity who is gathering experience, which is the activity of a self-centered mind. Don't say, "That is *samadhi*"—which is all nonsense, because you have only read of it in some book and have not discovered it for yourself. There is a vast difference between the word and the thing. The word is not the thing; the word *door* is not the door.

So, to meditate is to purge the mind of its self-centered activity. And if you have come this far in meditation, you will find there is silence, a total emptiness. The mind is uncontaminated by society; it is no longer subject to any influence, to the pressure of any desire. It is completely alone, and being alone, untouched, it is innocent. Therefore there is a possibility for that which is timeless, eternal, to come into being.

This whole process is meditation.

Generosity of the Heart
Is the Beginning of Meditation

We are going to talk about something that needs a mind that can penetrate very profoundly. We must begin very near because we cannot go very far if we do not know how to begin very close, if we do not know how to take the first step. The flowering of meditation is goodness, and the generosity of the heart is the beginning of meditation. We have talked about many things concerning life, authority, ambition, fear, greed, envy, death, time; we have talked about many things. If you observe, if you have gone into it, if you have listened rightly, those are all the foundation for a mind that is capable of meditating. You cannot meditate if you are ambitious—you may play with the idea of meditation. If your mind is authority-ridden, bound by tradition, accepting, following, you will never know what it is to meditate on this extraordinary beauty. . . .

It is the pursuit of its own fulfillment through time that prevents generosity. And you need a generous mind—not only a wide mind, a mind that is full of space, but also a heart that gives without thought, without a motive, and that does not seek any reward in return. But to give whatever little one has or however much one has—that quality of spontaneity of outgoing, without any restriction, without any withholding, is necessary. There can be no meditation without generosity, without goodness—which is to be free from pride, never to climb the ladder of success, never to know what it is to be famous; which is to die to whatever has been achieved, every minute of the day. It is only in such fertile ground that goodness can grow, can flower. And meditation is the flowering of goodness.

Meditation Is Essential to Life

To understand this whole problem of influence, the influence of experience, the influence of knowledge, of inward and outward motives—to find out what is true and what is false and to see the truth in the so-called false—all that requires tremendous insight, a deep inward comprehension of things as they are, does it not? This whole process is, surely, the way of meditation. Meditation is essential in life, in our everyday existence, as beauty is essential. The perception of beauty, the sensitivity to things, to the ugly as well as to the beautiful, is essential—to see a beautiful tree, a lovely sky of an evening, to see the vast horizon where the clouds are gathering as the sun is setting. All this is necessary, the perception of beauty and the understanding of the way of meditation, because all that is life, as is also your going to the office, the quarrels, miseries, the perpetual strain, anxiety, the deep fears, love, and starvation. Now the understanding of this total process of existence—the influences, the sorrows, the daily strain, the authoritative outlook, the political actions, and so on—all this is life, and the process of understanding it all, and freeing the mind, is meditation. If one really comprehends this life then there is always a meditative process, always a process of contemplation—but not *about* something. To be aware of this whole process of existence, to observe it, to dispassionately enter into it, and to be free of it, is meditation.

KEY TO SOURCE ABBREVIATIONS

COL   *Commentaries on Living, Series 1 and 2, Volumes 1, 2, and 3.* Wheaton, IL: Quest Books, 1956, 1958, 1960.

CW   *Collected Works of J. Krishnamurti,* 17 Vols. Dubuque, IA: Kendall/Hunt Publishing, 1991, 1992.

ESL   *Education and the Significance of Life.* Reprint. San Francisco: HarperSanFrancisco, 1953.

FLF   *First and Last Freedom.* Reprint. San Francisco: HarperSanFrancisco, 1954.

JKI   *Krishnamurti Interviews #1–92.* Krishnamurti Foundation of America Archives, Ojai, California.

LA   *Life Ahead.* Reprint. New York: Harper & Row, 1963.

TTT   *Think on These Things.* New York: HarperPerennial, 1964.

SOURCES

January 1—TTT, pp. 27–28

January 2—CW, Vol. VII, p. 213

January 3—COL, Series I, pp. 171–72

January 4—CW, Vol. XIV, p. 234

January 5—COL, Series II, pp. 147–48

January 6—LA, p. 85

January 7—CW, Vol. XV, p. 239

January 8—CW, Vol. XI, pp. 108–109

January 9—FLF, p. 156

January 10—CW, Vol. XVI, pp. 213–14

January 11—LA, Introduction, p. 8

January 12—CW, Vol. XIV, p. 238

January 13—CW, Vol. XV, p. 173

January 14—CW, Vol. XIV, p. 170

January 15—CW, Vol. XII, pp. 296–97

January 16—CW, Vol. XVII, p. 34

January 17—CW, Vol. XIV, p. 15

January 18—ESL, p. 60

January 19—CW, Vol. IV, p. 46

January 20—CW, Vol. IV, p. 44

January 21—COL, Series I, pp. 95–96

January 22—CW, Vol. VII, pp. 52–53

January 23—CW, Vol. V, pp. 334–35

January 24—FLF, p. 44

January 25—COL, Series I, p. 94

January 26—FLF, p. 47

January 27—CW, Vol. VII, p. 325

January 28—CW, Vol. XIV, p. 107

January 29—CW, Vol. VII, p. 55

January 30—CW, Vol. IV, p. 1

January 31—CW, Vol. IX, p. 137

February 1—FLF, p. 51

February 2—COL, Vol. I, pp. 196–97

February 3—TTT, p. 14

February 4—COL, Vol. I, pp. 94–95

February 5—CW, Vol. VI, pp. 274–75

February 6—CW, Vol. VI, pp. 272–73

February 7—CW, Vol. VI, p. 276

February 8—CW, Vol. V, p. 49

February 9—CW, Vol. XVI, p. 254

February 10—CW, Vol. VI, pp. 140–41

February 11—CW, Vol. VII, p. 130

February 12—CW, Vol. VI, pp. 140–41

February 13—FLF, p. 57

February 14—FLF, p. 58

February 15—CW, Vol. XIII, p. 33

February 16—FLF, p. 56

February 17—CW, Vol. VI, p. 260

February 18—FLF, pp. 52–53

February 19—CW, Vol. VI, p. 79

February 20—FLF, p. 54

February 21—CW, Vol. VI, pp. 261–62

February 22—CW, Vol. VIII, p. 318

February 23—CW, Vol. III, pp. 212–13

February 24—FLF, pp. 145–46

February 25—CW, Vol. IX, pp. 228–29

February 26—CW, Vol. VII, p. 49

February 27—CW, Vol. VII, pp. 232–33

February 28—CW, Vol. VII, pp. 153–54

March 1—CW, Vol. XIII, pp. 110–11

May 24—CW, Vol. IX, p. 35
May 25—COL, Series III, pp. 31–32
May 26—CW, Vol. XIII, p. 326
May 27—CW, Vol. IX, p. 35
May 28—CW, Vol. X, pp. 158–59
May 29—CW, Vol. XIV, p. 190
May 30—FLF, pp. 225–26
May 31—CW, Vol. XIII, p. 240
June 1—TTT, pp. 211–12
June 2—CW, Vol. XIV, pp. 289–90
June 3—CW, Vol. XIV, p. 290
June 4—CW, Vol. XIII, p. 109
June 5—CW, Vol. XII, p. 64
June 6—CW, Vol. XIV, p. 288
June 7—CW, Vol. XII, p. 67
June 8—TTT, p. 152
June 9—CW, Vol. IX, p. 280
June 10—CW, Vol. IX, p. 69
June 11—LA, p. 17
June 12—CW, Vol. X, pp. 139–40
June 13—LA, p. 18
June 14—CW, Vol. IX, p. 240
June 15—CW, Vol. XIII, p. 34
June 16—CW, Vol. III, p. 179
June 17—CW, Vol. XII, pp. 54–55
June 18—CW, Vol. IV, p. 209
June 19—CW, Vol. XII, p. 306
June 20—CW, Vol. IV, p. 209
June 21—JKI #87
June 22—CW, Vol. XVII, p. 259
June 23—CW, Vol. XVI, pp. 289–90
June 24—CW, Vol. III, p. 176
June 25—CW, Vol. XVII, pp. 170–71
June 26—CW, Vol. XVII, p. 142
June 27—CW, Vol. XVII, p. 256
June 28—CW, Vol. X, pp. 80–81
June 29—CW, Vol. III, pp. 154–55
June 30—CW, Vol. III, p. 203
July 1—FLF, p. 28
July 2—CW, Vol. VIII, pp. 117–18
July 3—CW, Vol. VII, p. 101
July 4—COL, Series I, pp. 240–41

July 5—CW, Vol. IV, p. 105
July 6—CW, Vol. VIII, p. 119
July 7—CW, Vol. VII, pp. 214–15
July 8—CW, Vol. XV, p. 226
July 9—CW, Vol. V, p. 46
July 10—FLF, p. 84
July 11—CW, Vol. VI, pp. 358–59
July 12—FLF, p. 170
July 13—CW, Vol. XII, p. 91
July 14—CW, Vol. XV, p. 221
July 15—CW, Vol. I, p. 141
July 16—CW, Vol. XII, p. 246
July 17—TTT, p. 204
July 18—CW, Vol. VIII, p. 105
July 19—CW, Vol. III, pp. 157–58
July 20—CW, Vol. VII, p. 224
July 21—CW, Vol. II, p. 68
July 22—COL, Series III, pp. 195–96
July 23—CW, Vol. XI, p. 284
July 24—CW, Vol. XIII, pp. 309–10
July 25—CW, Vol. XIII, p. 308
July 26—FLF, pp. 168–70
July 27—FLF, p. 170–71
July 28—CW, Vol. XII, pp. 94–95
July 29—CW, Vol. XIII, p. 311
July 30—CW, Vol. XIII, p. 255
July 31—CW, Vol. VI, pp. 312–13
August 1—CW, Vol. V, p. 205
August 2—CW, Vol. VI, p. 134
August 3—CW, Vol. VI, pp. 134–35
August 4—COL, Series I, p. 46
August 5—CW, Vol. VII, p. 265
August 6—CW, Vol. V, p. 124
August 7—CW, Vol. XI, p. 207
August 8—COL, Series III, p. 146
August 9—CW, Vol. XII, p. 50
August 10—COL, Series III, p. 253
August 11—FLF, pp. 264–65
August 12—FLF, p. 170
August 13—COL, Series I, p. 92
August 14—CW, Vol. XVI, pp. 177–80
August 15—CW, Vol. XVI, pp. 23–24

October 30—CW, Vol. IX, p. 56
October 31—CW, Vol. VII, p. 50
November 1—CW, Vol. VI, p. 56
November 2—CW, Vol. IV, p. 36
November 3—TTT, pp. 115–16
November 4—CW, Vol. V, pp. 145–46
November 5—CW, Vol. VIII, p. 252
November 6—CW, Vol. X, p. 83
November 7—CW, Vol. VII, p. 124
November 8—TTT, p. 173
November 9—COL, Series III, p. 303
November 10—TTT, p. 237
November 11—CW, Vol. XVI, p. 176
November 12—LA, p. 41
November 13—FLF, pp. 83–84
November 14—CW, Vol. VI, p. 68
November 15—CW, Vol. XV, p. 33
November 16—CW, Vol. V, p. 355
November 17—CW, Vol. II, p. 227
November 18—CW, Vol. VI, p. 68
November 19—CW, Vol. XV, p. 319
November 20—CW, Vol. VI, pp. 68–69
November 21—CW, Vol. VI, p. 69
November 22—CW, Vol. XV, pp. 71–72
November 23—CW, Vol. XV, p. 74
November 24—LA, pp. 97–98
November 25—CW, Vol. V, pp. 101–102
November 26—TTT, pp. 152–53
November 27—CW, Vol. XIII, pp. 296–97
November 28—CW, Vol. X, pp. 191–92
November 29—CW, Vol. X, pp. 192–93, 196
November 30—COL, Series II, p. 223
December 1—CW, Vol. XV, p. 32

December 2—CW, Vol. XIV, p. 220
December 3—CW, Vol. VI, p. 312
December 4—CW, Vol. XIII, p. 228
December 5—CW, Vol. XVII, p. 184
December 6—CW, Vol. VII. p. 221
December 7—CW, Vol. VII, pp. 219–20
December 8—CW, Vol. XV, pp. 90–91
December 9—CW, Vol. XII, pp. 81, 82
December 10—JKI #48
December 11—CW, Vol. VI, pp. 204–5
December 12—CW, Vol. VII, p. 131
December 13—CW, Vol. V, pp. 48, 49
December 14—JKI #95
December 15—CW, Vol. II, p. 34
December 16—TTT, pp. 142–43
December 17—CW, Vol. V. p. 4
December 18—CW, Vol. VI, pp. 140–41
December 19—CW, Vol. IX, pp. 112, 113
December 20—CW, Vol. IX, p. 112
December 21—CW, Vol. II, p. 34
December 22—CW, Vol. V, pp. 165–66
December 23—CW, Vol. XIII, pp. 263–64
December 24—CW, Vol. XI, p. 67
December 25—JKI #20
December 26—CW, Vol. VI, p. 176
December 27—CW, Vol. XIII, pp. 324–25
December 28—CW, Vol. XIII, pp. 98–99
December 29—CW, Vol. X, p. 229
December 30—CW, Vol. XIII, p. 150
December 31—CW, Vol. XI, pp. 138–39